The Collaborative
Public Manager

Public Management and Change Series
Beryl A. Radin, Series Editor

Titles in the Series

Challenging the Performance Movement: Accountability, Complexity, and Democratic Values, Beryl A. Radin

Charitable Choice at Work: Evaluating Faith-Based Job Programs in the States, Sheila Suess Kennedy and Wolfgang Bielefeld

The Collaborative Public Manager: New Ideas for the Twenty-first Century, Rosemary O'Leary and Lisa Blomgren Bingham, Editors

The Dynamics of Performance Management: Constructing Information and Reform, Donald P. Moynihan

The Greening of the U.S. Military: Environmental Policy, National Security, and Organizational Change, Robert F. Durant

How Management Matters: Street-Level Bureaucrats and Welfare Reform, Norma M. Riccucci

Managing within Networks: Adding Value to Public Organizations, Robert Agranoff

Measuring the Performance of the Hollow State, David G. Frederickson and H. George Frederickson

Public Values and Public Interest: Counterbalancing Economic Individualism, Barry Bozeman

The Responsible Contract Manager: Protecting the Public Interest in an Outsourced World, Steven Cohen and William Eimicke

Revisiting Waldo's Administrative State: Constancy and Change in Public Administration, David H. Rosenbloom and Howard E. McCurdy

The Collaborative Public Manager

New Ideas for the Twenty-first Century

Rosemary O'Leary and
Lisa Blomgren Bingham, Editors

Georgetown University Press
Washington, D.C.

Georgetown University Press, Washington, D.C.
www.press.georgetown.edu

Library of Congress Cataloging-in-Publication Data
   The collaborative public manager / edited by Rosemary O'Leary and Lisa Blomgren Bingham.
       p. cm.—(Public management and change series)
   Includes bibliographical references and index.
   ISBN 978–1–58901–223–3 (pbk. : alk. paper)
   1. Public administration—United States.   2. Intergovernmental cooperation—United States.   3. Public-private sector cooperation—United States.   I. O'Leary, Rosemary, 1955–   II Bingham, Lisa (Lisa B.), 1955–
   JF1351.C577 2008
   351.973—dc22

                                                                      2008012642

15 14 13 12 11 10 09 08   9 8 7 6 5 4 3 2
First printing

Printed in the United States of America

We dedicate this book
to our
mothers,
Mary Jane Kelly
and
Lola Blomgren

Contents

Illustrations

Acknowledgments

Most of the chapters in this book were first presented at a research conference. They have been revised to reflect developments in the field. Without the conference, this book never would have been developed.

The Collaborative Public Management Conference, sponsored by the Maxwell School of Syracuse University, was held in 2006 at the Syracuse University Greenberg House in Washington. It was funded by the Maxwell School's Dean's Office. It was sponsored by the Collaborative Governance Initiative, a part of the Program on the Analysis and Resolution of Conflicts (PARC) at the Maxwell School. All the participants were experts in public management but with very different areas of expertise: leadership, personnel, law, bureaucratic politics, intergovernmental relations, conflict resolution, environmental management, emergency management, volunteerism, contracting, and information technology. Some were from the public sector, some were from the private sector, and still others were from the nonprofit sector. Some were academics, some were practitioners, and some were "pracademics"—individuals who span both worlds.

The group was united, however, by one common interest: a desire to foster new knowledge and understanding about collaborative public management. The discussions ranged from the theoretical to the practical. Cost/benefit analyses, case studies, quasi-experimental designs, and meta-analyses were placed under the microscope.

We are grateful to Catherine Gerard, codirector of PARC, who helped mastermind the conference, kept our discussions on track, and provided wise counsel based on her years as a public manager and consultant. We are also grateful to the other conference participants who did not write chapters for this book but whose comments and insights while participating in the two-and-a-half-day conference were invaluable in crafting the final product: Terry Amsler (League of California Cities), Stu Bretschneider (Syracuse University), John Bryson (University of Minnesota), Chris Carlson (Policy Consensus Initiative), Terry Cooper (University of Southern California), Barbara Crosby (University of Minnesota), Sue Faerman (State University of New York at Albany), Richard

Feiock (Florida State University), George Frederickson (University of Kansas), Archon Fung (Harvard University), Heather Getha-Taylor (University of South Carolina), Maja Husar Holmes (American University), Patricia Ingraham (Binghamton University), Soon Hee Kim (Syracuse University), Malka Kopell (Stanford University), Harry Lambright (Syracuse University), David Matkin (Florida State University), Brint Milward (University of Arizona), Steve Page (University of Washington), Jim Perry (Indiana University), Carla Pizzarella (Syracuse University), Bill Potapchuk (Community Building Institute), Keith Provan (University of Arizona), and Jodi Sandfort (University of Minnesota). Many of the papers written by these individuals can be found in our companion volume, *Big Ideas in Collaborative Public Management*, published in 2008 by M. E. Sharpe.

We thank the PARC staff for their expert assistance in planning and implementing the conference, including Lisa Mignacca, Chris Praino, Rob Alexander, and Rachel Fleishman. We thank Laurel Saiz, Sarah Breul, and Luke Dougherty for their excellent editing and Carin McAbee for assembling the final manuscript. We thank the staff of Greenberg House, particularly Mary Anagnost, for providing a delightful conference setting and staff assistance.

We also thank our anonymous reviewers, as well as Beryl Radin, Gail Grella, and Don Jacobs, for their helpful suggestions for improvement. Finally, we are grateful to the contributors for their consistently excellent work and for their enthusiasm. We sincerely hope that the solid research, surprising findings, and thoughtful questions in this book will energize and deepen discussions among practitioners, academics, and students around the world about collaborative public management.

The Collaborative
Public Manager

Chapter 1

Public Managers in Collaboration

Rosemary O'Leary, Beth Gazley,

Michael McGuire, and Lisa Blomgren Bingham

With the evolution from government to governance, public management scholars have given renewed attention to forms of organization that cross agency boundaries. In this book, we focus on collaborative public management and, more particularly, on the latest empirical research by some of the leading scholars in the field of public management, public policy, and public affairs. Public managers who work collaboratively find themselves not solely as unitary leaders of unitary organizations. Instead, they often find themselves facilitating and operating in multiorganizational networked arrangements to solve problems that cannot be solved, or solved easily, by single organizations. This phenomenon has been the subject of an explosion of research in recent years.

This new collaborative public management scholarship responds in part to the growth of networks of public, private, and nonprofit organizations; the context, environment, and constraints within which they work; the situation of the public manager in a network; these networks' governance processes and decision rules; how they define their work, tasks, and goals; and their impact on public policy and the policy process. The collaborative public management literature uses a variety of "sound bites" to describe the importance of this phenomenon to our field. Sometimes, scholars talk about the public manager's "toolkit" or "strategies." Sometimes, they talk about collaborative public management as an "option" or a "choice." Sometimes, they refer to it as a "model" or a "structure" within which managers find themselves. There is a tension between the literature on a manager's (or his or her organization's) individual choice to participate in a network and the literature that looks at these networks as systems that are not the product of individual choice but instead emerge from intentional or fortuitous collective design.

On the ground, in the world of the practitioner, there has been an explosion of new developments in the area of collaborative public management in the last ten years. Some developments are high profile and are known by most of us. For example, when thousands of residents gathered in twenty-first century town meetings (see www.americaspeaks.org), using new electronic tools to design the future of Lower Manhattan after September 11, 2001, we all read about it in the popular press. But most examples are not so well known. Consider these real-world examples of public managers in collaboration:

- The state of Arizona initiates wilderness working groups in its counties. Their purpose is to bring together environmental advocates, ranchers and farmers, industry officials, and government representatives to create land management strategies for each local area.
- The Centers for Disease Control and Prevention work with health professionals, federal government agencies, industry, consumer advocates, state governments, and minority groups to plan a national response in the event of a flu pandemic.
- A task force comprising industry groups, concerned citizens, members of environmental protection advocacy groups, and other parties negotiates new livestock permitting regulations in Ohio to protect water quality. The regulations become law.
- A state agency, a city, a regional council, and a transit authority work collaboratively in Utah to evaluate transportation needs for 8.5 miles of state highway outside a large suburb of Salt Lake City. The project includes public and agency coordination, data collection, developing and evaluating alternatives, environmental analysis, environmental impact statement preparation, and concept-level design.
- On the Chesapeake Bay, a monitoring committee made up of members of the commercial fishing industry, scientists, public servants, and concerned citizens determines target outcomes, defines criteria and indicators to monitor these outcomes, determines the appropriate system for monitoring, participates in data gathering and analysis, and interprets data over time in order to provide recommendations to regulators. Government policies are changed based on the findings of this collaborative monitoring group.

Of course these are only a few of the hundreds of examples of collaborative public management today, and they are offered here only to whet your appetite and lure you into the fascinating analyses in each of this book's chapters.

FRAMING THE ISSUES: A COLLABORATIVE PUBLIC MANAGEMENT PRIMER

Collaborative public management is an idea that resonates with many in our field, yet it lacks a common lens or definition, and it is often studied without the benefit of examining parallel literatures in sister fields. Accordingly, we were forced to make choices as to how to define collaborative public management for the purposes of this book. Although scholars have forwarded numerous definitions of collaboration, each emphasizing the preconditions, process, or outcomes of the relationship, for this book we have adopted the following definition, which has been adapted from Agranoff and McGuire (2003a) as well as from O'Leary, Gerard, and Bingham (2006): "Collaborative public management is a concept that describes the process of facilitating and operating in multi-organizational arrangements to solve problems that cannot be solved or easily solved by single organizations. Collaborative means to co-labor, to achieve common goals, often working across boundaries and in multi-sector and multi-actor relationships. Collaboration is based on the value of reciprocity. Collaborative public management may include participatory governance: the active involvement of citizens in government decision-making."

Roots in the Literature

Public managers have practiced collaborative management for quite some time. Decades-old research on intergovernmental relations and policy implementation describes public management as being frequently collaborative in practice. American federalism, for example, is perhaps the most enduring model of collaborative problem resolution (Agranoff and McGuire 2003a), whereby "federal–state–local collaboration is the characteristic mode of action" (Grodzins 1960, 266). Empirical evidence suggests that intergovernmental relations in the United States have always been cooperative, such that nearly all the activities of government are shared activities, including their planning, financing, and execution (Elazar 1962). The grants-in-aid system, certainly the most prominent context within which collaboration has occurred since the nineteenth century, has long been characterized by the presence of bargaining and cooperation (Ingram 1977; Pressman 1975). The three levels of government and multiple types of nonprofit organizations cooperate, and have cooperated, both informally and officially, in many different ways and through many different mechanisms for generations.

There is also empirical evidence demonstrating the direct connection in the 1960s between federal policymaking in the United States and the development of implementation structures that involved multiple actors. Pressman and Wildavsky (1973) described policy implementation in terms of shared, collaborative management. Their empirical investigation of the Economic Development Administration's attempts in the 1960s to address the unemployment of minorities in Oakland referred to the "complexity of joint action" among the multiplicity of participants and perspectives from all levels of government pursuing policy goals that in practice may be conflicting. Hall and O'Toole's (2000, 2004) examination of institutional arrangements incorporated into legislation enacted by the 89th Congress in 1965 and the 103rd Congress in 1993 found that the majority of significant new legislation prescribed the involvement of collaborative structures for policy implementation. This research demonstrates empirically that, "in most cases [for both Congresses], the implementation of new programs at the national levels requires U.S. public administrators to be prepared to work with a variety of different kinds of actors both within and without government—actors drawn from different organizational cultures, influenced by different sets of incentives, and directed toward different goals" (Hall and O'Toole 2004, 189–90). Outside the United States, collaborative structures used for implementing personnel training in Germany and Sweden in the 1970s were characterized at that time in terms of multiple power centers with reciprocal relationships, many suppliers of resources, overlapping and dynamic divisions of labor, diffused responsibility for actions, massive information exchanges among actors, and the need for information input from all actors (Hanf, Hjern, and Porter 1978). Other public policy studies in the 1980s revealed the extent of collaboration in public policy implementation (Hull with Hjern 1987; O'Toole 1985).

Elements of Collaboration

Barbara Gray (1989), who has written extensively on collaboration in business management, distinguishes collaboration from other, lesser forms of cooperation by requiring these four elements:

- the interdependence of the stakeholders,
- the ability to address differences constructively,

- joint ownership of decisions, and
- collective responsibility for the future of the partnership.

Gray (1989) and Gray and Wood (1991) observe that "collaboration" between organizations is different from "cooperation" or "coordination" because these latter two terms do not capture the dynamic, evolutionary nature of collaboration. Collaboration from this perspective is best examined as a dynamic or emergent process rather than a static condition—a perspective that greatly complicates its empirical measurement (Sharfman, Gray, and Yan 1991; Takahashi and Smutny 2002). Selden, Sowa, and Sandfort's (2002) dimensional illustration of a collaborative "continuum" is based on earlier related literature and captures the distinction between collaboration and other relational forms (Austin 2000; Mattessich and Monsey 1992). In this model, shown here in figure 1.1, the right-hand side of the continuum describes the highest level of service integration and least autonomous relationships, while the left side describes relationships where the joint action is less central to organizational mission.

Cross-Sectoral Collaboration

Efforts have also been made to define the unique elements of "public–private" partnership or cross-sectoral collaboration, whether between government and businesses or with the voluntary sector. Fosler (2002, 19) observes that collaborators across the sectors aspire to be partners rather than simply contractors or recipients of government funding: "Collaboration generally involves a higher degree of mutual planning and management among peers; the conscious alignment of goals, strategies, agendas, resources and activities; an equitable commitment of investment and capacities; and the sharing of risks, liabilities and benefits. . . . Collaboration, therefore, suggests something less than authoritative coordination and something more than tacit cooperation."

Other scholars caution that public–private partnerships are best viewed as a closely related form of cooperation that is not necessarily collaborative

Figure 1.1 Continuum of Collaborative Service Arrangements

Cooperation   Coordination   Collaboration   Service integration

Source: Selden, Sowa, and Sandfort (2002).

by nature (Peters 1998). Public–private partnerships that are created by statutory authority or are dependent on public resources may lack the essential ingredients of shared decision making and institutional autonomy (Gazley 2008a). Much of this confusion over terminology stems from a lack of a consistent definition for the intersectoral relationships broadly defined as "public–private partnerships" (Becker 2001; Kooiman 1993; Pierre 1998; Stephenson 1991). Some definitions are conceptual or anecdotal, and few have been tested empirically. These limitations notwithstanding, public–private partnerships are understood to involve long-term partnership relationships in which organizations can bargain on their own behalf, and to which each organization makes material or symbolic contributions. All organizations share responsibility for the outcomes, and expectations may include a synergistic effect or greater gain than could be achieved through individual action (Kooiman 2000; Kouwenhoven 1993; Peters 1998).

Collaboration as a Multidimensional and Multitheoretical Construct

Many of these definitions of interorganizational or cross-sectoral collaboration hint at its contingent, multidimensional nature. At present, we see widespread conceptual and empirical efforts from a variety of perspectives and disciplines to explain various dimensions of collaborative activity. These efforts have grown increasingly integrative in nature as scholars from many fields and theoretical perspectives have attempted to identify the more or less cooperative and competitive dynamics that define intersectoral relations (Gazley 2008b). Many of these research efforts are aimed at helping public managers and policymakers understand the most useful or important elements of partnerships—the "glue binding them together" (Gazley 2008a, 150).

Potentially important collaborative features include structural and motivational dimensions (Thomson and Perry 2006), the nature of shared goals, the degree of risk or reward, and the degree of involvement (Becker 2001). The extent of interpersonal trust, shared norms, the quality and amount of shared resources, and the presence of formal agreements have also been examined as factors in the formation of partnerships that also influence their structure and outcomes (Becker and Patterson 2005; Chaserant 2003; Gazley 2008a; Huxham 2003; Isett and Provan 2005; Kooiman 2000; Thomson and Perry 2006; Vangen and Huxham 2003).

The Goals and Outcomes of Interorganizational Collaboration

The literature on collaboration is often celebratory and only rarely cautious (Berry et al. 2004). In their review of the scholarship on public–nonprofit partnerships, Gazley and Brudney (2007) observe that much of the literature establishes collaboration as a goal in itself rather than as a set of relationships that offer both risks and rewards. Studies of collaborative outcomes are difficult to summarize, given the normative cast of much of the scholarship, and wide variation in theoretical approaches, sampling frames, and methodological rigor. Generally, the potential benefits of interorganizational cooperation include achievements in both organizational effectiveness and efficiency, such as the ability to buffer external uncertainties, share risks, achieve competitive advantages, generate cost savings, improve organizational learning, and produce higher-quality services. Intersectoral alliances also have the potential to achieve greater public accountability by better meeting public expectations for results (Foster and Meinhard 2002a, 2002b; Gazley and Brudney 2007; Grønbjerg 1993; Huxham 1996; Linden 2002; Mulroy and Shay 1997; Provan and Milward 1995; Rapp and Whitfield 1999; Snavely and Tracy 2000).

We commenced this chapter with some examples to illustrate the many ways in which the greater complexity of societal problems, the blurring of intersectoral boundaries, and the organic nature of networked relationships place greater expectations on public managers to collaborate among themselves and across sectoral boundaries. Nonetheless, the empirical research on collaborative partnerships still suggests the need for caution in approaching partnerships, and great expertise in managing them. Little research has been conducted on partnership failure. Although environmental and institutional conditions vary widely, along with the potential benefits, the scholarship also identifies the potential for "mission drift, the possible loss of institutional autonomy or public accountability, cooptation of actors, greater financial instability, greater difficulty in evaluating results, and the expenditure of considerable institutional time and resources in supporting collaborative activities" (Gazley and Brudney 2007, 392; also see Ferris 1993; Gray 2003; Grønbjerg 1990; Shaw 2003).

Theories on Collaboration and Strategic Decision Making across Sectors

The principal influences on partnership formation—statutory, financial, and relational—correspond to the principal theoretical lenses through which collaborative activity has been viewed, as an organizational form emerging from political, economic, organizational, and interpersonal factors. Theories of collaboration have been built especially on explanations of strategic decision making within organizations; less scholarship has been devoted to the human element in collaborative decisions (Gazley 2008b).

Resource dependence theories have been especially prominent, with their ability to explain how a need to increase resources or reduce competition drives an organization's strategic decision to ally with another (Gazley and Brudney 2007; Grønbjerg 1993; Guo and Acar 2005; Pfeffer and Salancik 1978). DeHoog (1984) and Stiles (2001) also observe that it is possible for collaborative partners to cooperate and compete for resources at the same time. These cooperative and competitive intents should not be viewed as opposing options or motivations but rather as two related, coexisting elements in a larger group of strategic motivations. These partnerships, formed and sustained in a highly competitive environment, are more likely to disband once the desired objective has been achieved.

Exchange and transaction cost theories have also helped to explain the organizational efficiencies of collaboration as an activity that can reduce the time and effort needed for interorganizational negotiation (Saidel 1994; Williamson 1996). These theories can help to explain how the relative difficulty of doing business with another service unit, organization, or sector can drive managerial decisions (Willer 1999). Those scholars who have tested these theories cross-sectorally suggest that exchanges between different sectors may not achieve balanced outcomes for both partners, may be harder to accomplish, and may be less desirable (Gazley and Brudney 2007; Grønbjerg 1993; Williamson 1996). Public managers, therefore, may find themselves caught between two rather opposing forces: the pressure to outsource to cut costs, and the desire to accomplish this new transactional form as efficiently as possible. In the context of intersectoral relations, one result might be less interest (from either sector) in forms of exchange that require a great investment of staff time or resources, including the more involved forms of collaborative activity like joint case coordination. This perspective on efficient intersectoral relations may explain why many governments rely heavily on managed competition to accomplish their privatization goals; by limiting the number of bidders and their expectations regarding service quality, public managers can also control the transaction costs tied to finding and managing indirect service providers.

Antecedents to Collaboration

The internal and external conditions that may affect the formation of collaborative relationships are not yet entirely understood. When the existing scholarship includes both private- and public-sector research, the larger body of work suggests the influence of a number of institutional and interpersonal factors related to preexisting relationships or institutional capacities of various kinds, including political support and resources, organizational size, stability, and fiscal health (Agranoff and McGuire 1998; Foster and Meinhard 2002b; Gazley 2008a; Gazley and Brudney 2007; Greene 2002; O'Toole and Meier 2004b; Vigoda-Gadot 2003; Whitaker and Day 2001). The public management literature already recognizes the importance of strong managerial capacity when implementing indirect government (Kettl 1988a; Rainey 1997). Alternatively, other research suggests that collaborative activities can also represent a form of load shedding and that partnerships can be driven by financial need (Boyne 1998; Brudney et al. 2005). In other words, both the "push" of financial need and the "pull" of capacity can influence both the formation of partnerships and their subsequent nature.

Managing Collaborative Networks

Although not all collaborative relationships occur within multiactor networks, the literature on collaborative public management has been substantially strengthened by studies of such networks (Alter and Hage 1993; Goldsmith and Eggers 2004). Collaborative public management in networked settings has both vertical and horizontal dimensions, involving an array of public and private actors. A network manager may be involved simultaneously in managing across governmental boundaries, across organizational and sectoral boundaries, and/or through formal contractual obligations. In some cases, management takes place in highly formalized and lasting arrangements such as a network either encouraged (Schneider et al. 2003) or prescribed (O'Toole 1996; Radin et al. 1996) by law. In others, formal collaborative ties form within specific policy areas. Informal, emergent, and short-term networks are also common (Drabek and McEntire 2002).

Many different types of collaborative structures are used in public management. One type of "interorganizational innovation" identified by Mandell and Steelman (2003) is intermittent coordination, in which interaction is relatively low and commitment is at arm's length. A second type of collaborative arrangement is a temporary task force, which is established to work on a specific and limited purpose, and disbands when that purpose is accomplished. Similar to intermittent coordination, resource sharing is usually limited in scope. A third type of collaborative structure is permanent and/or regular coordination. Resource exchange is more extensive than the first two arrangements, but the risk is minimal.

The most tightly intermingled collaborative structures identified by Mandell and Steelman (2003) are coalitions and networks. Similar in structure, each involves interdependent and strategic actions, but the purposes of a coalition "are narrow in scope and all actions occur within the participant organizations themselves or involve the sequential or simultaneous activity of the participant organizations," whereas a network "takes on broad tasks that reach beyond the simultaneous actions of independently operating organizations" (Mandell and Steelman 2003, 204). Coalitions disband after the task is completed or the problem is solved, but networks have a long, even indefinite life span because the problems addressed by the network are either long term or become redefined as the network evolves. In general, a network is a structure involving multiple nodes—agencies and organizations—with multiple linkages. A public management network includes agencies involved in a public policymaking and administrative structure through which public goods and services are planned, designed, produced, and delivered (and any or all of the activities) (McGuire 2003).

Not all network structures are alike. Agranoff's (2007) study of fourteen networks in various policy areas delineates four different types of networks in terms of the scope of activities undertaken within the network. Informational networks involve multiple stakeholders that come together for the sole purposes of exchanging information and exploring possible solutions to a problem or set of problems. Any action that is taken occurs within the member agencies' home organizations. Developmental networks involve information exchange combined with education that enhances the ability of the member organizations to implement solutions within the individual organization. Outreach networks not only exchange information and improve the administrative capacity of the network members, but they also develop programming strategies for clients that are implemented elsewhere, usually by the partner organizations. The most extensive type of network is an action network. Unlike the other three network types, action networks engage in collective action by formally adopting network-level courses of action and often delivering services. Milward and Provan (2006) also describe four network types based on the purpose of the arrangement: service-implementation networks, information-diffusion networks, problem-solving networks, and community-capacity-building networks.

Clearly, there is no one best way to organize for collaboration, and public managers need to give careful consideration to the decisions associated with organizing collaborative activities (Imperial 2005). Smaller, flatter structures such as networks may be best in one situation, whereas a simple partnership between two actors may be best in another. Instead of a self-governed network, the presence of a lead organization, acting as system controller or facilitator, is often a critical element of network management (Milward and Provan 2006). Thus, a merging of hierarchy and collaborative networks is common. As Moynihan (2005a) shows, responses to a human-made disaster can take place through networks governed by command-and-control procedures. His study of the outbreak of Exotic Newcastle Disease in California describes the formation and management of a collaborative task force assigned with limiting the spread of the disease within the context of a top-down incident command system. The emergency response network was coordinated hierarchically, suggesting the existence of a "hierarchical network" (Moynihan 2005b).

Collaborative structures also take on features commonly associated with formalized agencies. Bardach (1998, 21) observes that "interorganizational collaborative capacity is very much like an organization in its own right." Collaborative organizations are "organizations composed of other organizations" that perform a variety of more traditional functions by institutionalizing rules, procedures, and processes into a coordinating organizational structure (Imperial 2005, 299). Collaborative partnerships have a great deal in common with conventional organizations, including a concern with routines, roles, norms, values, and a culture. Thacher's case study of a national effort designed to forge partnerships between police departments and community development corporations revealed that partnerships became "traces of a new organization in the space between those that already existed" that more accurately resembled inchoate hierarchies than purely networked collaborative arrangements (2004, 116). Managers thus must be cognizant of the types of collaborative structures they are attempting to manage or manage in (Milward and Provan 2006, 6).

THE CONTRIBUTION OF THIS BOOK

Research on collaborative public management offers a set of findings marked by rapid progress and a continuing focus on knowledge generation. Although collaborative management has been occurring for quite some time, the amount of empirical research on it has increased significantly over the past decade. Overall, there is a general understanding that there is still much to learn about it.

This book contributes to our knowledge of and theory development for collaborative public management by offering analyses and empirical research from some of the field's top thinkers. Many surprising findings and common themes run throughout the chapters to come, but perhaps the most surprising theme is that of the paradoxes inherent in collabora-tive public management. A paradox, of course, is a seemingly contradic-tory statement that may nonetheless be true.

These paradoxes of collaborative public management epitomize how challenging a time it is to be a public manager. Many public managers are both unitary leaders of unitary organizations *and* work with other organi-zations and with the public through networks.[1] As such, public managers must work with both autonomy and interdependence, and they must be both authoritative and participative. These paradoxes yield tensions, which, coupled with the challenges of working with a variety of organizations and with a diverse public, yield the ultimate public management paradox: Collaborative public management may bring conflict, particularly in its most common form, networked public management. Conflict within net-works is not inevitable, yet it is predictable if it is not managed.

This chapter has set the stage for the rest of the book by providing a brief review of the most salient literature and foreshadowing some of the surprising findings and questions raised by our authors. The chapters in part I focus on why public managers collaborate. The chapters in part II analyze how public managers collaborate. The chapters in part III take a hard look at how and why public managers get others to collaborate. Fi-nally, the concluding chapter examines the common themes, surprising findings, and paradoxes that run throughout this book, raising intriguing questions for future research in collaborative public management. Taken as a whole, the chapters in this book push us to rethink what we know about collaborative public management.

NOTE

1. As O'Toole (1997, 45) explains, "Networks are structures of interdependence involving multiple organizations or parts thereof, where one unit is not merely the formal subordinate of the others in some larger hierarchical arrangement. Networks exhibit some structural stability but extend beyond formally established linkages and policy-legitimated ties. . . . The institutional glue congealing net-worked ties may include authority bonds, exchange relations, and coalitions based on common interest, all within a single multi-unit structure."

Part I

WHY PUBLIC MANAGERS COLLABORATE

When the city of Menlo Park, California, adopted a collaborative budgeting process in 2006–7, city officials ended up working with 225 residents to try to figure out a way to allocate scarce resources. Why did they not just do it themselves? Why do public managers collaborate? Is it public relations? Is it because they are forced to do so? Is it to lessen the impact of budget shortfalls? Is it to make better decisions?

Why public managers collaborate and the challenges that ensue from that collaboration are the subjects of the chapters in part I. Each chapter attacks the issue from a very different vantage point. In chapter 2, Mary Tschirhart, Alejandro Amezcua, and Alison Anker lead off by examining why individuals and agencies share. They suggest that it is the specific activity of resource sharing that is at the root of some of the challenges encountered by agencies attempting to collaborate, and at the core of collaborations in which partners achieve outcomes beyond the ability of any partner to achieve alone. It is the combining of resources, not simply their exchange, that may result in synergy.

In chapter 3, Rachel Fleishman studies estuary partnerships and reveals her latest findings. Asking why organizations participate in networks, she finds that the importance of shared goals and advocacy motivations appears again and again in her study of nonprofit environmental organizations, indicating that partnerships provide a unique platform from which organizations can leverage resources to achieve common goals. Other reasons to collaborate cited in her research include access to informational, financial, and technical resources.

In chapter 4, Elizabeth Graddy and Bin Chen explore the consequences of partner selection on collaborative effectiveness in the social service agencies in the Family Preservation Program administered by the Los Angeles County Department of Children and Family Services. They analyze how the motivations involved in forming partnerships affect the perceived effectiveness of the resulting relationships. They develop a theoretical connection between partner selection and partnership effectiveness, and they then translate their findings into suggestions for improving collaborative public partnerships.

In chapter 5, Michael McGuire shares his research on collaborative activity in local emergency management. Evidence from his analysis shows that a professional county-level emergency management agency collaborates in an increasingly complex administrative environment. Both better training and a less-fragmented, more-focused organizational structure are associated with collaborative activity. As the level of training in an agency increases, so too does the level of collaborative activity. Similarly, if the organizational structure of an agency is based in first response capabilities and is responsible for duties beyond emergency management, the level of collaborative activity is lower than for agencies that do not have these characteristics. A new professionalism in the emergency management field thus appears to be linked to a more highly collaborative type of management. The practical and theoretical implications of this study for our understanding of collaborative public management are explored.

In chapter 6, Alissa Hicklin, Laurence O'Toole, Kenneth Meier, and Scott Robinson examine voluntary collaborative public management in the context of school districts managing unexpected influxes of high-need students on short notice. They find that organizational capacity clearly makes a difference in the ability to develop collaboration in multiple directions. The size of the unexpected shock to the organizational system also matters—positively—as a stimulus or prod toward the development of collaboration. The authors find that collaboration is less a function of stable relationships, and thus structural ties, and more a product of the manager's individual-level decisions. Thus, the presence of a manager who chooses to engage in networking during normal times—a truly collaborative public manager—contributes to how these organizations respond.

When examined as a whole, the five chapters in part I offer considerable insights for policymakers, public managers, and concerned citizens interested in improving collaborative public management.

Chapter 2

Resource Sharing: How Resource Attributes Influence Sharing System Choices

Mary Tschirhart, Alejandro Amezcua, and Alison Anker

Interorganizational collaborations are being promoted as a way to address complex social problems and achieve competitive advantages. But research studies find that collaborating can be a frustrating and disappointing experience or even be a partnership only on paper (Huxham and Vangen 2000; Lasker, Weiss, and Miller 2001). The management literature is awash with models attempting to define and describe collaboration and empirically identify antecedents and outcomes. The diversity in conceptualizations of collaboration and choice and in the measurement of study variables makes it difficult to compare empirical research findings and draw strong conclusions about how to foster and maintain effective collaborations.

To help provide some coherence to the unwieldy and growing literature, we focus on one common activity in collaborations—resource sharing—which, for some researchers (e.g., Kanter 1994), is one of collaboration's defining features. "Shared resources" is one of ten broad categories that Thomson (2001) used to cluster phrases found in definitions of collaboration from the public management literature. We suggest that the specific activity of resource sharing is at the root of some of the challenges encountered by agencies attempting to collaborate, and is at the core of collaborations in which partners achieve outcomes beyond the ability of any one partner. It is the combining of resources, not simply their exchange, that may result in synergy. By homing in on resource sharing, we hope to add clarity and depth to broad-ranging treatments of collaboration.

RESOURCE SHARING AS DISTINGUISHED FROM RESOURCE EXCHANGE

Although reciprocity or, more narrowly, resource *exchange* is a common feature of many models of collective action (e.g., Ostrom 1990), resource *sharing*, in which the same resources are used by collaboration partners, has received less specific attention. Our concern in this chapter is not with simple calculations of resource inputs and outputs as a way to show benefits for collaboration members—in other words, "I give and I get." Instead, we focus on the dynamics of the use of the same resource by more than one collaboration member—or "I share." For resource sharing to occur, a necessary and sufficient condition is that the resource is accessible for use by more than one partner in the collaboration, at least for a limited period of time. Use may be simultaneous or sequential, but no one member of the resource-sharing system owns the resource and/ or has independent control of its accessibility to others. Members of the system are seen as independent actors, who voluntarily accept and enter into resource-sharing arrangements.

Collaboration managers have options. They may seek to acquire a desired resource (obtain it by acquiring the unit in which the resource resides), trade for it (purchase or barter for it), or gain use of it through a sharing arrangement. The dynamics of collaborations may involve exchanging some resources and sharing others, and that sharing may affect and be affected by the dynamics of exchanging. In other words, the sharing of some resources may be a precursor, a side effect, or a desired consequence of the exchange of other resources. Collaborations involve packages of arrangements, any number of which may be specific to the sharing of a resource. Like resource exchanges (Levine and White 1961), we can think of resource-sharing arrangements as being made up of (1) the resource used; (2) the parties in the arrangement, that is, members of the sharing system; and (3) the agreement underlying the arrangement, that is, the resource-sharing norms, rules, and procedures. Focusing on resource sharing complements other work that delves deeply into key aspects of collaboration, such as member composition (e.g., Huxham and Vangen 2000), network structure (e.g., Provan and Milward 1995), and trust (e.g., Inkpen and Currall 2004). In this chapter, we provide a categorization scheme for differentiating among types of resources and systems of resource sharing, and we offer a set of propositions.

THE NATURE OF SHARED RESOURCES

In this section, we discuss the attributes of resources that we will link to types of sharing systems later in the chapter. Looking at the attributes of resources is nothing new. Economists have long differentiated among types of goods according to their substitutability, ease of monitoring use, and lumpiness and nature as rival goods. Resource dependence theory reminds us that the characteristics of resources, such as predictability and scarcity, affect the intensity and depth of dependencies. The literature on common-pool resources speaks to dimensions of resources that affect their depletion and renewal. We draw from these and other theoretical bases to examine resource attributes within the context of resource sharing.

We focus on four attributes of resources—functionality, importance, tangibility, and availability—any or all of which may interact. The more functional a resource is perceived to be, for example, the more important it may be to an organization. The more available it is perceived to be, the less it may be treated as a strategically important resource to monitor and manage with care. The more tangible the resource is perceived to be, the more the extent of its availability may be calculable by a potential sharer. We discuss each attribute separately, but a full model treats them as a dynamic set. The following subsections present the characteristics of the resource attributes and questions about them that a collaboration manager might consider in evaluating resource-sharing opportunities.

Functionality

Are there ways that my agency can use a resource that is diminished, maintained, or increased if others are also using it? The functionality of a resource is its usefulness. In considering the functionality of a resource in a sharing arrangement, one can look at the amount of the resource usable at any one time to meet demand and the existence of alternative uses for the same resource, both among the sharers and by one sharer. For example, a shared library among co-located organizations may serve a set of functions for users (e.g., a quiet place for writing, a storehouse of information for staff, a distribution center for client education, a repository for software, and a signal of legitimacy). In considering functionality, we can determine whether it is unaffected by sharing, increased by sharing, or decreased by sharing. A library room may reduce functionality for a user who needs a quiet place for writing when it is being used for a client education event. As a signal of legitimacy, the library's functionality may grow with increased sharing. Functionality may be unaffected by the sharing of software. An organization can make the same use of software stored on a library server no matter whether others are simultaneously using it.

There are special issues related to the sharing of strategic resources, that is, those that offer sustainable, competitive advantage to their holder. A prerequisite for a resource to be strategic is that it has imperfect mobility and imitability (Chi 1994). It can move to some extent and it can be duplicated, but with causal ambiguity. Some resources are perfectly immobile. They cannot move from one organization to another, and thus cannot be shared (e.g., a manager or physician with a contract that prevents his hiring or sharing by competitors, or an asset that has no functionality for other users, such as a highly specialized software program). Resources have causal ambiguity to the extent that it is unclear exactly what makes them useful and how to reproduce their functionality. Some tacit knowledge, for example, cannot be fully articulated and shared (Polanyi 1967). A particularly effective technique for dealing with challenging clients may be understood to be more of an art than a science. It may not be easy to explain what the technique is and how to use it. This type of resource is a less likely candidate for resource sharing than one that is more concrete in the understanding of how it can be used, such as a piece of physical equipment or a referral list.

Importance

Is the value to my agency of a resource diminished, maintained, or increased if others are sharing it? By the importance of a resource, we mean an organization's need for a resource to operate and achieve its organizational objectives. Unless something has at least some value, it cannot be considered to be a resource. A resource needed to deliver core programs and services is more important than a resource that can be forgone or substituted without ill effect on the program and service delivery. Importance may or may not be the same for all users of a shared resource. For example, co-located agencies may share parking areas, office equipment, signage, advertising, and other resources. The importance of the parking space resource to an agency with numerous visitors is likely to be greater than the importance placed on the parking spaces by an agency with few visitors. Valuations of resources provided and gained are part of cost/benefit calculations that influence willingness to collaborate (Alter and Hage 1993). No matter the importance of a resource, there may be benefits as well as drawbacks to sharing it, just as there are for exchanging one resource for another.

A possible consequence of resource sharing is that resource importance stays the same (remains low or high) or increases or decreases in value. The benefits and drawbacks of sharing a resource are affected by whether the resource is transformed through the sharing process. Its original value, before sharing, may not match its value once shared. Resources, once pooled, may create valuable synergy. For example, an augmentable database may gain value as each user adds more data. The sharing of expertise may result in the creation of new ideas and understanding. However, the sharing of a resource may result in a loss in the resource's value—when, for example, the sharing of a client base or technology gives other service providers a competitive advantage or reduces an agency's ability to distinguish itself from other providers. Sharing donor lists may result in donor fatigue and in fewer gifts due to the more numerous solicitations.

As part of the resource-sharing process, other resources beside the one shared may be obtained or lost. In calculating the importance of a shared resource, the importance of these secondary resources may be relevant. One resource that may emerge from sharing other resources is "collaborative know-how" (Simonin 1997; Boddy, MacBeth, and Wagner 2000; Huxham 1996). For example, organizations may gain knowledge about other members of the sharing system and develop a conflict resolution system that can be helpful to them in future collaborations. They may also develop skills in negotiation and cooperation. In addition, through participation in a sharing system, members may gain knowledge about technologies and develop contacts that can be used to improve their own plans and operations. They also may gain visibility and credibility with members that can be leveraged. Conversely, sharing resources may result in inadvertent leaks of information that can harm the competitive position of an organization.

Tangibility

Can my agency determine if, when, and how others are using a shared resource? The tangibility of a resource is its degree of physical existence. Resources that are easily measured and divided have high tangibility, for example, financial assets in a shared account, cars in a shared fleet, and books in a shared library distribution system. We might also think of work hours of shared volunteers and staff, storage space on a shared computer server, and names contributed to a shared donor or client prospect list as having a fair degree of tangibility—they can be counted. More amorphous are such shared resources as tacit knowledge and client information for integrated service systems. In thinking about what their agency is bring-ing to a collaborative project and what they are getting from it, managers may find it easier to focus on the tangible resources that can be quanti-fied. In addition, in comparing their use of resources with other agencies' use, it may be easier to think of resources that can only be used sequen-tially rather than simultaneously, and whose flow among users can be monitored. Still, intangible resources may be shared, even if it is more difficult for collaboration managers to see them.

Availability

If my agency shares a resource, are we likely to get more, the same, or less of it than if my agency does not share it? It is easy to find references to the availability and need for resources in the literature on collabora-tion, in particular in the work of Alter and Hage (1993) and Gray (1989). Often the references are vague, with little discussion of the nature of a resource or how it is secured and used. However, some scholars have emphasized the environment and norms surrounding resource exchange as a key antecedent, process, and/or outcome of collaboration. For ex-ample, Adamek and Lavin (1975) argue that resource munificence and norms of reciprocity, not resource scarcity, influence organizations to develop partnerships. Once developed, collaboration may be enhanced by the presence of adequate resources (Provan and Milward 1995). However, others (e.g., Levine and White 1961; Pfeffer and Salancik 1978) argue that resource scarcity motivates organizations to formalize their interactions and foster interdependencies in order to obtain needed resources. In this view, the focus is on the demand for scarce resources as a driver for coop-erative and collective behaviors.

Shared resources may be scarce or munificent, and depletion may or may not be possible. Sharable goods are those that have at least some ex-cess capacity (Benkler 2004). They can be utilized by more than one agent either simultaneously or sequentially. Benkler suggests that the most shar-able resources are those that are technically "lumpy" and "midgrained." By lumpy, he means that their functionality comes in discrete packages cre-ating slack; the resource is available whether or not it is needed. For re-sources whose value decays over time, such as perishable food in a food bank, capacity can be wasted through lack of use. If a resource is not de-pleted through use, and its value does not decay over time, it can be shared or remain unused in "storage" with no affect on its long-term availability.

The notion of granularity captures the distribution of the resource among owners who could choose to share it along with the shape of the demand for the functionality of the resource and the nature of the functionality. A "large-grained" resource is only available by aggregating demand for it. For example, it may be too expensive for an individual user to purchase alone, like a grain mill jointly owned by members of a cooperative. Without collective action, the resource is unavailable. A "midgrained" resource has individual owners who cannot use all the capacity of the resource, such as an academic paper, and therefore can share it with others with no loss to themselves. A "fine-grained" resource has individual owners who can buy just enough of the resource to meet their personal needs. Sharing fine-grained resources is a sacrifice; the owner forfeits the resource to make it available to others.

THE RELATIONSHIP OF RESOURCE ATTRIBUTES WITH SHARING SYSTEMS

There are numerous options for resource-sharing arrangements. The benefits and drawbacks of participation in a sharing system are influenced by design and implementation choices. Here we focus on two big questions for collaboration managers considering developing or participating in resource-sharing systems. First, what are the likely procedures, rules, and norms for sharing? And second, how inclusive is membership in a sustainable sharing system likely to be? Our answers are contingent on resource type. In thinking about options for designing and implementing sharing arrangements, we consider the possible benefits and drawbacks to members. Our fundamental argument is that the ability to maximize benefits while minimizing drawbacks partially depends on resource functionality, importance, tangibility, and availability. We have discussed the benefits of a sharing system indirectly in our discussion of resource attributes. Sharers may have access to more or less important and functional resources that may be more or less otherwise obtainable. The combination of resources can create synergies unachievable by organizations acting alone. The next paragraph elaborates potential drawbacks.

Potential drawbacks for resource sharers include (1) those related to coordination costs and loss of autonomy, which draws our attention to procedures, rules, and norms; and (2) those related to problems with other sharers, drawing our attention to the inclusiveness of membership and power distribution among the participants in the sharing system. The following are the potential drawbacks for participants in a partnership: "diversion of time and resources from their other priorities and obligations; reduced interdependence in making decisions about their own activities; a loss of competitive advantage in obtaining funding or providing services;

insufficient influence in the partnership's activities; conflict between their own work and the partnership's work; negative exposure due to association with other partners or the partnership; frustration and aggravation with the collaborative process; and insufficient credit for their contributions to the partnership" (Lasker, Weiss, and Miller 2001, 191). Writing specifically about resource sharing, Hughes (2001) suggests that obstacles include concerns about the quality of resources provided by another organization (e.g., likely performance of shared workers), equity issues involving differences in costs of the pooled resources (e.g., differences in the pay scales of shared workers and differences in the costs of utilizing shared equipment due to physical location), and commitment issues (e.g., willingness and ability to share).

A number of propositions—summarized in table 2.1—present the arrangements we are likely to find depending on the attributes of the resources that collaboration managers wish to exchange. These propositions assume that the managers are acting strategically, maximizing benefits and minimizing drawbacks. The resources are not being shared unknowingly as an unintended consequence of other activity. We are focusing on conscious decisions to develop or participate in a resource-sharing arrangement. First we focus on the coordination mechanisms in use, and then we turn to the exclusivity of membership in the system.

We can categorize resource-sharing arrangements according to the degree of coordination. Participants' assessments of likely risks and payoffs can influence their willingness to invest in and be subject to coordination and control mechanisms. Arrangements with higher coordination are likely to be those that impart more risk to participating organizations, or offer more potential value. Participants are more likely to be willing to sacrifice autonomy to reduce significant risk and enhance positive outcomes from sharing. Arrangements with low coordination may rely on general norms of reciprocity, and social pressures embedded in larger social network relations to ensure that sharing is done appropriately. When other sharers' behaviors have little effect on the participant's use of a shared resource and the resource has little importance, the participant is unlikely to devote much time or effort to encouraging sharing or restricting other sharers from gaining the greatest rewards from the sharing arrangement. The costs of high coordination outweigh the benefits.

The importance of a shared resource, the availability of alternatives, and the ability to compel provision of the resource affects an organization's dependence on a resource-sharing arrangement and, thus, its willingness to invest in the arrangement's design and maintenance. If an organization needs a resource to continue operating, and can only get it through

Table 2.1 Propositions on Links of Attributes to a Resource-Sharing System

Resource Attribute	Sharing System Characteristic
Functionality higher with sharing	High participation pressure, loose control over process, high monitoring, norm of equity or equality, inclusive system
Functionality lower with sharing	Tight control over process or high trust, high monitoring of process and participation, norm of equity or equality, exclusive system
Functionality same with sharing	Low trust importance, low control and monitoring of process and participation, norm of use as needed, inclusive system
Importance increases with sharing	Loose control over process, strong participation pressure, high monitoring of members, norm of equity or equality, inclusive
Importance decreases with sharing	Tight control over process or high trust, high monitoring of process and participation, norm of equity or equality, exclusive
Importance remains low with sharing	Low trust importance, low control and monitoring of process and participation, norm of use as needed, inclusive
Importance remains high with sharing	Low trust importance, loose control over sharing process, medium monitoring of participation, inclusive
Resource tangibility is high	Reliance on formal rules and procedures for sharing process, more monitoring of resource than member, inclusive system
Resource tangibility is low	Reliance on trust rather than formal rules and procedures, more monitoring of member than resource, exclusive system
Depletable, or resource scarce	Tight control over process or high trust, high monitoring of process and participation, norm of equity or equality, exclusive
Nondepletable, or resource munificent	Low trust importance, low control and monitoring of process and participation, norm of use as needed, inclusive
Disagreement on attributes	System less likely to be sustainable, likely to be more exclusive membership in eventual system

resource sharing, then the dependence is high and efforts to maintain the flow of the resource will be high (Levine and White 1961; Pfeffer and Salancik 1978). However, if the organization can compel, pressure, or force sharing of the resource, then the actual dependence on other sharers is less. For example, nonprofits may be able to compel governments to share certain types of information and provide equal access to public spaces. Nonprofits wishing to share these resources may be able to do so easily with little investment of their own in establishing coordination structures and norms.

Formal rules, as well as informal norms, can influence the behaviors of participants in a resource-sharing arrangement. The collaboration literature (including work on partnerships and alliances) offers numerous discussions of trust and contracts as control mechanisms. Gulati (1995a), for example, examines how the two mechanisms function in interaction. We propose that sharing systems are most likely to rely heavily on contractual controls or trust for resources that are scarce, have high importance, and whose functionality and value can be damaged by misuse or overuse.

The more intangible the resource, the more difficult it is to control and measure its input and use. Tangible resources may be easily monitored to ensure that no ill effects from sharing occur to their functionality, value, or supply. For intangible resources, sharing arrangements may focus more on monitoring participants' behaviors than the resources themselves. Sharing systems involving an intangible resource are also more likely to rely on trust than on formal control systems, due to the difficulty in constructing and implementing controls.

Trust among participants is frequently mentioned as an important requirement for effective collaborations. We propose that the degree of trust needed will vary by resource type. The ability of some participants to take advantage of others in a sharing system is much less if the shared resources are not scarce and are renewable. The less value placed on the shared resources, the less concern participants are likely to have that some participants may gain more from the shared resource pool and contribute less. Building relationships and fostering trust is a challenging and time-consuming task (Lasker, Weiss, and Miller 2001; Waddock 1988). Rather than invest in trust building, participants may prefer to accept that unequal benefits will occur in order to minimize their involvement in the sharing system and reduce participation costs. Knowledge that benefits stay the same or increase with sharing reduces the need for trust or other control structures such as explicit contracts. Though possibilities for opportunistic behavior may still exist, they will result in little direct harm to other users.

The procedural justice literature tells us that participants react nega-tively to perceptions of unfairness (Levinthal 1980). A sharing system is likely to be more sustainable if it is deemed to be fair, thus avoiding mem-ber frustration, sabotage, noncompliance with rules and procedures, dis-trust, and low commitment resulting from perceptions of unfairness. Some systems may establish a rule or norm that participants only take their "fair share" of a resource based on their contributions (equity principle) or that the resources are divided equally. In contrast, some systems may rely on the rule of use based on need, with no effort to prevent some from getting more use than others out of a resource.

A collaborative project may consist of different sharing principles for different types of resources, and the norms, procedures, and rules may change as the collaboration evolves (Jap 2001). Jap argues that the qual-ity of participants' relations with one another is affected by whether equality or equity norms are in place, in interaction with the degree of resource contribution symmetry, divisibility, and mobility (functionality outside the collaboration). Our goal in this chapter is to more simply point out that for some kinds of resources (the less important and scarce ones that are largely unaffected by sharing), participants in a sharing system may have little need or desire for equity or equality sharing principles, or even for monitoring. Participants may be comfortable with the idea that the re-source is free for use.

The previous propositions assume that all members in the resource-sharing arrangement will perceive the resource attributes in the same way. For example, if one collaboration manager participating in the system thinks functionality increases with sharing, the others do as well. How-ever, this may not always be the case. Managers considering resource sharing may wish to use the resources in different ways and this may af-fect how they evaluate each of the attributes. They might also have differ-ing amounts of information on the attributes, which affects their degree of certainty on the attributes. For example, one manager may believe that the resource is scarcer than another or may be less sure about its degree of availability.

In addition to predicting what the overall system will look like based on resource attributes, we can predict what type of system a collaboration manager would see as most desirable based on that manager's perception of the resource attributes. The most powerful participants in the system are most likely to have their preferences implemented. The degree of conflict among the collaboration managers participating in the system is likely to determine the sustainability of the system. If there is a high level of disagreement on what type of system to use, there is likely to be more tensions and satisfaction with the system. With greater heterogeneity in views, compliance with the system's rules and procedures may be reduced, unless the system is tightly controlled.

Sharing systems vary in the degree and type of exclusion of possible participants (Benkler 2004). For example, the Google Web search engine does not exclude users. Partial exclusion may be found in other types of sharing systems; for example, cooperatives may have equipment with capacity limits that are used on a first-come, first-served basis or that allow users in a particular membership category to have priority over others.

For resource holders, perceptions of excess capacity influence their sharing behaviors (Benkler 2004). Organizations are more likely to share slack resources widely than scarce or inadequate resources. There is little risk that they will not have adequate access to or amounts of the resource when it is plentiful. Therefore, we predict that the more munificent the resource, the more likely it will be shared with an inclusive group.

In some cases, the more participants in a sharing system, the greater will be the benefits to the sharers. For example, organizations may join with others in an insurance pool—the more members, the lower the insurance premiums and the greater the coverage. Organizations may also join with others to purchase supplies; the greater the volume of purchases, the better the discounts. There may also be economies in the scale of production that encourage wide use of the products, and thus the desire to bring in more users (Govindarajan and Fisher 1990). When the functionality and importance of a resource increase with use, we are likely to find inclusion in the sharing system.

When considering whether to engage in resource sharing, actors may be influenced by the degree of control they will have over resource allocation and the movement of resources among organizations. The design of the decision-making process may be a more important predictor of participation in a resource-sharing arrangement than the design of structures to facilitate the actual sharing of resources, as Charalambides (1984) found in studying the sharing of services among subunits within organizations. Though a resource may be made available to a wide sharing group, an inner circle of members—typically the core resource providers or those able to compel provision of the resource—may make the decisions about the resource-sharing arrangement and show greater commitment to it (Kanter 1994; Lasker, Weiss, and Miller 2001).

Organizations are embedded in a social network of relationships (Granovetter 1985), and experience in these networks can influence willingness to share with other organizations (Saxton 1997; Gulati 1995a, 1995b). A history of sharing strategically unimportant resources may open the door for more complicated strategic alliances, allowing wider access to other resources. Participation in a sharing network may build the values, norms, trust, and shared identity among members that can then support other types of collaborative behaviors. Reversing the dynamic, a history of successful resource exchanges may build trust and/or enforcement mechanisms that make resource sharing more likely.

The earliest participants in a sharing arrangement may play critical roles in shaping the membership of a sharing system. Through referrals, they may bring in others who are part of their networks. They may also draw on previous relationships and dense network ties to encourage sharing behaviors and curb opportunism (Granovetter 1985; Ahuja 2000). The greater the importance of the shared resources and the problems of opportunism, the more likely we are to see both the careful selection of participants who are known to have desired qualities or can be pressured to exhibit desired behaviors and the greater exclusion of "strangers."

To make a system feasible and sustainable, some exclusion may be necessary (Huxham and Vangen 2000). Even Internet listservs that allow diverse individuals to share their thoughts without specific goals for what outcomes will result from the sharing are likely to remove participants who are disruptive or break ethical standards. Diversity within a sharing group can make it difficult to create shared goals and synergies. Systems for sharing ideas and perspectives among diverse participants to develop and improve services, products, and programs require higher levels of leadership and coordination than such systems for more homogenous groups (Mitchell and Shortell 2000; Lasker, Weiss, and Miller 2001). If resources shared are intangible ideas and perspectives, then there is likely to be at least some partial selection of membership in order to reduce tension and conflict due to differences in attitudes and interests and credibility.

For more tangible resources, a sharing system may rely more heavily on screening inputs to the system than on the individuals who input them. For example, some areas have systems for sharing brochures and other promotional information, for example, a community calendar of events or a shelf or bulletin board for the display of materials. Coordinators of the sharing system may allow anyone to add material as long as it meets certain criteria. Community calendars, therefore, typically, list only events open to the public, of wide public interest, and not commercial in nature. The greater ability to monitor and control tangible resources makes inclusion more likely for the sharing of tangible resources than intangible ones.

In discussing membership in a resource-sharing arrangement, it is important to acknowledge that participants may be unclear or disagree on who are the other participants in the system. Ambiguity in membership may be more common than the general collaboration literature suggests (Huxham and Vangen 2000). In addition, we wish to return to our earlier point that resource sharing may be occurring within a more complex set of resource exchanges. As Huxham and Vangen (2000) explain, collaborations may be part of other collaborations, adding to the complexity and ambiguity of membership structures.

When possible resource sharers do not agree on resource attributes, there is a greater likelihood that they will not be able to agree on what type of system is best for sharing. We expect that they are likely to seek to share resources only with those with similar views in order to increase the likelihood of reaching agreement on the system and conformity to it. Of course, this is independent of any other resource exchange or sharing relationships they may have.

FINAL THOUGHTS

We have provided a set of propositions on one aspect of collaborative relationships. Some of the mixed findings on collaborations may exist because analysts are largely studying the forest rather than the trees. By focusing on the dynamics of resource sharing, we hope to provide useful insights that have practical as well as theoretical value.

If collaboration managers find themselves struggling to develop or sustain a resource-sharing arrangement, we recommend that they consider how much of their difficulty is related to differences of opinion on the attributes of the resource that they are attempting to share. By discussing these differences, they may be able to modify opinions or construct systems that better foster the perceived benefits and reduce the perceived drawbacks for individual members.

In our review of resource sharing, we included examples that some researchers may be reluctant to label as collaborations. An example is situations in which sharing has no effect on the sharer's assessment of the functionality, importance, and availability of the shared resource. The sharing may then be seen to occur as a nonstrategic act, with no or very little direct risk or payoff to the sharer of the resource, and little need or desire for coordination or monitoring of the sharing. However, as implied earlier in the chapter, this type of resource sharing may set the stage for more collaborative acts or be an outcome of previous collaborations, and thus is worthy of discussion and further empirical examination. It also is worthy of attention because it calls into question the predominance in the collaboration literature of building trust and selective collaboration membership. Though perhaps not as grand as other types of interactions that result in synergy, these types of acts do occur and are part of the landscape of resource use and flows among organizations.

A second situation calling for more attention is when organizations directly suffer from sharing a resource. If the functionality, importance, and supply of a resource decrease due to sharing, why share? It seems irrational to do so. Most of the literature on collaboration takes a decidedly rational, strategic perspective. Taken alone without a larger context of connected resource exchanges, this kind of behavior does not easily fit under this umbrella, except perhaps as a consequence of poor information and prediction. Seen as one of many arrangements involving flows of resources, this sharing may make more sense. In addition, collaboration scholars may find it productive to look at this situation through the lens of gift giving or altruism. Another potentially useful lens, unexplored in this chapter, is identity dynamics. It may be that the conception of who is the sharer may be wrong. By taking an expanded view of identity, we may find that collaboration members appearing to lose from sharing actually gain when seen as belonging to a larger group.

Collaboration managers would be wise to look carefully at the attributes of the resources they are sharing as well as those they are exchanging. Accurate views of these attributes can help in judging how much coordination is needed and who should participate in a collaborative project. Most collaboration managers are involved in the use of more than one resource. That does not negate the value of looking at each resource individually. Once each resource is understood, a collaboration manager may determine acceptable trade-offs for systems where the sharing or exchange of one resource is linked to the sharing or exchange of other resources.

Chapter 3

To Participate or Not to Participate? Incentives and Obstacles for Collaboration

Rachel Fleishman

Collaboration is more than a management buzzword. For many government agencies, collaboration has become the primary means of coping with modern problems, such as complexity in the policy process, turbulent environments, dispersion of resources and expertise, and the constant flow of new information. One highly integrated collaborative structure is the "interorganizational network"—a web of organizations that engage in collaborative activities, often bound together by relationships of mutual dependency. Interorganizational networks are becoming increasingly common in policy areas where resources are dispersed and jurisdictions are shared and overlapping, such as health services (Provan and Milward 1995), social services (Selden, Sowa, and Sandfort 2006; Graddy and Chen 2006), environmental policy (Wondelleck and Yaffee 2000), economic development (Agranoff and McGuire 2003a), and emergency management (Waugh and Streib 2006). Many government agencies in these policy areas are simply unable to accomplish their goals unilaterally, either because they do not exercise complete authority over the policy area or because they lack important resources.

This research focuses on one task that faces the manager of an interorganizational network: how to motivate individual organizations to join and/or remain in the network. The purpose of this research is to better understand the motivations and obstacles facing organizations in their decision to join an interorganizational network, as well as participants' decisions to maintain their chosen level of involvement. In a practical sense, these insights are critical. For a collaborative manager, it is essential to understand what motivates different types of organizations to participate in order to "activate" and "mobilize" the right participants at the right time (Agranoff and McGuire 2001). On a more theoretical level, this research advances theories of network structure by observing which factors facilitate or impede the formation of network linkages. It has implications for the stability and longevity of network linkages, which is particularly important in light of evidence linking network stability to performance (Provan and Milward 1995).

The context of this research is watershed management in the United States. It is expected, however, that the lessons may be applied to organizational networks in other countries and focused on other policy areas. Watershed management was chosen because of the diversity of organizational networks and associations working in this area and the rich body of scholarship that describes them (e.g., Wondelleck and Yaffee 2000; Koontz et al. 2004).

The next section reviews theories of organizational participation in interorganizational networks, focusing on resource dependency. Research questions and the methodology follow. Finally, findings from the research are presented and discussed.

ORGANIZATIONAL PARTICIPATION IN NETWORKS

Scharpf (1978, 350) stated that "it is the task of interorganizational policy studies to identify . . . the empirical factors facilitating or impeding necessary interorganizational coordination in actual policy processes." Unfortunately, not enough progress has been made since Scharf made this statement over thirty years ago. Although several different theories have been proposed to explain why organizations participate, there is no consensus on which motivations are most important and under what conditions some may be more salient than others.

Resource Dependency and Exchange

Resource dependency is probably the most well-developed theory of interorganizational partnership. The basic assumption is that individual organizations do not have all the resources they need to achieve their goals and rely on inputs from the environment, which itself consists of a "collection of interacting organizations, groups, and persons" (Van de Ven, Emmett, and Koening 1975, 19). Since every organization is in the same position of dependency, exchange relationships develop. Levine and White

(1961, 588) have defined organizational exchange as "any voluntary activity between two or more organizations which has consequences, actual or anticipated, for the realization of their respective goals or objectives." More than just a way to acquire needed resources, interactions based on exchange are "a stabilizing force in the life space of organizations" (Alter and Hage 1993, 45). Exchange relationships stabilize interorganizational linkages by reducing uncertainty about the future provision of resources (e.g., Galaskiewicz 1985) and by maintaining consistent interaction patterns (Kickert, Klijn, and Koppenjan 1997b).

Most scholars of interorganizational coordination agree that organizations prefer autonomy to dependence (e.g., Rogers and Whetten 1982). In times of scarce resources, however, organizations must balance autonomy with resource needs. To do this, organizations attempt to maximize their power in exchange relationships by avoiding dependence on other organizations and by making others dependent on them (Aldrich 1979). The power of an actor within an interorganizational network is explicitly linked to his or her control over resources (Klijn 1997; Aldrich 1979). Moreover, power relations that develop out of resource dependencies form the basis of a network structure (Benson 1975). This is the conceptual connection between resource dependency and the formation of network linkages. In fact, some researchers have empirically shown that resource interdependencies and complex environments do in fact lead to decentralized, flexible, and informal (or "network-like") structures (for a short description of some studies, see Van de Ven, Emmett, and Koening 1975, 21).

Although resource exchange theory is based on the notion of dependency, even relatively independent organizations may participate in networks to take advantage of available resources. Organizations may actively seek out funds within existing network structures or seek to initiate collaboration to tap into funding sources (Agranoff and McGuire 2003a; Alter and Hage 1993).

Competing Theories

Several other theories have been introduced to explain organizational participation in networks. Although this study focuses on resource dependency, alternatives were considered during data collection and analysis. The citations point to more theoretical depth, but briefly these theories are:

1. *Common purpose:* Organizations form network linkages to achieve similar, compatible, or congruous goals (e.g., Gray 1989; Rogers and Whetten 1982).

2. *Shared beliefs:* A similarity in values and attitudes makes the formation of interorganizational linkages more probable (Aldrich 1979; Alter and Hage 1993) or makes these linkages more stable over time (Van de Ven, Emmett, and Koening 1975). A common "belief system," including norms, values, perceptions, and common worldview, "[provides] the principal 'glue'" to hold together networks of actors (Sabatier 1993, 27).

3. *Political interests:* Organizations sometimes pursue their political interests through networks (Sabatier 1993; Heclo 1978; Kickert, Klijn, and Koppenjan 1997b). Through participation in a policy network, organizations can (1) promote the views or desires of their members or constituency, (2) gain access to political officials or decision processes and/or cultivate political alliances, (3) gain political legitimacy or authority, and (4) promote organizational policies or programs.

4. *Catalytic actors:* Leadership both within the organization and by network leaders or coordinators can be important for the formation of network linkages (Agranoff and McGuire 2001; Kickert and Koppenjan 1997; Bardach 1998).

RESEARCH QUESTIONS

This research examines organizational participation through the lenses of resource exchange and the alternative theories described above. Two strategic decisions were made to narrow the project's scope. First, in the spirit of public policy research, the target population of organizational networks includes only government-sponsored partnerships: partnerships funded by and at least partly administered by a government agency. Second, to be relevant for scholarship on citizen participation and public–private partnerships, the focus was narrowed to a particular type of organizational participant: nonprofit organizations (NPOs). The final research questions are:

1. What factors motivate NPOs to participate in government-sponsored partnerships? What factors limit or impede NPO participation?
2. Is resource exchange theory helpful for understanding NPO participation patterns?
3. What alternative theories may be important for understanding NPO participation patterns?

METHODS

This research was exploratory. The purpose was not to formally test hypotheses but to generate directions and questions for future research. There were a few unique characteristics of this research project. First, information was collected from *both* participants and nonparticipants in the network, reducing a common source of bias. Second, standardized data were collected from multiple networks.[1] Finally, detailed empirical data were collected (if only for a small sample), including a mixture of quantitative and qualitative data, data on different types and levels of participation, and data on both motivations and obstacles facing organizations in their participation decisions.

Research Context: U.S. EPA Estuary Program

The interorganizational networks selected for study are partnerships sponsored by the U.S. Environmental Protection Agency (EPA) National Estuary Program. The primary mission of the Estuary Program is to protect the ecological health of "nationally significant" estuaries through long-term planning and management (EPA National Estuary Program homepage).[2] Established under the 1987 amendments to the Clean Water Act, the Estuary Program sponsors twenty-eight partnerships located on both coasts and the Gulf of Mexico. EPA funding is funneled through a local administering agency, responsible for managing all partnership activities. These administrative units are not uniform between partnerships and include state environmental agencies, nonprofits, universities, and local/regional government agencies.

Typical participants in the estuary partnerships include local and state government agencies and elected officials; individual citizens, and NPOs representing environmental, regional planning, recreational, agricultural, and business interests. Most estuary partnerships utilize a board and advisory committee structure that ensures broad participation. In addition, many partnerships have committee bylaws requiring representation from certain interests—such as conservation or regional planning. For any *particular* nongovernment organization, however, participation is voluntary.

The main activities of estuary partnerships include water-quality monitoring and research, restoration projects, education programs, and public awareness. Partnership activities are governed by each estuary partnership's Comprehensive Conservation and Management Plan, a master plan developed collaboratively over three to eight years and signed by the governor. Small grants are dispersed (often to NPOs) for projects related to the implementation of this plan.

Sampling and Data Collection

Four estuary partnerships (of twenty-eight) were selected based on the following criteria: a current website, an online membership list (i.e., a list of participating or affiliated organizations), and at least ten NPO participants.[3] For each partnership, these online membership lists furnished the preliminary set of survey respondents. Added to this were nonprofit environmental organizations located in the partnership's focus area (called the "study area") but not listed as members.[4]

Data collection included a small set of interviews and an Internet survey. Four telephone interviews with executive directors of participating NPOs, as well as e-mail interviews with leaders of the estuary partnerships, helped in the development of the Internet survey. This survey was sent a total of 140 potential respondents, who were generally executive directors, presidents, or managers of programs/projects related to water quality. Branching of the survey allowed respondents to self-select as participants or nonparticipants depending on their response to the following question: "Over the past year, has your organization participated in the [partnership name] in any way?"

Key survey questions are shown in the appendix.[5] Survey questions differed somewhat for participants and nonparticipants. Both participants and nonparticipants received questions about "integrative factors" (the perceived levels of compatibility and trust between the respondent's organization and others in the partnership) and "obstacle statements" (the perceived seriousness of certain obstacles to participation). However, only participants were asked to describe their organizations' involvement in the partnership (questions focused on committee activity, meetings/events, grant funding, etc.). Participants were also asked about "motivation factors" (the motivations that were most important in their organization's decision to participate).

Response Rates and the Distribution of the Data

The overall response rate for the survey was 51 percent, with response rates for the individual partnerships ranging from 25 to 69 percent. Table 3.1 shows the distribution of the data among the four partnerships and between participants and nonparticipants. A large majority of the data comes from the Delaware Estuary and Galveston Bay partnerships, likely because

Table 3.1 The Distribution of the Data

Partnership Name	Participants	Nonparticipants	Nonawares[a]	Total Respondents	Response Rate (percent)
Charlotte Harbor National Estuary Program	5	1	1	7	25
Partnership for the Delaware Estuary	11	17	1	29	48
Galveston Bay Estuary Program	16	9	2	27	69
New Hampshire Estuaries Project	3	4	1	8	62
Overall	35	31	5	71	51

[a]"Nonawares" means that they had never heard of the partnership and were left out of the quantitative analysis.

of large cities located within their study areas (Philadelphia and Houston, respectively) that are home to many NPOs. Overall, there were about the same number of participant and nonparticipant respondents (thirty-five and thirty-one, respectively).

RESULTS AND DISCUSSION: DESCRIPTIVE DATA

Because of the small sample size, quantitative analysis was limited to descriptive statistics and correlations. Although preliminary, these results will provide direction for larger-scale quantitative analysis in the future. Regression analysis, in particular, would be useful for empirically testing the theoretical models against one another. I start by presenting descriptive results, focusing on the motivations and obstacles identified by the survey and interview respondents.

Motivations

Table 3.2 shows an overall ranking for the thirteen "motivation factors," listed in order of mean score on a zero-to-three scale of importance. The most important motivations for participation were resource availability (especially informational resources), being part of a network, and working with other organizations toward common goals.

The interview data and the open-ended survey responses support the findings about top motivation factors. One interviewee, when asked about the benefits of participation in the partnership, enumerated several *resources* the partnership provides: "Sharing databases [and] contact info is a huge advantage. Obtaining broader ranges of expertise [is] also a benefit." Another interviewee noted that being on a partnership committee allowed him to educate himself about estuary issues, the policies that affect the estuary, and the organizations involved—all informational resources. Similarly, a survey respondent noted that the most helpful aspect of the partnership was "information about the estuary as a whole and the groups working in it, through the scientific conferences and the newsletter."

The qualitative data clarify respondents' interpretation of motivation factors such as "the opportunity to be part of a network of environmental organizations." When asked about the benefits his organization received from participation in the partnership, one interviewee responded that he valued just being part of the consortium, and working with other environmental groups in the area. He explained that there is strength in numbers and that the environmental groups in the region have to stick together.

Table 3.2 Motivations for the Participation of Nonprofit Organizations

Motivation Factor[a]	N	Mean (0–3)[b]
Access to useful information	27	2.19
Be part of environmental network	29	2.14
Work with other orgs that share our goals	29	2.07
Financial resources	24	1.96
Technical expertise	27	1.89
Express views to citizens/community	27	1.78
Initiative of person in organization	25	1.68
Influence policy	27	1.67
Get name out to funders	27	1.44
Express views to government	26	1.42
Effort by partnership leaders	22	1.27
Attract volunteers or members	23	1.13
Efforts by other partners	22	0.64

[a]Motivation factors followed the question (to participants only): Over the past year, how important were the following factors in your organization's decision to participate in [the partnership]?
[b]The mean of responses, where not at all important = 0, somewhat important = 1, very important = 2, extremely important = 3.

Another survey respondent wrote: "[Their] network is more diverse than our own. Communication with [the partnership] enables our organization to make contacts with businesses, universities and the right person within a particular agency more efficiently."

A high ranking for the motivation factor "the opportunity to work with other organizations that share our goals" is also supported by the qualitative data. One interviewee found "an increased ability to work cooperatively on areas of mutual concern" to be a key advantage of participation in a large network of environmental organizations. Another interviewee described the opportunities that arise from common missions: "[Participation in the partnership] is a great opportunity for our organization to . . . tap into the existing base that's there. The goals that are set forth for [our organization fall] hand in hand with the program that's already in place. . . . So it's very important for us, again, not to recreate the wheel, so to speak, but to get involved with what they're already doing and we thought we could be . . . an advocate of what they're doing as well as bring in more activities along those lines."

Obstacles

Table 3.3 displays descriptive data regarding potential obstacles to participation. Because these obstacle statements were measured on an agree/disagree scale from +2 to –2, it is important to point out that some items were phrased negatively (e.g., "reporting requirements take too long") and others positively (e.g., "we can achieve our policy goals through the partnership"). Except for the first two statements listed in table 3.3, the average respondent agreed with positive statements and disagreed with negative statements, indicating a positive perception of most aspects of the partnership. However, respondents, on average, agreed that reporting requirements are too burdensome and disagreed that the partnership helps their organization achieve its policy goals.

The qualitative data echo this dissatisfaction with reporting requirements for grants sponsored by estuary partnerships. One survey respondent wrote that a "bad experience with mini-grant requirements" was the main reason her organization discontinued its participation. The executive director of another NPO that has regular contracts with an estuary partnership noted: "When I initially undertook to apply for grant money

Table 3.3   Possible Obstacles to Participation

Obstacle Statement[a]	N	Mean (2 to –2)[b]
Burdensome reporting requirements [c]	19	0.32
Can achieve policy goals	37	–0.22
Partnership has power/authority	35	0.11
Meetings and events too far	36	–0.25
Inconvenient meeting times	25	–0.32
Useful information available	41	0.61
Financial opportunities available	35	0.80
Participation takes more time than its worth	35	–0.86
Partnership is effective	39	0.90
Partnership is well-respected	39	1.10
Technical expertise available	41	1.17
Partnership is well-managed	33	1.27
Participation may limit our autonomy	40	–1.60

[a]Obstacle statements followed the request: Please indicate the extent to which you agree or disagree with the following statements.

[b]The mean of responses, where agree strongly = 2; agree somewhat = 1; disagree somewhat = –1; disagree strongly = –2.

[c]Asked only of participants.

from them, one of the members of my advisory committee said 'Oh, you're not gonna like it if you get that money because . . . you're gonna spend so much time writing reports' and I laughed it off at the time, but every time I was writing one of those darned reports I . . . thought, 'Yep, he was right.'"

In fact, general "inconvenience factors" rank high on the list of obstacles to participation. Qualitative evidence supports this finding. Of thirty-one responses to an open-ended question on obstacles, twelve responses (or 46 percent) focused on the NPO's lack of time to engage with the partnership or geographical distance to meetings or activities. Of four responses to an open-ended question on why the NPO stopped participating in the partnership, two cited a lack of time and staff. In response to a question on the costs of participating, another interviewee promptly answered "time and gas money," explaining that he sometimes drives three hours to attend a two-hour meeting, a practice that is prohibitively expensive for citizen volunteers. Although these "inconvenience factors" may seem trivial to a collaborative manager, they have derailed watershed management programs in the past (e.g., see Thomas 1999).

The second primary obstacle was the perception by NPOs that they will not achieve their policy goals through the estuary partnerships. Estuary partnership activities tend to focus on research and public education rather than advocacy, perhaps due to the fact that they are funded and often administered by government agencies. This "steering away" from a strong political stance may frustrate environmental interest groups. For instance, one interviewee representing a local Audubon society chapter felt that they sometimes had to "bite their tongue" and not get as opinionated or political as they wanted to when working with the partnership. He explained that the partnership is generally more moderate, and very dependent on scientific facts. But, he added, you want to stay involved and be a voice in what they do because they are one of the more powerful environmental organizations in the area, in terms of money, staff, energy, and political connections.

Two other respondents—both representing environmental advocacy groups—expressed similar sentiments. In response to an open-ended question on obstacles to participation, the representative of a local Riverkeeper chapter said: "Our adversarial positions on many river issues are too strong for the Partnership due to their need to maintain a greater degree of neutrality". A local Sierra Club chapter representative said of the estuary partnership: "[It] does not seem to be working on definite goals, other than supporting the health of [the Bay]. I see it as an entity that dispenses grants and holds innocuous update seminars every two years. It seeks not to offend and succeeds."

Another finding was respondents' lack of concern about a loss of autonomy. On average, respondents strongly disagreed with the statement "participation in the partnership limits what we can do or say as an organization." Resource dependency theory predicts a high level of concern over organizational autonomy in situations of interdependence. Perhaps organizations in estuary partnerships are not highly interdependent? If so, this lack of interdependence could be a function of the small size of grants offered to NPOs through the partnership and/or the availability of resources from outside. Another possibility is that the estuary partnerships place only minimal demands on their members in terms of conforming to partnership values, ideas, and goals. Indeed, the committee structure of the estuary programs, bylaws that emphasize diverse representation, and the programs' mission statements point to a great tolerance for a diversity of views.

There is also a theoretical argument, based on the idea that autonomy is a more subtle and dynamic concept than presented in resource exchange theory. When forming network linkages, organizations may simultaneously lose and enhance their autonomy, giving up control in some areas but developing or strengthening new sources of power. In estuary programs, the loss of autonomy may be minimal due to limited demands on network members to conform, while the opportunities for developing new sources of autonomy (a broader volunteer base, a stronger position in the community) are great. Thus, participation may actually *increase* autonomy overall.

RESULTS AND DISCUSSION: CORRELATIONS

Scores for motivation factors, obstacle statements, and integrative factors were correlated with measures of participation. This was a preliminary step to understanding which categories of motivations (e.g., resource exchange, political interests, common goals) tend to be associated with higher levels of participation.[6] Three measures of participation were used: (1) a binary participation variable; (2) a summative measure called "activity level," which accounted for several different types of participation;[7] and (3) approximate hours per month spent on partnership activities.

Resource Motivations

Table 3.4 examines the relationship between *resource motivations* (i.e., availability of financial, technical, informational, or human resources) and participation. If resource dependency were a strong predictor of participation and participation levels, we would expect to see high and significant correlations. Although some were significant, there was little consistency; for instance,

Table 3.4 Pearson's Correlations between Measures of Participation and Resource Exchange Motivations (Financial, Technical, Information, and Human)

Measure of Resource Exchange Motivation[a]	Participation Measure			
	Participation (0/1)[b]	Activity Level[c]	Hours per Month[d]
Financial opportunities available (obs)	.173 (N = 35)	.189 (N = 24)	.244 (N = 23)
Financial resources (mot)		.275 (N = 24)	.307 (N = 23)
Get name out to funders (mot)		.160 (N = 26)	−.185 (N = 26)
Technical expertise available (obs)	.084 (N = 41)	.439[e] (N = 27)	.193 (N = 27)
Technical expertise (mot)		.261 (N = 26)	.170 (N = 26)
Useful information available (obs)	−.056 (N = 41)	.091 (N = 24)	.283 (N = 24)
Access to useful information (mot)		.331[f] (N = 26)	.260 (N = 26)
Attract volunteers or members (mot)		.134 (N = 23)	.188 (N = 22)

[a]These are coded responses to selected "motivation factors" (mot) and "obstacle statements" (obs). See tables 3.2 and 3.3 for the entire list of these statements.

[b]Binary measure of organizational participation (yes or no).

[c]A summative measure of participation ranging from 0 to 14. It sums the frequency of attending partnership meetings, attending partnership events, and contacting partnership staff (each coded from 0 to 4, for a maximum score of 12) plus the value of the binary variables "being on a partnership committee" and "receiving a grant or contract from the partnership."

[d]The total hours per month spent on partnership activities, as estimated by the respondent.

[e]Correlation is significant at alpha = .05 level (2-tailed).

[f]Correlation is significant at alpha = .1 level (2-tailed).

none of the resource exchange items were significant across more than one participation measure. The preliminary conclusion is that resource dependency is *not* a prominent motivation for participation in estuary partnerships.

This seems to contradict the earlier finding that NPOs rank resources as highly important motivations for participation (see table 3.2). There are two critical differences. First, the motivation rankings represent the *perception* of participants but do not take into account *actual* participation patterns. Second, the descriptive analysis did not differentiate between *levels* of participation. Although "access to informational resources" is an important motivation, for instance, it may lead to only low levels of engagement, such as checking the website or signing up for a newsletter. Less universally important motivations, such as "the opportunity to influence policy as it is made or implemented," may lead to high levels of engagement in terms of time and activities.

The qualitative data support the finding that resource motivations—particularly funding—are not as critical to NPO participation as the rankings suggest. In response to the open-ended motivation question, one respondent said that "[the partnership's] grant program is too modest to be useful, given the conditions imposed on the grants, and the constantly changing focus of the grant program." Another respondent finds that partnership "grant proposals are time consuming to prepare and their acceptance is uncertain." In response to an open-ended question to nonparticipants asking which incentive(s) would encourage them to participate, funding was mentioned only once out of fifteen responses.

The qualitative data also reveal that a significant portion of NPOs lack the necessary resources, especially time and paid staff, to initiate participation in the partnership. There may be a certain "activation energy" necessary to get to the point at which an NPO can assimilate resources from a partnership. Ironically, some NPOs consider themselves too resource-poor to initiate a search for resources (e.g., "We don't have the time or resources to seek out a lot of partnerships"). This may further dampen the effect of resource motivations.

Alternative Motivations: Political Interests and Integrative Factors

The top half of table 3.5 examines the relationship between *political motivations* and participation. If political interests were a strong predictor of participation and participation levels, we would expect to see high and significant correlations. In fact, three out of four measures of political interest show a positive and significant correlation with more than one participation measure.

Participation and Integrative Measures (Shared Beliefs, Common Goals, and Social Integration)

| Measure | Participation Measure | | |
	Participation (0/1)[a]	Activity Level[b]	Hours per Month[c]
Measures of political interest[d]			
Influence policy (mot)	.315[f] (N = 37)	.499[e] (N = 26)	.394[e] (N = 26)
Can achieve policy goals (obs)		.345[f] (N = 24)	.314 (N = 24)
Express views to government (mot)		.255 (N = 25)	.351[e] (N = 25)
Summative political measure[g]		.355[f] (N = 24)	.379[f] (N = 24)
Integrative Measures[h]			
Work with orgs that share our goals (mot)	.403[i] (N = 44)	.442[e] (N = 28)	.338[f] (N = 28)
Compatible goals and objectives (int)	.130 (N = 33)	.217 (N = 27)	.157 (N = 27)
Can rely on other orgs in partnership (int)		.475[e] (N = 23)	.344[f] (N = 24)
Like other people in partnership (int)	.053 (N = 38)	.354[f] (N = 26)	.235 (N = 26)
Trust people in partnership (int)	.194 (N = 39)	.254 (N = 24)	.361[f] (N = 24)

Note: Only measures that correlated significantly with at least one participation measure are shown.

[a] Binary measure of organizational participation (yes or no).

[b] A summative measure of participation ranging from 0 to 14. It sums the frequency of attending partnership meetings, attending partnership events, and contacting partnership staff (each coded from 0 to 4, for a maximum score of 12) plus the value of the binary variables "being on a partnership committee" and "receiving a grant or contract from the partnership."

[c] The total hours per month spent on partnership activities, as estimated by the respondent.

[d] These are coded responses to selected "motivation factors" (mot) and "obstacle statements" (obs). See tables 3.2 and 3.3 for the entire list of these statements.

[e] Correlation is significant at alpha = .05 level (2-tailed).

[f] Correlation is significant at alpha = .1 level (2-tailed).

[g] A sum of three motivation factors related to political/advocacy goals (Cronbach's alpha = .93): "the opportunity to express our views to citizens or community leaders" + "the opportunity to express our views to government officials" + "the opportunity to influence policy as it is made or implemented." Each was coded on a 0 to 4 scale for a maximum score of 12.

[h] These are coded responses to selected "motivation factors" (mot) and "integrative factors" (int). See the appendix to this chapter for the entire list of these statements, including question and item wording.

[i] Correlation is significant at alpha = .01 level (2-tailed).

These results indicate that NPOs motivated to participate by political interests tend to be more highly engaged in terms of activity level and/or hours. This makes sense, because achieving policy goals through the partnership likely requires higher levels of commitment than other goals, such as obtaining information. The interview data indicate that the political legitimacy and reputation of the estuary partnership are indeed important to potential NPO participants. For instance, one survey respondent praised the partnership's rapport with her community: "The staff is extremely active in the community. Not only do they have the technical expertise, but they interface with the whole community in a personal and professional manner. . . . [The partnership] makes every effort to bring consensus and cohesion to a very diversified watershed."

The bottom half of table 3.5 examines the relationship between certain "integrative factors," that is, those that express shared goals, compatibility, and trust and participation.[8] Correlations with measures of *common goals* were significant. One measure—the motivation factor "the opportunity to work with other organizations that share our goals"— showed a positive and significant correlation with two participation measures. The other—the integrative factor "my organization's goals and objectives are compatible with those of the partnership"—was positively and significantly correlated with the binary measure of participation, meaning that participants were much more likely than nonparticipants to agree with the statement.

The qualitative evidence supports the importance of overlapping or compatible missions. Of thirty-one responses to an open-ended question on obstacles to participation, eight responses (or 26 percent) mentioned differences in mission or geographical focus (e.g., "different goals/interests," "our missions only slightly overlap," "outside our watershed of concern"). In response to an open-ended question to nonparticipants asking which incentive(s) would encourage them to participate, seven of the fifteen responses (or 47 percent) were mission oriented (e.g., if the partnership worked on [this sort of project]; "a project that both parties were interested in"; "grants, programs, etc., related to our mission"; "direct relevance to the goals of our organization").

CONCLUSION

This study has aimed to better explain the motivations and obstacles facing organizations in their decision to join and/or remain in an interorganizational network. Although it is not possible to draw firm conclusions due to the small sample size, the results indicate directions for future research.

Regarding motivations for organizational participation, resources (especially informational resources), networking, and common goals ranked highest among participants. Inconvenience factors and the partnerships' failure to help NPOs achieve their policy goals may be key deterrents to participation.

Although respondents indicated that resource availability was an important motivation to participate, there was no consistent evidence that it was correlated with actual participation patterns. In contrast, measures of "political interest" (e.g., achieving policy goals through the network, influencing policy) and "shared goals" (e.g., compatible goals and objectives and the desire to work with organizations that share one's goals) correlated positively and consistently with participation.

The failure to confirm resource exchange theory as a basis for participation in this analysis could indicate that resource exchange is less important than is commonly thought in determining network structure. A more dynamic explanation is that, although resource needs are important as an initial motivator to participate, they fail to translate into highly active levels of engagement. But there is another possibility that points to a potential fault in the research design: By focusing on government-created estuary partnerships, this analysis may fail to capture the true, organic network of interdependencies that encompass NPOs. That is, the NPOs surveyed may be part of a larger network of organizations outside the sphere of the partnership and may be resource-dependent on these external actors (this is certainly possible considering the small size of the grants available through the partnership). Sorting out these possibilities is an empirical task that requires further data collection and analysis.

Nonetheless, this study has pointed out that a variety of motivations and integrative factors, over and above resource exchange, are important in organizations' decisions to participate. For instance, the importance of shared goals and networking appears again and again, indicating that partnerships provide a unique platform from which organizations can leverage resources to achieve common goals.

Collaborative managers in particular may take away several lessons from this study. First, some of the top motivations for NPO participation in networks are things that they cannot easily change or manipulate. For instance, the existence of *shared goals* among organizations in the network was a top motivation cited by respondents and correlated to participation patterns. Collaborative managers can "frame" the network's goals in ways that seem compatible with potential participants (Agranoff and McGuire 2001); they can also actively seek common ground and look for shared interests (Gray 1989). However, it will be frustrating and, in the end, impossible to engage organizations whose goals and objectives are truly incompatible. Second, collaborative managers may be able to reduce obstacles to participation by streamlining burdensome bureaucratic procedures. Any inconvenience is a potential deterrent for organizations, especially NPOs taxed with too many projects and not enough staff. Collaborative managers should also be attentive to the different political needs of their organizational members, including advocacy groups that seek policy change. To continue to attract diverse members, it is important to maintain legitimacy and political vitality in the community. Finally, collaborative managers need to be aware of the shifting needs and interests of the organizations in their network, as well as the complexity and integrated nature of organizational motivations.

APPENDIX: SELECTED QUESTIONS FROM THE INTERNET SURVEY INSTRUMENT

Branches were set up in the Internet survey to distinguish between participants and nonparticipants on the basis of their response to the following question: "Over the past year, has your organization participated in the [partnership name] in any way?" In presenting the key survey questions below, I divide them into those questions answered by both participants and nonparticipants, those questions answered only by participants, and those questions answered only by nonparticipants. They are further divided by my analysis categories, such as obstacle statements, integrative factor statements, and motivation factors.

Questions Answered by Participants and Nonparticipants

"Integrative factor" statements (item order was randomized)

Please indicate the extent to which you agree or disagree with the following statements (agree strongly = 2; agree somewhat = 1; disagree somewhat = −1; disagree strongly = −2):

____ 1. My organization's goals and objectives are compatible with those of [partnership name].

____ 2. My organization's culture (norms, standard operating procedures, and general perspective) is compatible with the other organizations in [partnership name].

____ 3. It is easy to work with the other organizations in [partnership name].

____ 4. I trust the other people involved in [partnership name].

___ 5. The other organizations in [partnership name] can be relied upon to get work done.

___ 6. I like the people in [partnership name].

___ 7. I have fun at [partnership name] events. (This statement was given only to participants)

"Obstacle" statements (item order was randomized)

Please indicate the extent to which you agree or disagree with the following statements (agree strongly = 2; agree somewhat = 1; disagree somewhat = −1; disagree strongly = −2):

___ 1. [Partnership name] offers useful information that we can't get ourselves.

___ 2. [Partnership name] offers useful technical advice and expertise.

___ 3. [Partnership name] offers significant financial opportunities, such as grants or contracts.

___ 4. My organization can achieve its public policy goals through [partnership name].

___ 5. [Partnership name] has power and authority.

___ 6. [Partnership name] is well managed.

___ 7. [Partnership name] is effective.

___ 8. [Partnership name] is well respected in the community.

___ 9. Participation in the partnership limits what we can do or say as an organization.

___ 10. Participation in [partnership name] requires more time than it is worth.

___ 11. It's hard to get to partnership meetings and/or events because they occur at inconvenient times.

___ 12. The partnership meetings and/or events are too far away.

___ 13. The reporting requirements for partnership grants or contracts take too much time. (This statement was given only to participants)

Open-ended obstacle question: Please briefly describe the main obstacles to your organization's participation in [the partnership], if any.

Questions Answered by Nonparticipants Only

What incentives, if any, would motivate your organization to participate in [the partnership]?

Questions Answered by Participants Only

Type and amount of participation

Over the past year, about how many times has someone from your organization done the following? (0 = not at all; 1 = 1–2 times; 2 = 3–6 times; 3 = 7–11 times; 4 = 12 or more times):

    ____ 1. Attended a partnership meeting.
    ____ 2. Attended a partnership event (i.e., educational program, festival, restoration project).
    ____ 3. Contacted partnership staff via phone, email, or in person.

Over the past year, has someone from your organization served on a committee for [partnership name]? Yes/No

Over the past THREE YEARS, has your organization received a grant or contract from [partnership name]? Yes/No

On average over the past year, about how many HOURS PER MONTH did your organization spend on partnership activities?

For how many years has your organization participated in [partnership name]?

Motivation factors (item order was randomized)

Over the past year, how important were the following factors in your organization's decision to participate in [the partnership]? (0 = not at all important; 1 = somewhat important; 2 = very important; 3 = extremely important):

    ____ 1. Grants, contracts, or financial resources available through the partnership.
    ____ 2. Gaining access to technical advice or expertise.
    ____ 3. Gaining access to potential volunteers or members.
    ____ 4. Useful information available through the partnership.
    ____ 5. The opportunity to work with other organizations that share our goals.
    ____ 6. The opportunity to be part of a network of environmental organizations.
    ____ 7. The opportunity to influence policy as it is made or implemented.
    ____ 8. The opportunity to express our views to government officials.

____ 9. The opportunity to express our views to citizens or community leaders.

____ 10. The opportunity to "get our name out" to potential supporters or funders.

____ 11. The initiative of one or more persons in our organization who wanted to participate.

____ 12. Efforts by other partners to get us to participate.

____ 13. Efforts by partnership leaders to get us to participate.

Open-ended motivation question: Are there any additional reasons why your organization participates in [the partnership]?

At any point in the past, did your organization stop participating in [the partnership], or significantly reduce its level of participation? Yes/No

If yes, what were the main reasons that your organization stopped participating or significantly reduced its participation?

NOTES

1. Collecting standardized data from multiple networks was accomplished by creating four different Internet surveys—one for each of the four partnerships—that were exactly the same except for the name of the partnership.

2. An estuary is a semi-enclosed coastal body of water which has a free connection with the open sea and within which seawater mixes with freshwater (e.g., a bay, mouth of a river, salt marsh, or lagoon). They are unique ecosystems and carry out a myriad of unique ecological functions—they serve as feeding areas for migratory birds, provide spawning grounds for many species of fish, regulate floodwaters; and filter out pollutants.

3. These criteria create some selection bias but are justifiable for two reasons: First, the research is exploratory; and second, the unit of analysis is the nonprofit organization rather than the partnership. Seven partnerships actually fit the selection criteria, but three were dropped before the data were collected—two because of their large watershed area and complicated administrative structure that spanned multiple states, and one due to resistance from the network leadership.

4. Identifying nonprofit environmental organizations that are located in the partnership's focus area but not listed as members was accomplished in two steps. First, geographic information system maps of each estuary watershed were used to identify all zip codes within the program's "study area." Second, 2001 Internal Revenue Service data were used to identify all environmental NPOs located in those zip codes. NPOs were classified as "environmental" using the National Taxonomy of Exempt Entities codes.

5. The survey was piloted with a small set of potential respondents (four) and a larger set of faculty and graduate students (twenty). Real-time feedback was solicited from one former NPO director. Feedback from pilot respondents was incorporated into the final survey design. Administration of the survey generally followed Dillman (2000) and included a pre–e-mail, first wave, and four follow-up waves of thank you and reminder messages, all via e-mail.

6. Regression analysis would be a preferable means of analysis, but the lack of cases means that no more than two variables could be included.

7. Activity level is a summative measure of participation ranging from 0 to 14. It sums the frequency of attending partnership meetings, attending partnership events, and contacting partnership staff (each coded from 0 to 4, for a maximum score of 12) plus the value of the binary variables "being on a partnership committee" and "receiving a grant or contract from the partnership."

8. Some of the "integrative measures" are quite blunt considering the subtlety of concepts like "trust" and "compatibility" and should not be considered more than a rough first cut.

Chapter 4

Partner Selection and the Effectiveness of Interorganizational Collaborations

Elizabeth A. Graddy and Bin Chen

Two themes have characterized public management research and practice over the past two decades: an emphasis on interorganizational partnerships and a focus on performance. As governments have faced more complex problems and increased demand for their limited resources, they have turned to external partners for help. In many services and many governments throughout the world, these partnerships of public and private service providers are replacing the traditional model of direct service delivery by public agencies. As a result, the role of public managers has been transformed from direct service providers to facilitators and coordinators of networks and collaboration across public, nonprofit, and even for-profit organizations. Public managers are thus becoming more "collaborative" than "directive" in their work.

The goals of these collaborative ventures are presumably to enhance the effectiveness of public-sector activities. Partnering with others is believed to contribute to increased efficiency and innovation, local adaptation, increased flexibility, and enhanced community ties. And, to the extent this is true, this movement intersects with and supports the increased focus on performance. Governments at all levels have made performance measurement a core component of public-sector reform. Taxpayers, politicians, and program stakeholders have created a mandate for outcome-based performance measurement in public programs to promote more effective, efficient, and responsive service delivery (Heinrich 2003).

However, an alternative explanation for the focus on collaboration is ideological. Increased reliance on the private sector to deliver public services was also expected to reduce the size of government. If this is the goal, the expected impacts on effectiveness are less clear. In either case, the costs associated with managing the partnerships may outweigh their benefits. And, in the absence of effective management, any benefits to effectiveness may be lost.

It is the connection between partnerships and their effectiveness that we seek to explore. The formation and management costs of such interorganizational structures are high. It is thus important for public managers to understand the consequences of formation decisions and how the collaboration is structured. Despite strong scholarly interest in both collaborations and performance measurement, their interplay has not been widely studied. Collaboration remains a somewhat elusive concept, and we know little about when and how these efforts are likely to be successful. What factors contribute to well-functioning interorganizational partnerships? The failure rates of strategic alliances have been found to be high (Nilsson 1997; Devlin and Bleackley 1988). Understanding the association between collaboration characteristics and their effectiveness should also enhance the likelihood of their survival. Therefore, empirical work that seeks to understand this relationship is important for public management research and practice.

Here, we are interested in the consequences of partner selection on collaborative effectiveness. How do the motivations involved in forming partnerships affect the perceived effectiveness of the resulting relationships? Effectiveness can be assessed from different perspectives—for example, the community, the partnership, the client (Provan and Milward 2001). We focus here on the partnership—how effective is it perceived to be by its component organizations?[1] The resulting insights should enable public managers to more effectively initiate, design, operate, and manage interorganizational collaborations and networks.

In the next section, we develop the theoretical connection between partner selection and partnership effectiveness. Then we explore our model with data on the delivery of family preservation services collected in Los Angeles County. We conclude with a discussion of the implications of our findings for public management and policy.

PARTNER SELECTION

Partnerships are inherently risky endeavors. Their integral characteristic is mutual interdependence, and this interdependence implies vulnerability to the behavior of one's partner (Graddy and Ferris 2006). Therefore, organizations seeking a collaborative partnership must assess the trade-off between the benefits of cooperation and this vulnerability. This suggests that potential partners will be assessed based on both the strategic benefits they bring and the risks associated with their behavior. The latter can be mitigated by selecting partners the organization views as trustworthy. Such trust can be viewed as incorporating both the intentions of a partner and its competence (Das and Teng 2001). Can and will the potential partner behave as expected?

The literature suggests two broad categories of benefits that organizations seek from collaborative partners. They may seek a resource that they need for their activities but do not possess (resource exchange), or they may seek associational advantages from a well-respected or well-connected partner (organizational legitimacy). When comparing partners with similar benefits, they are likely to seek those with lower associated partnership costs (transaction costs). This requires knowledge about the potential partner, which might come from previous partnerships or other relationships, common missions, or third-party links. Such information should reveal whether the potential partner is expected to be trustworthy or not in the broad sense described above.

In our research, we have integrated these theoretical perspectives of interorganizational alliances and developed a network formation model for social service delivery (Graddy and Chen 2006). Here, we adapt this model to the formation of dyadic partnerships and explore its connection to the expected effectiveness of the collaboration. Specifically, we identify three factors that we believe explain the choice of partners in collaborative arrangements: programmatic needs that promote resource exchange; organizational legitimacy goals; and efforts to reduce the transactions costs associated with partnership formation and management.

Resource/programmatic needs. Complex programmatic needs in social service delivery could drive the formation of partnerships. Individual organizations are constrained by technological, political, and cognitive limits in the face of complex, many-sided problems. A resource exchange view suggests that organizations will establish alliances when one organization has resources or capacities beneficial to, but not possessed by, another organization (Dyer and Singh 1998). Establishing strategic alliances between organizations may afford an organization access to tacit knowledge and complementary skills, new technologies or markets, and the ability to provide a wider range of products and services beyond its organizational boundaries.

We identify five types of resource acquisitions that are likely to be important in helping providers of social services meet their programmatic needs: extra provision capacity for case overload, specific service expertise, geographic coverage, local knowledge and client access, and cultural and linguistic competence. A single social service agency may not have the capacity to handle growing caseloads alone. An individual agency is constrained in the number and types of services they can provide to clients due to agency tradition and specialization. There may be spatial restrictions on a social service provider's ability to serve clients scattered over a large geographic area. An organization may lack local knowledge and access to targeted clients. Its service staff may not be trained to provide services that must be adapted to accommodate language, culture, and racial/ethnic distinctions. Therefore, some partners will be strategically selected for their ability to provide such complementary resources.

Organizational legitimacy. Organizations may seek partners that enhance their legitimacy. We identify three such motivations: to meet funding agency requirements, to enhance organizational reputation, and to build future relationships. Local funding agencies are increasingly requiring or strongly promoting a partnership plan as a condition for receiving service delivery contracts. If public funding is, or appears to be, contingent upon a collaborative plan, then social service agencies, which are dependent on public contracts, will comply. Such dependency on external resources has long been recognized as affecting an organization's strategic decisions (Aldrich 1976), including its willingness to form partnerships (Oliver 1990). Having remained at the forefront of social service provision, nonprofit social service agencies are increasingly engaging in networks and partnerships as a response to mandates from various public funders.

Partnerships can convey legitimacy in other ways. Institutional theory suggests that strategic alliances can originate from an organization's motives to improve its reputation, image, prestige, or congruence with the prevailing norms in its institutional environment (Aldrich 1976; DiMaggio and Powell 1983). Social service organizations may thus choose to affiliate with a reputable organization to enhance their own reputation. This in turn may make it more competitive for public funding. Organizations may also seek partners because they want to build future relationships with them, either to enhance their ability to gain future contracts or to achieve other organizational goals.

Transaction costs. Whether organizations seek to form partnerships for resource exchange or for legitimacy, they should seek to reduce the associated transaction costs. To reduce the threats of opportunism, organizations must identify partners they can trust. By trust, we mean positive expectations of both their intentions and their competence. If organizations can identify such partners, they can reduce the monitoring costs associated with collaboration and significantly enhance the chance for effective partnerships. It is difficult to directly measure the informational costs associated with identifying desirable partners and with managing successful partnerships. We have identified three proxy indicators of such costs. First, organizations should seek partners that share their organizational vision or mission. Partnerships between organizations with different visions are difficult to initiate and sustain because fundamentally different missions can create interorganizational conflicts. For example, nonprofit service delivery organizations often distrust the profit motives of business organizations.

Second, organizations should seek partners with which they have experience. One has the best knowledge of organizations with whom you have past partnering experience. Thus, organizations should be more willing to form future partnerships with those with which they have prior working relationships, and Gulati (1995a) finds evidence to support this. In addition, with prior partnering experience, an organization builds expertise in its effective management. This expertise reduces transaction costs and thus increases the willingness of an organization to form more partnerships.

Finally, there are search costs associated with finding partners. Social network theory introduces an organization's relationships with other organizations as facilitating or constraining its internal and external capacity to join an alliance (e.g., Gulati 1998). Gulati (1995) argues that an organization's external capacity to join an alliance is constrained by its social network. So organizations face supply side constraints on their ability to form alliances. In their study of network formation, Graddy and Chen (2006) found that even if organizations were willing to comply with a funding requirement to form a provider network, they were constrained by the availability of potential partners. In some cases, an organization may select a particular partner simply because they are not aware of alternative service providers.

COLLABORATIVE EFFECTIVENESS

We expect that these three motivations for partner selection—gaining programmatic resources, enhancing organizational legitimacy, and reducing transaction costs—can have an impact on collaborative effectiveness. The expected nature of that impact and its relative influence will depend on the dimension of effectiveness explored.

We consider here three dimensions of effective collaboration—client goal achievement, improved interorganizational relationships, and organizational development. These different dimensions reflect the different types of goals organizations might seek from interorganizational collaboration.[2]

The first—client goal achievement—refers to the primary purpose of most public-sector efforts to increase collaboration, that is, to gain resources that will improve service delivery. The second—improved interorganizational relationships—captures both potential collective and organizational benefits of collaboration. If the organizations in the collaborative work well together, this may enhance the social capital in the community served. Better working relationships among organizations enhance the opportunity for problem solving and pave the way for better future relationships. Organizations themselves may also benefit if these relationships enhance their legitimacy.

The third dimension—organizational development—most directly benefits the organization. If the collaboration enhances the organization's development, this may increase its capacity to effectively compete for future contracts and may improve its ability to achieve its mission and goals. The mechanism for such development is often the organizational learning that comes from working with another organization in developing a shared understanding of the problem and reaching a consensus on how to address it (Gray 2000).

When partners are selected to meet programmatic needs, we expect a strong positive association with client goal achievement. Because the partner is viewed as providing programmatic components that are necessary for successful service delivery, the expectation is that the resulting service provision will be enhanced. If organizations come to rely on the specific expertise and capacity of their partners, this can lead to better collaborative processes and thus better outcomes (Doz and Hamel 1998). Moreover, working together to meet programmatic needs requires some investment in mechanisms for coordination, the management of information, and accountability. As these relation-specific assets develop, partners establish trust, learn (Cohen and Levinthal 1990), and thus improve their working relationship. Therefore, we also expect a positive association with improved interorganizational relationships. However, enhanced organizational development may not be correlated with partners selected to meet programmatic needs. Therefore, we have no expectations about an effect on this dimension of effectiveness.

When partners are selected to enhance organizational legitimacy, we expect a positive effect on organizational development and on improved interorganizational relationships. Organizations seek to build their collaborative relationships with a respected organization not only to enhance their own reputation and gain greater legitimacy but also to develop a foundation for future collaboration. Given these expectations, this motivation should be positively associated with these measures of effectiveness. However, when an organization is seeking a partner to position itself to receive funding rather than because it views the partner as necessary to meet client goals, the collaboration is presumably less likely to yield effective client outcomes. Therefore, we do not expect a positive impact on client goal achievement.

The expected impact of a transaction cost focus in partner selection varies by indicator. When an organization seeks to reduce transaction costs by identifying trustworthy partners, we should observe lower monitoring costs, easier communication, and more joint decision making. All these should enhance partnership performance and thus improve client goal achievement and interorganizational relationships. Such well-performing partnerships are also likely to provide spillover benefits to organizational development. Thus, all dimensions of effectiveness should improve.

If, however, the organization has high search costs due either to capacity limitations in the community or to its own lack of a social network, then all indicators of effectiveness should suffer. If organizations select partners based solely on their availability, the resulting partnership is unlikely to be associated with improved client outcomes, stronger interorganizational ties, or enhanced organizational development.

These expected effects are summarized in table 4.1.

EMPIRICAL SPECIFICATION

We now empirically explore the relationship between partner selection and collaborative outcomes in the context of social service delivery in Los Angeles County. Here we discuss our data and variable measurement. In the next section we present our analysis and the results.

Table 4.1 Expected Effects of Partner Selection on Collaborative Effectiveness

Resource/programmatic needs
- → Increased client goal achievement
- → Improved interorganizational relationships

Organizational legitimacy
- → Improved organizational development
- → Improved interorganizational relationships

Reduced transaction costs
- → Increased client goal achievement
- → Improved interorganizational relationships
- → Improved organizational development

Study Population

The population for this study is the social service agencies in the Family Preservation (FP) Program administered by the Los Angeles County Department of Children and Family Services (DCFS). In the context of rising foster care caseloads and increasing foster care costs, both federal and state governments became interested in time-limited, intensive home-based services for families in crisis. The aim of the interventions is to improve family functioning when children are at imminent risk of placement in foster care and to prevent this placement. The FP Program in Los Angeles County is the largest of its kind in the United States.

Los Angeles County has a population of 10 million living in about ninety incorporated cities and numerous additional neighborhoods, many of which are multiethnic communities. Children and family-related social services are both substantial and diverse. The FP Program is based on a lead-organization network model. DCFS created thirty-eight Community Family Preservation Networks (CFPN) in defined geographic areas throughout the county. For each area, DCFS contracts family preservation services to a lead agency through a request-for-proposal process. The lead agency receiving the contract, which can be either a public or a nonprofit organization,[3] is asked to partner with other service providers to deliver a broad range of services to children and families.

Data Collection

We collected the data for this study (for the survey instrument questions, see the appendix). The Los Angeles County DCFS provided us with access to relevant official documents on the FP Program, identified key informants in the DCFS and in each CFPN, and endorsed our survey of the CFPNs. Based on information obtained in our review of program documents and interviews with DCFS staff, and the executive directors and FP Program directors from three lead agencies, we developed a survey instrument to collect data on CFPN lead agencies and their network partners. The full fifteen-page survey included sections on the lead agency, the network structure, the partner organizations, and network management. Here, we use data collected on partner organizations. The survey data were supplemented as necessary with contract information provided by DCFS.

In the FP Program, each service contract covers one CFPN in a specific geographic area. The DCFS allows an organization to bid on more than one service contract. As a result, the DCFS granted multiple contracts to five lead agencies. Three of these agencies chose to manage their multiple contracts as one CFPN. Therefore, thirty-five lead agencies were slated for study. The survey was mailed to the executive director or the family preservation program manager in each of the lead agencies/networks.[4] The response rate was 77 percent, with twenty-seven of the thirty-five lead agencies completing the survey. All the lead agencies except one are nonprofit social service providers (the exception is a public agency). Three agencies have religious affiliations.

The unit of analysis for this study is the dyadic relationship between a lead agency and each of its network partners. One lead agency is not involved in any collaboration and was dropped from the study. The remaining twenty-six lead agencies formed 139 partnerships to deliver up to eleven different family preservation services. Among these partners, 10 percent (14) are public organizations, 79 percent (110) are nonprofit organizations, 2 percent (3) are faith-based organizations, and 9 percent (12) are for-profit organizations.

Variable Measurement

We asked the lead agencies to rate how important each of the eleven programmatic and organizational factors specified in our model was in their choice of a specific partner. More precisely, we used a 7-point Likert scale (with 1 representing "not at all" and 7 representing "very important") and asked the lead agency to select the number that best indicated how important each reason was in its choice of a specific organization as a partner. Table 4.2 presents the summary statistics on the responses.[5]

Among programmatic reasons to choose a particular partner, specific service expertise was the most important. For those seeking organizational legitimacy, reputation enhancement was the most important goal. For the transaction costs variables, shared vision was the most important. Gaining capacity to cope with case overload was the least compelling rationale for selecting a partner. But all the indicators seem to resonate to some extent as motivations for partner choice.

Our dependent variables—the three collaborative outcomes—were measured with the three questions given in table 4.3. Again, we used a 7-point Likert scale (with 1 representing "not at all" and 7 representing "very effective"). Respondents were asked to select the number that best indicates their assessment of the collaboration with each partner organization on each of the three outcomes. Table 4.4 presents the descriptive statistics of their responses. On average, the partnerships were

Table 4.2 Descriptive Statistics on Partner Selection Variables ($n = 139$)

Variable	Mean	Standard Deviation	Minimum	Maximum
Resource/programmatic needs				
Extra caseload capacity	2.20	2.04	1	7
Specific service expertise	5.33	2.40	1	7
Geographic coverage	3.92	2.67	1	7
Local knowledge and client				
access	3.78	2.52	1	7
Cultural and linguistic needs	3.68	2.75	1	7
Organizational legitimacy				
Funding agency requirement	3.30	2.43	1	7
Reputation enhancement	5.00	2.09	1	7
Building future relationships	4.81	2.31	1	7
Transaction costs				
Shared vision	4.94	2.34	1	7
Successful past collaboration	3.83	2.59	1	7
Few available partners	3.03	2.33	1	7

viewed as effective in achieving these outcomes. Client goal achievement has the highest overall mean (and the lowest variance in responses), indicating that this was the most successful outcome on average. Our measure of organizational development—broadened views—was on average the least successful outcome (with the largest variance), but even this outcome was rated highly. We turn now to the estimation and analysis of our model.

Table 4.3 Questions for Measuring the Three Collaborative Outcomes

Outcome	Question
Client goal achievement	Overall, how effective is this collaboration in achieving the expected goals of serving Family Preservation Program clients?
Quality of working relationship	Overall, how would you rate the quality of working relationships that have developed between your organization and this partner organization as a result of this collaboration?
Broadened views	Overall, to what extent has your organization's view on how to better serve Family Preservation Program clients been broadened as a result of listening to this partner organization's views?

Table 4.4 Descriptive Statistics on Collaborative Outcome Measures ($n = 139$)

Variable	Mean	Standard Deviation	Minimum	Maximum
Client goal achievement	6.35	0.91	2	7
Improved interorganizational relationships	6.27	1.10	3	7
Broadened organizational views	5.53	1.61	1	7

ESTIMATION AND ANALYSIS

The two-level structure of our data makes it inappropriate to apply a traditional linear regression analysis. Recall that the 139 dyadic relationships in our study are clustered in twenty-six networks. Relationships in the same network are presumably more similar than those in different networks. Thus, it is not reasonable to assume independence across pairs within a network. Dyadic collaborations operating in the same network are likely to share values on several variables. Some of these variables will not be observed, and their presence in the error term would violate estimation assumptions in the classical multivariate regression model. Therefore, we estimate a fixed-effects model to control for the network components of the error term.

Table 4.5 presents the fixed-effects regression estimates of the impact of partner selection decisions on subsequent collaborative effectiveness. We assess statistical significance based on a two-tailed test. The results reveal that the model is a good fit for the data for all three collaborative outcomes, thus providing support for the importance of partner selection in perceived collaborative effectiveness. The different reasons for partner selection have different types of impact on effectiveness. We now consider each in some detail.

Resource/programmatic needs. Selecting partners to meet programmatic needs is positively associated with all three indicators of collaborative effectiveness. As expected, the most important influence is on the achievement of client goals. Partners selected to meet caseload capacity, to gain specific service expertise, and to obtain desired geographic coverage are all positively associated with achieving client goals. Selecting partners to meet programmatic needs also proved, as expected, to promote improvements in interorganizational relationships. Partners selected to obtain geographic coverage and specific service expertise improved interorganizational relations. Obtaining specific service expertise from a partner

Table 4.5 Fixed-Effects Regression of Partner Selection on Collaboration Outcomes

| | Collaboration Outcome | | |
	Client Goal Achievement	Improved Interorganizational Relationships	Broadened Organizationa Views
Reasons for Partner Selection			
Resource/programmatic needs			
Extra caseload capacity	.09**	.05	.04
Specific service expertise	.05*	.09**	.05
Geographic coverage	.14***	.12**	.12*
Local knowledge and client access	.01	.05	−.03
Cultural and linguistic needs	−.00	−.03	.05
Organizational legitimacy			
Funding agency requirement	.02	.09**	.19***
Reputation enhancement	.11**	.07	.05
Building future relationships	−.11**	−.04	−.03
Transaction costs			
Shared vision	−.01	.08*	.22***
Successful past collaboration	−.02	−.07**	−.03
Few available partners	−.06	−.11**	−.22***
Number of observations	139	139	139
Probability > F (36, 102)	.00	.00	.00
R^2	.77	.75	.82

* $p < .1$; ** $p < .05$; *** $p < .01$.

requires interaction and learning, and this may promote communication and coordination across organizations. Communication and some joint decision making are normally needed to coordinate geographic coverage, and this may explain the positive impact of these partnerships on interorganizational relationships and on organizational development. Resource-based partnerships are the least likely to have an impact on organizational development—only one measure had an impact, and that is consistent with our expectations.

Organizational legitimacy. The three indicators of partners selected to achieve organizational legitimacy each had an impact on at least one of the collaborative outcomes. As expected, selecting partners to meet a requirement by the funding agency was positively associated with improving interorganizational relationships and with organizational development. The other two indicators of this motivation, however, did not affect these two outcomes. Therefore, the impact of this motivation was less than expected. We did not expect partners selected to enhance organizational legitimacy to affect client goal achievement, but the results suggest that it does. Partners selected to enhance the reputation of the organization are positively associated with client goal achievement. Perhaps organizations select these partners at least in part due to their expertise, and there are associated spillover benefits to service provision. Partners selected to lay the foundation for future relationships are negatively associated with achieving client goals. There is no reason to expect this motivation to have a positive effect on collaboration outcomes, and the negative impact may simply reflect the presence of multiple goals by the organization that may undermine its focus on service delivery.

Transaction costs. Partners selected because of a shared vision have the expected positive impact on interorganizational relationships and on organizational development. Such partners appear to reduce transaction costs and thus improve the operation of the partnerships as expected. The impact of successful past collaborations, however, was not as expected. These partners had a negative impact on interorganizational relationships. Perhaps multiple collaborations with the same partner raise concerns about dependency. This relationship may be a nonlinear one—reducing transaction costs up to a point, and then raising other concerns that undermine the effectiveness of the relationship. Gulati (1995a, 1995b) found such a pattern. Our last indicator of transaction costs, the high search costs associated with few available partners, had the expected negative impact both on interorganizational relationships and on organizational development. Not surprisingly, partners selected largely because they are the only alternative do not produce effective collaborations. None of the transaction cost indicators had an impact on client goal achievement.

CONCLUSION

The use of partnerships among public agencies and private organizations to deliver publicly funded services is a growing reality throughout the world (Goldsmith and Eggers 2004). However, little scholarly attention has been devoted to understanding the factors that promote well-functioning collaborations. There have been very few attempts to understand the causal links between formation conditions, such as how partners are selected and how the collaboration functions. In an era when working together is often required, it is thus not clear how to do so effectively. Both public and private organizations would benefit from more systematic empirical investigations of the factors that have an impact on collaborative performance in practice. Here, we considered the role of partner selection.

Organizations form partnerships for a variety of reasons. In this study, we considered three broad categories of motivations: resource/programmatic needs, organizational legitimacy, and reducing transactions costs. All three factors were found to affect collaborative outcomes, but their effects differed. These differences have policy implications for funding agencies seeking to promote partnerships, for the component organizations, and for those seeking to understand collaboration.

Managers in public agencies are often interested in the ability of organizational collaboration to improve client outcomes or to aid the development of the social network of communities to enhance their problem-solving capacity. Our results have direct implications for how they can design contracts that will achieve these goals. These results suggest that client outcomes are more likely to be improved when organizations choose their collaborative partners based on programmatic needs. Therefore, when this is the goal of the funding agency, managers may find contract requirements to be an effective tool. For example, if they issue requests for proposals covering larger contracts, which cover multiple services and broad geographic areas, this may encourage partnerships that ultimately benefit clients, presumably through more integrated service delivery and richer service choices.

Conversely, if the funding agency is primarily interested in establishing denser social networks within the community, then they may find a simple directive effective, as we found that the contractual requirement to partner is associated with improved interorganizational relationships. Our results indicate that contract characteristics requiring multiple services and broader geographic coverage should also help achieve this goal.

For managers in organizations seeking to enhance their own development via such partnerships, our results suggest that seeking partners with a shared vision is very important. For both the organization and its funding agencies, efforts to increase knowledge about available partners are likely to yield important dividends, because partners "of convenience" do not produce successful collaborations.

Finally, for those who study collaboration, this research suggests an important link between the formation of the interorganizational arrangement and its likely effectiveness. The reasons behind partner selection have an impact on the perceived effectiveness of the collaborative arrangement by its component organizations. Presumably other factors such as decision-making structures, how activities are coordinated, and how the relationships are managed are also important, but this work suggests that who participates in the collaborative exercise and why they were chosen to be part of it matters as well. Future research will need to sort out the relative importance of these different factors.

Some caveats, however, are needed. It is difficult to discern causality from cross-sectional data such as those we analyzed. The use of time-series data would allow the observation of changes in assessments of outcomes over time and thus inform the causality question. Another concern is the potential "social desirability bias" in the self-reported data that were used to construct the dependent and independent variables. There might be a tendency for organizations to overvalue their collaboration outcomes. The observed variation might be smaller than the actual variation. Therefore, the effects studied in our analysis may be underestimated. Finally, our analysis is focused on a single type of services, family preservation services, and a single location, Los Angeles County. There are eleven different social services included in our study, but the effectiveness of collaborations may vary for services with characteristics that are substantially different from these social services. Los Angeles County houses a complex and diverse set of communities. This complexity may make partnerships more necessary and seen as more valuable than might be the case in more homogeneous settings.

Nevertheless, our results provide considerable support for the importance of partner selection in collaborative outcomes and specificity about the nature of that role. This work offers policy design guidance for public agencies interested in using partnerships to achieve client and community goals. Finally, it contributes to our understanding of the factors that determine effective collaborations, and it should provide guidance for both public and private managers as they consider how to structure successful partnerships.

APPENDIX: SURVEY QUESTIONS

1. Below are possible reasons for selecting this organization as your Family Preservation Network partner. We selected this partner . . .
   a. Because DCFS required us to collaborate with other organizations to get funding.
   b. Because we share a common vision about how to serve families and children in need.
   c. Because we successfully collaborated in the past.
   d. Because we could not find other alternative service providers.
   e. Because caseloads are too heavily for us to handle alone.
   f. Because this partner organization has a better knowledge of local community and access to targeted population.

g. To obtain access to their expertise in providing *specific* family preservation services, which would help us better meet the needs of our clients.
h. To serve family preservation clients whose geographic area the lead agency is not able to cover.
i. To meet specific cultural and linguistic needs of family preservation clients.
j. To build a relationship because we expect to interact with this organization again in the future.
k. To enhance our organization's reputation by working with a partner with a strong reputation for quality services.

On a seven-point scale, select the number that best indicates how important each reason was in choosing one particular organization as your partner.

Not at All   Very Important

▼   ▼

1   2   3   4   5   6   7

2. On the 7-point scale below, select the number that best indicates your overall assessment of your collaboration with each partner organization.

Not at All Effective 1   2   3   4   5   6   7   Very Effective

a. Overall, how effective is this collaboration in achieving the expected goals of serving Family Preservation Program clients?
b. Overall, how would you rate the quality of working *relationships* that have developed between your organization and this partner organization as a result of this collaboration?
c. Overall, to what extent has your organization's view on how to better serve Family Preservation Program clients been broadened as a result of listening to this partner organization's views?

NOTES

The research for this chapter was partially supported by a summer research grant from the Bedrosian Center on Governance and the Public Enterprise at the University of Southern California. We greatly appreciate the cooperation of the

Los Angeles County Family Preservation Program, and especially Rhelda Shabazz and Walter Yu-lung Kiang for their considerable help and expertise.

1. Ultimately, service delivery collaborations should yield measurable improvements in client outcomes. But, the connection is difficult to demonstrate because clients often depend on services provided by multiple agencies, and client outcomes involve many other antecedent and mediating factors than those we address here.

2. These dimensions of collaborative effectiveness are consistent with those proposed by others. Gray (2000) reviews this literature and suggests five—problem resolution, generating social capital, creating shared meaning, changing network structures, and shifting power distributions.

3. Only public entities or nonprofit social service organizations that are tax exempt under 501©(3) of the Internal Revenue Code are qualified to bid on the RFPs.

4. We used a mail survey because of the large amount of detailed information requested. This format allowed respondents to consult with other staff or colleagues for assistance in answering questions when necessary.

5. The reasons were not organized according to our model categories and were listed in a random order. The specific questions used to determine the motivations for partner selection and the assessment of collaborative effectiveness are reproduced in the appendix.

Chapter 5

The New Professionalism and Collaborative Activity in Local Emergency Management

Michael McGuire

The changes in the field of emergency management signal the development of a distinct profession. A "profession" emerges as occupational groupings mature and there is an identifiable body of technical knowledge. Members begin to identify with colleagues in other jurisdictions or even nations, develop standards of conduct and professional practice, and establish minimum professional qualifications and experience. That process is well under way in the field of emergency management and, in the twenty-first century, emergency management agencies and policy making will increasingly be guided by professionally trained and educated officials. (Stanley and Waugh 2001, 697)

Disasters, by their very disruptive and dynamic nature, create such significant demands on the affected community that well-executed, multiorganizational responses become not only necessary, but essential. In other words, . . . no single department or agency has sufficient resources to deal with the disaster at hand. In addition, disasters often require the assistance of outsiders and multiple levels of government, thereby leading to multijurisdictional response operations. (Drabek and McEntire 2002, 206)

As the first passage above by Stanley and Waugh suggests, much is changing in the world of emergency and disaster management. The scale of emergencies has grown—as demonstrated by the recent hurricanes, tsunamis, wildfires, and terrorist attacks—and the concomitant demands placed on emergency managers are growing as well. The increasing size and scope of disasters and emergencies suggest that no longer can a community rely on untrained nonprofessionals to prepare for, mitigate against, respond to, and recover from disasters. As Drabek and McEntire argue above, today's emergency managers are multiorganizational managers who must operate across intergovernmental and intersectoral boundaries. Recent case studies document the critical role of networks in planning and responding to disasters (Kendra and Wachtendorf 2003; McEntire 2002; Moynihan 2005a). By implication, the new professional emergency manager is a collaborative public manager.

Various observers refer to a professional (McEntire 2007) or human resources model (Neal and Phillips 1995) that portrays the new emergency manager as a facilitator, as one who shuns a paramilitary approach to emergency management, and as one who operates in both a horizontal and vertical collaborative environment in all functions of emergency management. This professional model of emergency management has several features (McEntire 2007, 97–98). For example, most scholars and practitioners in the field agree that adopting an "all-hazards" approach to disasters—meaning that there are more types of disasters than civil hazards—is most appropriate. The professional emergency manager also understands that he or she cannot deal with emergencies and disasters alone, and that hierarchical, command-and-control relationships are rarely effective and sometimes impossible. Such a professional manager views multiorganizational collaboration as essential to emergency management planning and response, and therefore adopts a strategic approach to coordination (Drabek 2001). The model also assumes that the professional emergency manager performs different functions than do first responders such as firefighters, police officers, and paramedics.

However, there is little in the empirical research literature that measures what is meant by *professionalism* in emergency management, how the emergency management field is becoming *professionalized*, and the role of professionalization in *collaboration*. Is professionalization actually associated with collaborative activity? Does the status of being "professional" induce collaboration? More specifically, does a professionalized emergency management agency collaborate more than a nonprofessional agency? These questions are addressed in the following pages. Using data from a large study of U.S. counties, a quantitative association is made between professionalization and collaboration. The models presented in this chapter thus have implications for understanding the importance of education, training, and organizational change in developing collaborative capacity in public managers.

PROFESSIONALIZATION AND LOCAL EMERGENCY MANAGEMENT

The assumptions of the professional model and the assertions of leading emergency management scholars suggest that professionalizing the emergency management field occurs in two different ways: through education and training, and through altering the organizational structure and scope of emergency management agencies. With respect to the former, one emergency manager long ago implored others to "get as much training as you can from whatever source" (quoted by Drabek 1987, 242). Such training occurs in many different venues. A multitude of training courses and exercises are offered by state governments in the United States, which typically are part of a certification training program or standalone courses. For example, the Georgia Office of Homeland Security offers training courses in emergency preparedness as well as courses specializing in bus extrication, infection control, and rescue operations. The Governor's Division of Emergency Management in Texas offers courses organized around the four general functions of emergency management (mitigation, preparedness, response, and recovery). The Indiana Department of Homeland Security offers first responder courses. Other examples abound.

In the U.S. federal government, the Emergency Management Institute (EMI) is the training and education arm of the Federal Emergency Management Agency (FEMA). As stated in its materials, "EMI serves as the national focal point for the development and delivery of emergency management training to enhance the capabilities of federal, state, local, and tribal government officials, volunteer organizations, and the public and private sectors to minimize the impact of disasters on the American public." Approximately 5,500 participants attend resident courses at the EMI facility in Emmitsburg, Maryland, each year, while 100,000 individuals participate in nonresident programs sponsored by EMI and conducted by state emergency management agencies under cooperative agreements with FEMA. Another 150,000 individuals participate in EMI-supported exercises. In addition to courses in specific substantive areas such as natural and technological hazards, EMI also provides courses in leadership, professional development, and how to design effective training exercises. Specialized courses are offered on such topics as cost/benefit analysis, building design, and emergency management software. EMI also offers a series of courses called the Professional Development Series. The seven courses that make up the series include fundamental courses in principles of emergency management, emergency planning, effective communication, decision making and problem solving, and others. It should be noted that specific courses on collaboration or intergovernmental relations are not part of the course list.

The International Association of Emergency Managers (IAEM) also sponsors a rigorous training program known as the Certified Emergency Manager. Admission into the program requires a baccalaureate degree and considerable on-the-job experience. Requirements for the certification include a minimum of 100 hours of training in emergency management and 100 hours of general management training, making major contributions to the field such as through published articles or public speaking, a written essay designed to respond to various hypothetical scenarios, and a 100-question multiple choice exam.

The structure and scope of local emergency management agencies are also being professionalized. Until recently, emergency management functions typically were performed by agencies associated with first responders from fire and/or police departments. Public safety was viewed as the equivalent of emergency management. Traditional models assumed that emergency management should be located in emergency service departments (McEntire 2007). It was also common for traditional emergency managers to undertake other activities such as building inspection or public works. Emergency operations plans were once commonly written by the fire chief or the nominal emergency management director, if one existed at all. Increasingly, however, there is an assumption that the most effective (i.e., most professional) emergency management agency is either a standalone agency or located in an office that reports to executives separate from police and fire departments.

The new professionalism approach is thus based in education, training, and changing organizational forms. These concepts are defined and operationalized in the next section.

DISCUSSION OF VARIABLES AND HYPOTHESES

The data for this analysis were drawn from a national survey of counties conducted by the National Center for the Study of Counties at the Carl Vinson Institute of Government on behalf of the National Association of Counties. The unit of analysis of this study is the emergency management agency and director located within a county government. There is an emerging belief that emergency management agencies should be based in a county government (Waugh 1994). Counties can act as the important regionalizing force that is critical to coordinating the many resources that encompass emergency management. Counties generally are spatially and geographically close to environmental problems, have greater resource bases than do cities, have administrative structures that encourage inter-governmental collaboration, act as administrative arms of state government, and provide forums that represent local interests (Waugh 1994, 253).

A Web-based questionnaire addressing emergency management issues was submitted to emergency management directors in all 3,066 counties in the United States. The intent of the survey was to establish the capac-ity of counties to prepare for and respond to emergencies and disasters in their community. In addition to questions on collaboration, the survey covered budgeting issues, public organization and management structures, citizen readiness, and volunteerism, among other issues. The final data set of 564 cases represents more than 18 percent of the total number of counties in the country, with the final analysis consisting of 331 counties with complete data.

Although the response rate is low, the distribution of the population and socioeconomic characteristics of the sample closely resemble the nation as a whole (table 5.1). The data set includes a slightly greater proportion of

Table 5.1 Comparison of Sample Counties with U.S. Counties (percentage of population)

Classification	All Counties	Sample Counties
Population group		
Over 500,000	3	5
250,000–499,999	4	7
100,000–249,999	9	16
50,000–99,999	13	14
25,000–49,999	21	20
10,000–24,999	29	21
Under 10,000	22	18
Census region		
1	6	9
2	35	35
3	45	39
4	14	16
Socioeconomic		
Median household income	$41,990	$36,060
Percent below poverty line	12.4	12.6

Source: Web-based questionnaire on emergency management issues submit-ted to emergency management directors in all 3,066 U.S. counties.

large counties (i.e., larger than 100,000 population) and a lower proportion of small counties (smaller than 25,000 population) compared with the total county population. All states with counties are represented in the sample with the exception of Connecticut, Hawaii, and Vermont.

Another means to assess the generalizability of the sample is to compare how closely the sampled counties resemble the nonsampled counties and the nation on a measure known as the Social Vulnerability Index (SoVI). The SoVI measures the social vulnerability of U.S. counties to various hazards. It is useful as an indicator in determining possible recovery from disasters. The index synthesizes forty-two socioeconomic and built environment variables that the research literature suggests contribute to a community's ability to prepare for, respond to, and recover from hazards. The 2000 index uses principal components analysis to reduce the number of variables into a smaller set of eleven indicators, which include personal wealth, ethnicity, occupation, and infrastructure, among others. Cutter, Boruff, and Shirley (2003) determined the vulnerability of counties by calculating their SoVI scores based on standard deviations from the mean into five categories ranging from –1 at the lower end to +1 at the upper end. According to this index, table 5.2 shows that the sampled counties appear to be representative of the nonsampled counties and the nation as a whole.

The dependent variable of the analysis is the total amount of collaborative activity undertaken by county emergency management agencies. Survey respondents were asked to choose which of nineteen actors in the governmental and nongovernmental sectors they work with for eleven specific activities in their emergency planning, mitigation, response, or recovery (see table 5.3 for the list of actors and activities). Thus, all four phases of emergency management were addressed in the survey question. These potential actors included eleven agencies from federal, state, and local governments, as well as eight from nongovernmental organizations such as the American Red Cross and hospitals. The activities for which collaboration occurred include formal interactions such as mutual aid agreements, memoranda of understanding, grant applications and management, and funding transactions, as well as informal cooperation, technical assistance, equipment provision, and joint planning. The additive scale for the measurement of this variable thus ranges from 0, indicating no collaboration with any of the actors, to 209, indicating collaboration with all nineteen actors for all eleven activities. To confirm the scale measure of collaboration, a Cronbach alpha coefficient was calculated for the 209 items, and the coefficient is .954. The mean amount of collaborative activities for the sample counties is 33.9, with a maximum of 166.

Table 5.2 Comparison of Nonsampled Counties, Sampled Counties, and National SoVI Scores

Measure	Nonsampled Counties		Sampled Counties		National SoVI Scores	
	No.	%	No.	%	No.	%
≤1 std. dev.	295	11.4	61	10.8	356	11.3
−1.0 to .5 std. dev.	473	18.3	105	18.7	578	18.4
−.5 to .5 std. dev.	1,154	44.8	273	48.5	1,427	45.4
.5 to 1.0 std. dev.	336	13.0	67	11.9	403	12.8
>1 std. dev.	320	12.4	57	10.1	377	12.0
Total	2,578	100	563	100	3,141	100.0

Note: SoVI = Social Vulnerability Index; std. dev. = standard deviation. The number of total sampled counties in this table (563) is different from the total data set (564) due to missing data. The number of total counties in this table (3,144) is different from the survey (3,066) due to the discrepancy in years (2000 compared with 2006).

Source: Hazards and Vulnerability Research Institute, University of South Carolina.

Table 5.3 Types of Collaborative Organizations and Activities Surveyed (percentage of counties collaborating with each type of organization)

Collaborative Organizations	Collaborative Activities
State emergency management agency (88.7)	Informal cooperation (81.4)
Other county (86.3)	Mutual aid agreements (76.8)
American Red Cross (85.3)	Provides training (73.3)
Federal Emergency Management Agency (84.1)	Joint planning (71.2)
City (83.3)	Technical assistance (67.2)
School districts (82.6)	Grant application (65.9)
Hospital (81.1)	Memoranda of understanding (64.4)
Other Department of Homeland Security agency (77.2)	Receives funding (63.5)
Other state government agency (62.7)	Provides funding (58.8)
Faith-based organization (62.0)	Grant management (50.5)
Other nonprofit agency (60.3)	Provides equipment (50.4)
State environmental protection agency (55.6)	
Other federal government agency (54.2)	
Radio Amateur Civil Emergency Service (51.7)	
Township (49.0)	
Environmental Protection Agency (48.3)	
Amateur Radio Emergency Service (47.1)	
Regional alliance (46.6)	
Council of governments (45.1)	

Source: Web-based questionnaire on emergency management issues submitted to emergency management directors in all 3,066 U.S. counties.

Establishing a valid measure of collaboration is a difficult task. Although operationalizing collaboration as a set of actors and activities is common (Agranoff and McGuire 2003a; Meier and O'Toole 2003), McGuire (2002) suggests with regard to network management that collaboration is an elusive target to properly measure. Similarly, Bardach (1998, 20) notes that "not all collaborative activities are equal." Research that measures activities as the outcome variable "would be obliged to weight these different sorts of activities relative to one another" (Bardach 1998, 20). However, though an index of contacts and the types of contacts may constitute "an imperfect and rough measure of managerial networking," it has been shown empirically that such a measure "taps important components of managerial action in valid and reliable ways" (Meier and O'Toole 2005, 536). The measure of the dependent variable for this analysis does not incorporate such networking activities as "exchanging business cards" or "sitting through planning meetings," as Bardach (1998, 20) warns. Instead, only emergency management-specific actors and activities are incorporated into the measure, and the number of potential actors exceeds those used in previous analyses of economic development and education. This exhaustive measure is not all-inclusive, but it taps into a wide variety of actors and activities.

Professional emergency management education and training are operationalized as five different variables, all of which are hypothesized to be positively associated with the level of collaboration (see table 5.4 for the descriptive statistics of these variables). The first education and training variable is measured as the education level of the top emergency management official in the county. If the lead official has a postgraduate degree of any type, emergency management related or otherwise, the dichotomous variable takes on a value of 1; if the official has any other level of education, the variable has a value of 0. Just 13.5 percent of the sample has such a degree.

Three additional variables measure whether the lead emergency management official has taken part in any of three specialized formal training activities. The first corresponds to state certification training. If the lead emergency management official has state certification training, a dichotomous variable has a value of 1; if not, the variable is measured as 0. The second specialized training variable is measured by whether the lead official has participated in the FEMA Professional Development Series. If so, the dichotomous variable is measured as one; if not, it takes on a value of 0. Like the other two, the third specialized training variable is valued at 1 if the lead official has been trained as a Certified Emergency Manager by the IAEM, or 0 if not. A total of

Table 5.4 Descriptive Statistics for Explanatory Variables (percentage responding in the affirmative, unless otherwise specified)

Variable	Descriptive
Education and training	
Postgraduate degree	13.5
State certification training	44.1
FEMA training	41.1
IAEM training	19.1
Training functions	Mean = 6.23
National Incident Management System	70.2
Incident command	69.1
Terrorism response	65.6
Hazardous materials	63.6
Communications	54.2
Volunteer resource management	52.9
Fire	48.5
Emergency medical	46.9
Meteorological	46.5
Grant writing	45.8
Police	38.2
Military	21.9
Structural	
Public safety agency	34.9
Duties beyond emergency management	57.1
Task force prepared plan	20.5
Control	
Total population	Median = 36,016
Urban population	46.24
Expected budget increase	39.0
Average concern about terrorism	Mean = 3.26

Source: Web-based questionnaire on emergency management issues submitted to emergency management directors in all 3,066 U.S. counties.

44.1 percent of the lead officials in the sample have state certification training, 41.1 percent have participated in FEMA training, and 19.1 percent have IAEM certification.

The fifth education and training variable measures the total number of functions for which the county emergency management agency has received training. The survey asked the respondent to select whether the agency received training for twelve specific functions, including training in police, fire, incident command, the National Incident Management System, terrorism response, and other related emergency functions. Values for this continuous variable range from 0 if the agency received no outside training for any of the functions to 12 if the agency received training for all the functions. The Cronbach's alpha for this 12-item scale is .902. The mean number of training functions for the sample counties is 6.2.

Three variables address the level of professionalization of emergency management in the county by measuring the managerial structure of the agency. As noted above, the recent literature suggests that an emergency management agency that is not a "standalone" organization separate from law enforcement and fire fighting is not consistent with the requirements of the emerging profession. To test the hypothesis that a purely public safety agency is negatively related to the level of collaborative activity, a variable was created with a value of 1 if the county agency is a unit within public safety along with police and fire or 0 if not. More than one-third (34.9 percent) of the sample counties were structured that way.

The second structural variable measuring the level of emergency management professionalization in the county addresses whether employees of the agency have any duties beyond emergency management. Some ostensibly emergency management agencies are also charged with duties such as code enforcement, facilities management, building inspections, or public works. I hypothesize that agencies performing duties in addition to emergency management will be less collaborative. If the respondent noted that there are additional duties beyond emergency management, a value of 1 is assigned; if no additional duties, the variable is measured with a 0. The relationship between this variable and collaborative activity is thus hypothesized to be negative. A total of 57.1 percent of the sample counties report agency duties beyond emergency management.

The third structural variable measures how the county's emergency operations plan was prepared—whether by the office itself, a multiagency task force, a contractor, or by some other means. If the plan was prepared by a task force, the variable is assigned a value of 1; if not, a 0 is assigned. I hypothesize that counties with a plan that was prepared by a task force will have a greater level of collaborative activity. Approximately one-fifth (20.5 percent) of the counties used such a task force to prepare the emergency operations plan.

In addition to the eight professionalization explanatory variables, four control variables are used in the model, two of them dealing with the county population. Because community size was found to have been associated with interagency collaboration for emergency management in previous research (Drabek 1987), and because table 5.1 shows that there are some minor discrepancies in the sample population distribution in relation to the totality of counties in the United States, population size is employed as a control. A previous analysis of city-level collaboration in economic development has demonstrated that urban cities are more collaborative (Agranoff and McGuire 1998). Thus another control variable used is the percentage of the county population that is classified as urban. It is expected that the greater the population and the greater the percentage of urban population, the greater the degree of collaboration.

Two final control variables deal with the future concerns of the emergency manager. One addresses the agency's budget and whether the respondent expects a budget increase for the next fiscal year. Previous research demonstrates the effect of the budget on collaborative activity (McGuire 2000), suggesting that an increase in an agency budget can sometimes be the result of an increase in intergovernmental funds. If the respondent from the county emergency management agency anticipates a budget increase, the variable is measured with a 1; if the respondent expects the budget for the next fiscal year to stay the same or decrease, the variable is measured with a 0. A total of 39 percent of the counties expect their budget to increase. A positive relationship between an expected budget increase and the level of collaboration is hypothesized.

The other control variable measures the extent to which the agency is concerned about possible future emergencies and disasters. The respondent was asked to declare, on a 7-point scale, whether he or she was extremely concerned (measured with a 7), not at all concerned (measured with a 1), or somewhere between these extremes, about twenty-four different types of emergencies and disasters. Because terrorism presents the most alarming, if not the most immediate, concern for counties, and because a great deal of government attention and financial resources have been given to terrorism preparedness for local communities, the final control variable measures the agency's concern for terrorism. The responses for three questions about nuclear, biological, and chemical terrorism have been averaged into a single number that ranges from 1 to 7. The mean value for the terrorism concern variable is 3.26. I hypothesize that the greater the level of concern about terrorism, the greater the level of collaborative activity.

This analysis attempts to capture many different facets of professionalization through the use of eight different measures. The primary question to address is whether collaboration is associated with these factors. The next section attempts to answer this question.

ANALYSIS

The relationship between collaborative activity and professionalization is examined with both ordinary least squares (OLS) regression analysis and a technique known as substantively weighted least squares (SWLS) analysis (Meier and Gill 2000). The purpose of using SWLS is to explore the level of collaborative activity for those counties that are the most collaborative. Officials in county emergency management agencies interested in learning how education, training, and structural features affect one's propensity to collaborate are concerned with performance, with preparing for and responding to emergencies and disasters in the most efficacious way possible. OLS regression is used to determine the set of variables associated with counties that have average collaborative activity, thus demonstrating only how the "normal" or average county was affected by professionalization. Alternatively, SWLS analysis is an ideal mechanism for isolating those county agencies that are the most professional, as measured by the education, training, and structural variables. SWLS analysis assigns greater weight to the cases with above-average values of the dependent variable compared with the rest of the cases. We can observe and evaluate changes in the slopes across iterations to determine the characteristics of the most active counties that are different from the average county. Therefore, the results of the OLS analysis are used as an empirical bridge to a more substantive analysis.

The OLS results are shown in table 5.5. The table reveals that the level of collaborative activity by county emergency management agencies is a function of at least some of the professionalization variables. A bit more than one-third of the variance in the level of collaborative activity is explained by the twelve independent variables (adjusted $R^2 = .341$). Clearly, other factors contribute to collaborative activity, yet the results demonstrate a significant relationship between education, training, and collaboration.

The variable measuring the level of education is statistically significant at the .01 level. Those agency directors with some type of graduate degree report higher levels of collaborative activity and the coefficient indicates that, on average, seven more activities are associated with possessing such a degree. This result supports the hypothesis that greater levels of education are positively related to collaborative activity. The results are mixed for the variables measuring participation in formal, specialized training programs. Taking part in a state's certification training program is positively and significantly related to the level of collaborative activity by a county emergency management agency. Similarly, the variable that measures courses taken in FEMA's Professional Development Series is positively and significantly associated with collaborative activity. An agency director who has participated in both training programs, on average, can be expected to collaborate with more partners for more activities than those directors who have taken part in neither program.

Table 5.5 Ordinary Least Squares Regression of Collaboration on Professionalization

Explanatory Variable	Slope	Standard Error	Standardized Coefficient	t-score	Significance
Postgraduate education	7.274	2.784	.125	2.613	.009
State certification training	4.802	2.088	.117	2.300	.022
FEMA training	6.153	2.003	.150	3.072	.002
IAEM training	-.495	2.334	-.010	-.212	.832
Training functions	1.617	.262	.284	6.160	.000
Public safety agency	-2.821	1.956	-.066	-1.442	.150
Duties beyond emergency management	-2.674	2.003	-.065	-1.335	.183
Task force prepared operations plan	4.496	2.333	.089	1.927	.055
Total population (per 1,000)	.003	.002	.075	1.544	.124
Urban population	.069	.036	.104	1.941	.053
Expected budget increase	4.054	1.893	.098	2.141	.033
Average concern about terrorism	3.394	.659	.248	5.150	.000
Number of observations	331				
Adjusted R^2	.341				
F-statistic	15.21*				
Standard error	16.64				

* $p < .001$.

Interestingly, the variable measuring participation in the IAEM certification program, thought by some to be the centerpiece of the professionalism movement, is not significantly related to collaborative activity. Finally, as hypothesized, the fifth variable measuring education and training—the additive scale of functions for which the county has received training—is positively and significantly related to collaborative activity. Those counties with the mean number of functions (just more than six) will have, on average, nearly ten more collaborative activities than counties with no training in any function.

The coefficients for the three professionalization structural variables are in the hypothesized direction. Administratively locating emergency management in a public safety agency is negatively related to collaborative activity, as is an agency that performs duties other than emergency management, but neither of the variables is statistically significant. The variable denoting that a task force prepared the operations plan was positively but not significantly associated with the dependent variable. These findings suggest that the organizational prescriptions of emergency management professionalization do not contribute to the collaborative activity of the average county agency.

Contrary to earlier research on interagency collaboration in emergency management (Drabek 1987), the size of the county as measured by the total population is not a statistically significant determinant of collaborative activity in the average-performing county. The percentage of the population that is urban is also not significant. The other two control variables perform in the model as expected. There is a statistically significant relationship between an anticipation of an increase in the next fiscal year's budget and collaborative activity, and a county's concern for terrorism is positively related to such activity.

The results from the OLS provide some confirmation for the general hypothesis that the professionalization of emergency management is associated with greater levels of collaborative activity. In summary, all the education and training variables except one are statistically significant and positively related to collaboration. That is, when the director of an emergency management agency possesses a graduate degree and/or has participated in various training programs, that agency's level of collaboration with multiple intergovernmental and intersectoral actors for multiple activities is greater than for those directors who have not. Also, the greater the number of functions for which the agency has trained, the greater the level of collaborative activity undertaken by that agency. Conversely, there is little to suggest that structural aspects of professionalization contribute to collaboration. The variable measuring the use of a task force for preparing an operations plan approaches significance at the .05 level, but the variables addressing the administration location and duties of the emergency management agency are not statistically significant.

We can learn about the role of professionalization in collaboration by studying the high-performing county agencies, that is, the most actively collaborative ones. Counties where collaborative activity was higher than expected, given the values of the independent variables, were identified. Consistent with recent formulations of substantively weighted least squares (Meier and Gill 2000), the highest-performing counties are considered to be those counties with studentized residuals of .7 or more (approximately 22 percent of the cases). The original OLS regression model was run iteratively by weighting the counties with studentized residuals of less than .7 to count as .5 counties (thus weighting the highest performing counties by two times), .2 counties (highest-performing counties weighted five times), .1 counties (highest-performing counties weighted ten times), and finally, .05 counties (highest-performing counties weighted twenty times).

Changes in the coefficients (slopes) for the twelve variables have been calculated by dividing the SWLS regression slopes by the original OLS regression slopes. The numbers reported in table 5.6 indicate the change in each slope at each iteration compared with the original slopes. Values that are greater than one indicate that the slope for the variable has increased for that specific SWLS model relative to the original OLS slopes. Slope values that are less than 1 indicate a decrease in the slope relative to the OLS slope. Negative slope values indicate a change in direction for the coefficient. Substantively, the slope values for each variable indicate the impact of that variable on collaborative activity for the most active counties, holding all other variables constant, compared with the average county. The results for the final model with the high-performing counties weighted twenty times are reported in table 5.7.

The SWLS model that highlights the most active counties provides additional evidence that the professionalization of emergency management induces collaborative activity and offers some interesting contrasts to the original OLS model. As shown in table 5.6, the slope for the state certification training increases by more than 42 percent when the most active counties are weighted twenty times the other counties. The slopes for the FEMA training and for the training functions remain about the same through the iterations, with the FEMA slope decreasing by nearly 8 percent, suggesting that FEMA training is a slightly less important factor in determining collaboration in the most active counties. The SWLS model

Table 5.6 Change in Slopes for Explanatory Variables Using Substantively Weighted Least Squares (Weights for High-Activity Counties)

Explanatory Variable	Unweighted	2X	5X	10X	20X
Postgraduate education	1.000	.795	.539	.415	.352
State certification training	1.000	1.031	1.154	1.292	1.425
FEMA training	1.000	1.108	1.137	1.049	.922
IAEM training	1.000	.408	-.913	-2.067	-3.046
Training functions	1.000	1.028	1.036	1.016	.987
Public safety agency	1.000	.937	.974	1.071	1.172
Duties beyond emergency management	1.000	1.267	1.595	1.729	1.769
Task force prepared operations plan	1.000	1.067	1.205	1.290	1.334
Total population (per 1,000)	1.000	.713	.269	-.039	-.279
Urban population	1.000	1.390	1.841	2.072	2.203
Expected budget increase	1.000	1.245	1.515	1.635	1.699
Average concern about terrorism	1.000	1.100	1.213	1.257	1.273

Table 5.7 Substantively Weighted Weighted Least Squares Regression of Collaboration on Professionalization (High-Activity Counties Weighted 20 Times Other Counties)

Explanatory Variable	Slope	Standard Error	Standardized Coefficient	t-score	Significance
Postgraduate education	2.562	2.472	.042	1.036	.301
State certification training	6.841	1.868	.165	3.663	.000
FEMA training	5.671	1.779	.135	3.187	.002
IAEM training	1.508	2.049	.029	.736	.462
Training functions	1.596	.219	.293	7.291	.000
Public safety agency	-3.307	1.668	-.078	-1.982	.048
Duties beyond emergency management	-4.729	1.783	-.113	-2.653	.008
Task force prepared operations plan	5.996	2.080	.119	2.882	.004
Total population (per 1,000)	-.000	.000	-.012	-.272	.786
Urban population	.152	.032	.225	4.737	.000
Expected budget increase	6.889	1.704	.165	4.043	.000
Average concern about terrorism	4.319	.545	.325	7.926	.000
Number of observations	331				
Adjusted R^2	.515				
F-statistic	30.23*				
Standard error	7.41				

* $p < .001$.

in table 5.7 shows that all three variables remain statistically significant, with the t-score increasing for each variable.

Conversely, the slope for one of the statistically significant variables in the OLS analysis, postgraduate education, drops by nearly 65 percent when the most active counties are weighted twenty times the other counties. The SWLS model shows that the variable is no longer statistically significant. Contrary to the original hypothesis, this finding indicates that the level of collaboration in the most active counties is not affected when the director of the county emergency management agency possesses a graduate degree. The slope for the fifth education and training variable, participating in training with the IAEM, actually changes direction but the coefficient is not statistically significant.

Although none of the three structural professionalization variables perform in the OLS model according to the hypotheses, the slopes for all three increase substantially when the most active counties are weighted and each is statistically significant at the .05 level. If a county agency must take on duties beyond emergency management, its ability to collaborate is clearly inhibited. The slope for that variable increases by nearly 77 percent when the most active counties are weighted twenty times the other counties, an increase that is more than any of the other eight professionalization variables. Similarly, an agency that houses emergency management functions in a public safety agency responsible for police and fire is negatively associated with collaborative activity in the most active counties. Finally, the slope increase for the variable that measures whether the county used a task force to prepare an emergency operations plan indicates that the variable contributes significantly to collaborative activity in the most active counties.

As shown in table 5.7, the coefficient for the total population variable changes direction and the t-score decreases, remaining statistically not significant. The population size does not appear to limit the degree to which a county engages in collaborative activity. Although size does not appear to have an impact on collaborative activity in the most active counties, the context of the population does. The slope for the other population control variable, the percentage of the population that is urban, more than doubled in the final SWLS model and became statistically significant at the .001 level. Urban counties often have greater political linkages with state and federal agencies and are typically eligible for more funding opportunities than are rural communities. The slopes for the control variables measuring an expected budget increase and a county's average concern about terrorism increased substantially and became significant at the .001 level.

DISCUSSION AND CONCLUSION

The preceding analysis offers an empirical and quantitative test of the professional model of emergency management. Is such management collaborative? The answer is yes. The models estimated for this analysis demonstrate that in the field of emergency management, the agencies most capable of working with multiple jurisdictional and organizational partners are those that are considered to be the most professionalized, as conceptualized in terms of education, training, and organizational structure. Using an index of collaborative activity that measures the number and types of collaborative contacts made by a county emergency management agency, the findings suggest that the more professionalized such an agency is, the higher its level of collaborative activity. The results of the model have many implications for the field of emergency management specifically and for collaborative public management in general.

Although most training courses available to emergency managers do not explicitly teach about interorganizational relationships or collaboration, the capacity to collaborate still increases as professionalization increases. How so? There are multiple emergency managers in the training courses, presumably some who have had previous experience with disasters. It is improbable that future collaborative partners are in an Emmitsburg classroom at the same time, but shared learning can occur among strangers. Through this process, a type of transitory social capital is developed. Developing social capital is critical for collaboration; it is the stock that is created when a group of organizations develops the ability to work together for mutual gain (Fountain 1998). Although the emergency managers undergoing training at the same time may not work together personally, they assume roles that lend themselves to a collaborative effort. As Stanley and Waugh (2001) point out, the managers begin to identify with colleagues in other jurisdictions. Collaboration with likeminded colleagues becomes more likely because "it is doubtful that coordination will take place among organizations if they are unaware of each other" (McEntire 1998, 3). Bardach's (1998, 20) concept of interagency collaborative capacity is relevant here; he argues that such capacity "is the potential to engage in collaborative activities." One component of interagency collaborative capacity concerns the "relevant individuals' expectations of others' availability for, and competency at, performing particular collaborative tasks" which are in turn "built around the legitimacy and desirability of collaborative action directed at certain goals, the readiness to act on this belief, and trust in the other persons whose cooperation must be relied on for success" (Bardach 1998, 21). Through training and education, emergency managers develop the potential to collaborate, and do so in their home jurisdiction.

Formal education at a university is not significantly associated with collaborative activity in the highest-performing counties. The variable measuring education level used in the preceding analysis did not differentiate between postgraduate work in emergency management and postgraduate work in another field, but other models were run that isolated only emergency management degrees and there was no change in the findings. It may be that higher education is less vocational than federal and state training, and thus is perceived as less directly relevant to the future or current working professional. However, with the increase in emergency management graduate programs over the last few years, a similar analysis performed five to eight years hence may reveal greater collaborative capacity among those with graduate degrees. College textbooks have begun to address the collaborative nature of emergency management more explicitly (Lindell, Prater, and Perry 2006; McEntire 2007), and some have recently proposed standards for training and education in emergency management (Alexander 2003; Neal 2000).

Three other features of the professional model that are tested in this analysis address the organizational context of emergency management. According to the professional model of emergency management, the professional manager performs different roles than first responders and must not remain isolated from decision makers and other department heads (McEntire 2007, 97). The findings on organizational structure suggest that a command-and-control model of management, often associated with a public safety department where the manager works in an organization of first responders, is not associated with collaboration. Control is much harder to come by in collaborative efforts, but many suggest that asking the question "Who is in charge?" is meaningless in emergency situations (Quarantelli 1997). In reality, it is nearly impossible to impose control in such a collaborative enterprise—and not even desirable to do so (Dynes 1994).

There are practical and theoretical implications of this study for our understanding of collaborative public management. First and foremost, collaboration can be learned and collaborative capacity can be developed. As the emergency management field turns to training and education as a means to enhance the profession, managers not only recognize the value of collaboration but also pursue it as a necessary administrative activity. The future development of collaborative management theory should focus on the development of collaborative capacity over time rather than exploring it categorically as "present" or "not present." Second, where one sits in an organization may partially determine whether or how one collaborates outside that organization. Emergency management directors whose primary responsibility is first response collaborate less than directors from other types of agencies. Our understanding of collaborative management may be enhanced by studying the relationship between the structure of the "home" agencies and the network itself. In some cases, lack of collaboration could possibly be explained simply by showing that there is an internal organizational barrier to such collaboration.

Future research should focus on at least four other areas. First, the counties that are most active in collaboration could be studied as cases. An in-depth look at the highest-performing county agencies may teach us about the association between professionalism and collaboration. For example, is the level of collaboration driven by the personal qualities of the leader of the agency? That is, can leadership, however measured, be an important explanatory variable (Rubin 1985)? Or, as suggested in this analysis, does the agency itself embody a capacity to collaborate? There are other questions as well that can be addressed with a case study: What types of relationships exist between the agency and its collaborative partners? And what are the social mechanisms that link training and education with collaborative activity?

Second, as in other policy fields and programmatic areas, some emergency management collaboration is mandated by another level of government. For example, many counties participate in federal grant programs —such as the Hazard Mitigation Grant Program and FEMA's Environmental and Historic Preservation program—that require multiorganizational planning and administration. Similarly, state grant dollars often depend upon a local plan and, sometimes, drills and exercises that involve multiple governmental and nongovernmental actors. Although this analysis does not differentiate between "forced" and "voluntary" collaboration, it can be surmised that much of the collaboration reported in the survey is not mandated by another government but is indeed a necessary component of emergency management and is recognized as such by the manager. However, that is an empirical question that should be explored.

Third, where possible, the quality of the education and training should be taken into account in future models. For most variables in this analysis, just the presence of education and training was measured. However, more needs to be known about the training programs and the quality of the degrees that are being attained by emergency managers. What courses and exercises lend themselves to more collaboration? Is there higher quality and thus more collaborative training in some states compared with others?

Finally, as Bardach (1998, 23) suggests, additional analyses should focus on "How good?" rather than on "How much?" Collaborative activity can be the critical explanatory variable in a performance analysis of local emergency management. Of course, the dependent variable in such an analysis is not easily measured prior to an emergency. For example, an agency's response to and recovery from a disaster is clearly a function of its preparedness. And collaboration, in turn, may result from that agency's response. Empirically modeling such complexity is a necessary task if we are to understand the impact of collaboration in local emergency management.

What does it mean to be a collaborative public manager? In the world of the emergency manager, it means operating across organizational and sectoral boundaries that are not easily traversed. In many respects, the emergency manager may have the most complex organizational field within which to work; many nongovernmental organizations are at the heart of successful emergency and disaster management. In addition, emergency managers must work with professionals who come from agencies with strong, well-established cultures defined more in terms of command and control, such as police officers and firefighters. Emergency management collaboration also transcends other programmatic areas—including health, public safety, and community development—requiring managers to seek out information and expertise from multiple sources for multiple purposes. Whereas in some endeavors collaboration may be an activity that should be avoided (Huxham 2003), this is not the case in emergency management.

NOTE

I would like to thank Beth Gazley and the anonymous reviewers for their helpful comments.

Chapter 6

Calming the Storms: Collaborative Public Management, Hurricanes Katrina and Rita, and Disaster Response

Alisa Hicklin, Laurence J. O'Toole Jr.,
Kenneth J. Meier, and Scott E. Robinson

As scholars have explored the relationship between public management and organizational performance, a considerable body of work has identified interorganizational collaboration as an effective strategy to improve performance. These studies show a number of benefits that can be linked to the presence of a more collaborative public manager. As managers build relationships with other groups in the interdependent environment, these links often result in higher levels of support for the organization, joint ventures in pursuing policy goals, avenues for the acquisition of additional resources, and opportunities to proactively address some possible threats to the organization and its programs. Given the evidence, it would seem that networking to build collaborative relationships is a managerial activity with very few drawbacks—aside from the opportunity costs necessarily involved.

However, most of this evidence examines collaboration at times when the organization is functioning as it typically operates—carrying out its core functions and addressing somewhat predictable problems. Researchers in public management know much less about patterns of collaboration in times of sharp, unpredictable organizational crisis. This gap in our knowledge is problematic for two reasons. First, times of short-term crisis often have long-term effects on the organization and the people involved. As we have seen in a number of major crises (the September 11, 2001, terrorist attacks; Hurricane Katrina; etc.), effective management can help an organization to overcome the crisis and even grow stronger, but poor managers can cause lasting and irreparable damage. Second, the immediacy required in responding to a crisis may change the ways that managers view collaboration. Though networking can be expected to be beneficial for problem solving, there are reasons to expect that building these collaborative relationships during times of disruption and distraction could be very time consuming and costly. In times of externally imposed crisis, when the organization must respond quickly to a major environmental shock, what explains the extent of collaboration with others in the interdependent environment? In particular, do established patterns or styles of management externally contribute to the development of interorganizational collaboration during crisis periods?

These questions speak to the broader issue of the determinants of collaboration. Do managerial choices shape collaborative results? Is the decision to engage in collaboration strategic? Is it problem-specific? Or could collaboration develop as a product of a more diffuse management style emphasizing external interactions with others? This chapter addresses these questions by drawing on recent work in public management to develop hypotheses about what could drive the development of collaborative ties in response to a major organizational shock. These hypotheses are tested in a natural-experiment design by investigating the response during the aftermaths of Hurricane Katrina and Hurricane Rita, when school districts not directly hit by the hurricane nonetheless had to respond quickly when bombarded with an influx of displaced students.

WICKED PROBLEMS AND COLLABORATIVE ACTION: DISASTERS AND THEIR PUBLIC MANAGEMENT

Partnerships, interorganizational programs, and collaboratives are all the rage. The interest in these sorts of patterns is not confined to the United States but is also visible in the United Kingdom, other Westminster settings (Lowndes and Skelcher 2004; Rhodes 1997, 2002; Stoker 2004; Sullivan and Skelcher 2002), continental Europe (Bogason and Toonen 1998; Van Bueren, Klijn, and Koppenjan 2003; Kickert, Klijn, and Koppenjan 1997a, 1997b; Klijn 1996; Raab 2002), and elsewhere. Many forces have driven this upsurge in attention (O'Toole 1997), even though one can question whether such arrangements are particularly new or have become unusually visible in recent years (Hall and O'Toole 2000, 2004).

The importance of public management to successful collaboration is a theme that has been emphasized by several scholars (e.g., Agranoff and

McGuire 2003a; Meier and O'Toole 2003; O'Toole 1997; O'Toole and Meier 2003; Provan and Milward 1991). Among the reasons why interorganizational arrays have been adopted as a means of executing public purposes, and why public management can be a key element in their successful operation, is the prominence of so-called wicked problems (Rittel and Webber 1973) on the public agenda. When the kinds of issues demanding policy and management attention cannot be neatly compartmentalized in one sector—and one public organization—but instead span fields, sectors, specialties, and extant institutional arrangements, new and often collaborative cross-organizational forms may be the preferred structural choice. Many of today's most pressing challenges, from homeland security to HIV/AIDS to climate change, exhibit wicked-problem features.

One of the most obvious of such challenges is governmental response to natural disasters (Comfort 2006). Often appearing without warning, disasters like earthquakes, floods, major storms, and wildfires can unleash devastating forces that cause massive destruction and loss of life, along with severe disruption and dislocation in the lives of many. Natural disasters also touch upon many policy fields and governmental responsibilities simultaneously. Such events are no respecters of jurisdiction, and they can be considered shocks to multiple social, ecological, and physical systems simultaneously—with reverberations that can reach across time and even huge distances. Consider, for example, the tsunami in South Asia in December 2004, or the prospect of significant melting in the Greenland ice field that many experts anticipate in the coming years. Clearly, natural disasters can require responses that integrate efforts and organizational activities from many fields, often in intricate fashions. Multiple levels of government, multiple agencies of government, multiple governments at the same level, as well as multiple organizations in the private and not-for-profit sector, may all need to be mobilized and may even be required to work closely with each other in tight patterns of coordination if the myriad issues generated by major disasters are to be addressed.

Some of these types of collaboration, involving certain of these organizations, can and should be anticipated and planned for in advance. This is one of the principal premises underlying efforts at disaster preparedness, as called for by national policy, as well as the plans and policies in many states. Still, if the scale of the disaster is great and especially if the timing cannot be anticipated, some of the resulting needs, including needs for collaboration, cannot be programmed in advance—certainly not in intricate detail. In such circumstances, coordinated responses may have to be mobilized quickly and under pressure, and public managers can be called upon to mesh multiple streams of intricate effort—virtually overnight.

When such efforts fail, the costs can be enormous. Witness the devastatingly ineffectual responses at virtually all levels and by many individuals and organizational actors during and after the September 2005 hurricanes on the U.S. Gulf Coast. Hurricane Katrina and Hurricane Rita exposed huge weaknesses in the systems of disaster response in the United States, the states of Mississippi and Louisiana, and communities like New Orleans. Researchers will be probing the experiences related to these disasters for some time to come.

Still, some systematic investigation can be undertaken even now, at least on some of the salient questions. Of particular interest here is the question of whether and why some organizational responses triggered by Katrina and Rita were marked by substantial interorganizational, collaborative activity in the interests of addressing unexpected disruption, while others produced very little. We focus specifically on one discrete slice of the overall picture and explore in particular whether prior patterns of active networking by top managers helped to facilitate a more vigorous collaborative response to unexpectedly disruptive shocks in the service delivery system.

In doing so, we build on earlier work on public management, collaborative processes, and performance (O'Toole and Meier 1999).[1] We adapt that work to the realm of disaster response, a field in which specialists have understandably paid attention to collaborative patterns. In researching organizational response to disasters, scholars have long seen the importance of interorganizational coordination. Wenger, Quarantelli, and Dynes (1986, 10–11), for instance, found that many organizations discussed collaboration as a goal of their efforts but seldom included coordination in their actual activities. Drabek showed that coordination was part of the emergence of a multiorganizational network in the cases of disaster response that he studied (Drabek et al. 1982; Drabek 1983, 1985). More recent work has focused on the role of intergovernmental networks in responding to disasters. Schneider (1995) examined the coordination of federal and state relief in multiple natural disasters. A key factor in the perceived success of government efforts was clarity about the division of responsibility between the levels of government. Even today, the division of responsibility is unclear, as the severely bungled disaster response in New Orleans has made apparent.

Later work has refocused attention on the emergent nature of organizational networks (Comfort 1999). In researching organizational preparedness in Saint Louis, Gillespie and Streeter (1987) found that an organization's structure, the environment in which it operates, and its history with emergencies influenced its preparedness efforts. In addition, the quality of its interorganizational relations was an important contributor to its emergency preparedness. In light of this research, Tierney and her colleagues suggested that research on emergency preparedness networks is a "particularly promising approach" (Tierney, Lindell, and Perry 2001, 60). This set of studies also suggests that public management may be a critical element in this field, as it is for collaboration and coordination in other policy sectors.

Explaining the emergence of collaboration, therefore, is a key question generally in wicked-problem contexts and takes on particular salience in settings where collaboration is needed in unexpected and often widespread fashion. Specialists on disaster management recognize the issue as central. We examine one portion of the topic here by taking advantage of extensive prehurricane and posthurricane research conducted in one set of contexts: Texas school districts.

EDUCATING AND ASSISTING EVACUEES

Collaboration by public managers and their organizations is obviously an expected response to natural disasters, which typically overwhelm those immediately affected and also impose major, and often long-term, externalities on others, including other communities. During September 2005, Hurricane Katrina and Hurricane Rita provided vivid examples. These disasters caused untold devastation and also triggered the movement of millions of evacuees to other jurisdictions, indeed to other parts of the country. Even before the landfall of Hurricane Katrina, thousands of people fled the Gulf Coast and parts of Northeast Texas also in the hurricane's path, with many traveling west to unaffected cities across Texas, which organized to accommodate them.

One set of effects on Texas local governments and public managers occurred in public school systems, which had to take on the challenge of handling many additional, high-need students with almost no notice. These systems were faced with the unique task of absorbing a large number of students who had diverse, extensive needs reaching well beyond what school districts are normally expected to address. This complexity was further compounded by the fact that many decisions and constraints in the arena of public education are framed, in effect, at one remove, because the bulk of the regulations, curricula, and operating procedures implemented locally are set at the state level. With most evacuees having migrated across state lines, the interstate dimension produced additional management challenges that were not able to be resolved without cross-jurisdictional efforts.

Indeed, numerous aspects of this wicked-problem challenge called for these public organizations to collaborate with other actors—police, fire, and first responders; nonprofit and relief organizations; other school systems; governmental relief and welfare organizations; business organizations; and local, community, and religious organizations. Within days after Katrina, it had become obvious that people displaced from the most heavily affected areas of the Gulf Coast would not be able to return to their original homes any time soon. These victims were forced to look for long-term housing—and children in these families would not be able simply to wait out the displacement. They needed schooling, and more. To compound the situation, parts of East Texas had to evacuate as the second storm, Hurricane Rita, flooded many areas. A result was the long-term displacement of many students into school districts in Texas just weeks after the start of the new school year.

In November 2005 we initiated the administration of a mail survey directed at top managers—superintendents—of Texas school districts. The survey, administered in three waves between November and January, achieved a 47.7 percent response rate ($N = 600$). Data were collected on a number of issues related to how the districts responded to the sudden influx of these students and how the unexpected perturbation to the educational system affected the district's own emergency planning. The scale of the externally generated shock varied considerably among Texas school districts. Many districts took in only a handful of students with little disruption, while other districts felt a considerable impact, with larger districts finding themselves required to deal overnight with as many as 3,500 new students and smaller districts receiving enough evacuees to raise their enrollments considerably.

Those districts that absorbed a substantial number of evacuated students needed to integrate them into their classrooms as soon as possible, a challenge that in turn required the districts to address a number of additional needs, some directly related to education and others important but more indirectly connected to the core task. Many superintendents reported that their districts provided a number of goods and services to the evacuated students. Some elements provided were directly related to the educational process (crafting orientation programs, providing textbooks, opening new buildings, hiring additional teachers), and others were not (offering health care, shelter, food, Federal Emergency Management Agency information, etc.). Not surprisingly, addressing this broad array of student-centered needs led superintendents to look to other groups and organizations in the community that might be able to assist in ameliorating some of the problems and providing relevant services.

COLLABORATION IN EMERGENCY RESPONSE

The decision of many superintendents to look outward to other groups and organizations to aid in the response is unsurprising, given the diversity of needs that emerged. However, districts varied considerably in the extent to which they were stimulated to collaborate with other actors. This variation is interesting, because it touches on a number of issues related to managerial networking and interorganizational collaboration. In particular, it allows us to consider the determinants of collaboration.

General treatments of networking and of collaboration often point to the emergence of interorganizational and intergovernmental patterns of interdependence, including that, because of expectations, governments address tendentious wicked problems (Agranoff and McGuire 2003b; Klijn 2005; Lynn, Heinrich, and Hill 2001; O'Toole and Meier 1999). One would expect more complex problems to require more innovative and comprehensive managerial approaches and organizational strategies, but we have little systematic empirical evidence to support the asserted link between heightened complexity and collaboration (Klijn 2005). Indeed, as the ensuing discussion suggests, some of the literature might encourage an expectation that environmental shocks might sometimes actually reduce external connections. Most instances of the emergence of networked patterns in the public sector reflect incremental changes that organizations and their contexts undergo over extended periods of time. However, the challenges faced by public organizations and managers from a major, unexpected shock to the system could stimulate fundamentally different dynamics than those triggered by small fluctuations in organizational processes, especially when this disruption is not something that the organization has faced before. We explore this type of situation here.

Whereas the research literature on collaboration and networks clearly argues that wicked problems are likely to encourage more interorganizational ties and more externally oriented networking, other arguments suggest that matters may not be so straightforward. In his discussion of how public organizations react to major shocks from the environment, for example, Kaufman (1985) argues that such units can be expected to respond by, in effect, either expanding or contracting. In a decision to expand, the organization deals with environmental forces by "joining with [external actors] in confederal systems or federations" (see also Thompson 1967), whereas a decision to contract, or insulate, would prompt a "reduction of exchanges across boundaries in an effort to satisfy most needs and wants internally" (Kaufman 1985, 43). Although Kaufman builds on this logic to predict that the vast majority of organizations are incapable of dealing with these kinds of shocks—a notion that has very little empirical support—we can apply this basic logic to consider individual managerial choices and behavior.

When managers are confronted with a large-scale disruption, they may be faced with a decision about whether to be proactive and externally oriented in addressing the disruption or to become much more insular, in an effort to shut out external perturbations.[2] These two options, on their face, lead to competing expectations. If a manager chooses to connect with other actors, we could expect more external networking and more building of collaboration, whereas a decision to buffer and insulate would result in fewer collaborative relationships in an effort to protect the organization (for recent investigations of buffering and internal protective responses by managers, see Meier and O'Toole 2008, forthcoming). One question, therefore, is whether wicked-problem shocks in natural disaster settings stimulate or inhibit collaboration. Given the preponderance of the theoretical arguments, our expectation is in the former direction, particularly given sufficient organizational capacity:

> Hypothesis 1: Controlling for organizational capacity, districts which receive a larger number of evacuees (as a proportion of the regular student body) will be likely to engage in more collaborative relationships.

Another issue has to do with managerial patterns of interaction—networking—as such patterns establish themselves *prior* to an unexpected crisis period. Do these shape collaborative interorganizational arrays during the stressful postdisaster period? Networking can include a variety of managerial functions, including efforts to form longer-term cooperative relationships and to block potentially threatening influences (O'Toole and Meier 1999; Klijn 2005; Meier and O'Toole 2008). These options suggest that managers could be working with other organizations either to leverage resources and support or to sort out jurisdiction and responsibility to avoid being overwhelmed by events.

MANAGERIAL NETWORKING

Examining collaboration in response to an organizational shock offers the opportunity to ask questions about the nature of managerial networking. In particular, it is possible to consider how patterns of managerial networking may be related to interorganizational collaboration in response to disasters. How might externally oriented managerial behavior, predisaster, be related to the extent of organizational collaboration achieved, postdisaster? Three somewhat simplified alternative possibilities can be sketched: (1) Managers network to deal with particular problems, so patterns of networking behavior prior to an unexpected disaster should be essentially unrelated to the development of organizational collaborations, postdisaster. (2) Managers network efficiently, so they can be expected to build on their extant interactions selectively in response to a disaster, thus minimizing transaction costs necessitated when building interorganizational ties de novo. (3) Managers develop an external networking style or habit of behavior, and the general level of networking activity, predisaster, should thus be related to the extent of interorganizational collaborations developed to deal with unexpected environmental shocks, postdisaster. Each possibility leads to an hypothesis. We shall first sketch the causal logics in a bit more detail and then outline the corresponding three additional hypotheses.

First, as Kaufman (1985) suggests, networking could be a problem-specific response, one in which managers network only when triggered to do so by the problem-solving requirements immediately at hand. If networking is largely a problem-specific managerial behavior, there should be little or no relationship between past levels of networking and collaborative efforts following an environmental shock, when controlling for the extent of the shock itself and the extent of organizational capacity present in the system. Thus:

Hypothesis 2: The level of managerial networking activity in noncrisis times will be unrelated to the extent of interorganizational collaboration during crisis periods.

A second possibility is suggested by some of the literature on the emergence and maintenance of networks, which points to the large transaction costs involved in setting up collaborative partnerships (Agranoff and McGuire 2003a; Bardach 1998; Klijn 2005). Here, networks are viewed as complex relationships that take considerable time and effort to build and maintain. This logic would lead to the expectation that managers will be more likely to build collaborations in response to an organizational shock in instances for which the transaction costs are relatively low. Stated differently, managers who network in noncrisis times will be more likely to build interunit collaborations with the same interaction partners in response to organizational shocks, *because working with extant relationships lowers the transaction costs incurred when building and tapping collaborative relationships*. This possibility will be evaluated by testing the following:

Hypothesis 3: Collaborations are more likely in response to disasters in instances for which managers have developed a history of interaction with these actors/organizations.

Finally, a third possible explanation is that managerial networking could be a fundamental (learned or innate) part of an individual's managerial style; if so, levels of networking will be relatively stable; and interorganizational collaborations to deal with environmental shocks are more likely to be developed, in general, if top managers' established networking style involves more activity and involvement externally. Previous work provides some evidence in support of this expectation (Meier and O'Toole 2005), because a manager's level of networking in one year is found to be a significant predictor of his or her level of networking at a later time. If networking is stable across time, it could also be a stable component of management strategy to build collaboration in both crisis and noncrisis times. Managers who network in noncrisis times will be more likely to build collaboration in response to organizational shocks, *but this networking activity will not necessarily be focused on those organizations with which they have established relationships.* Formally stated:

Hypothesis 4: Organizational collaboration with others, including particular actors/organizations, will be a function of the top manager's overall propensity to engage in networking, not a function of a history of collaboration with that particular actor/organization.

DATA AND METHODS

Some of the data for this chapter are drawn from two surveys of Texas superintendents. In late 2005 and early 2006, after the hurricanes, we administered the Survey of Emergency Preparedness and the Impact of Hurricanes Katrina and Rita on Texas Public School Districts. This questionnaire, described briefly earlier in the chapter, collected data from school district superintendents throughout Texas on how the hurricane evacuees affected their school districts, including the extent of the impact, the nature of the district's response, the patterns of collaboration in response, and how the hurricanes affected the district's own emergency planning.

The data from this posthurricane survey have been combined with data from an earlier, prehurricane survey of Texas public school district superintendents that we administered in January 2005. This prehurricane survey, one in a series of several implemented regularly starting in 2000 by Meier and O'Toole, collected data on managerial strategies and behavior of superintendents, with an emphasis on their networking activity. The districts ranged widely on a variety of dimensions, including student composition (race, ethnicity, etc.), resources, setting (urban, rural, suburban), and performance. The response rate for the prehurricane survey was 58.0 percent ($N = 729$). In combining the data from the prehurricane and posthurricane surveys, we had considerable overlap, with 450 districts responding to both surveys. All nonsurvey data were drawn from the Texas Education Agency.

Our analyses were aimed at two general objectives: (1) seeing whether the size of the environmental shock helps to explain the extent of collaboration developed in school districts following the arrival of evacuees, while controlling for the organizational capacity of the district; and (2) determining which of the several possible causal relationships between earlier managerial networking and postdisaster school district collaboration seems to be supported by the evidence. For the second objective, the availability of data from the two surveys provided an unusual opportunity to execute a natural-experiment design.

Dependent Variables

The dependent variables for this study measure the extent to which—and, for some of the analyses, whether—school districts collaborated with other organizations as a part of their efforts to respond to the influx of displaced students in their districts. The top managers were asked which of the following types of organizations they collaborated with to provide for displaced students: police, fire, and first responders; nonprofit and relief organizations; other school districts; government relief and welfare organizations; business organizations; and local, community, and religious organizations. The primary dependent variable is the total number of types of organizations that the school district worked with in response efforts, ranging from 0 to 6.

Because Hypotheses 3 and 4 explore the extent to which superintendents were strategic (or influenced by transaction costs) in choosing collaborative partners, we examined in particular links with two individual types of nodes in the environment of the school districts: other school districts and business organizations. These were chosen for attention because they represent actors, the interaction with whom at the individual level (i.e., with other superintendents and local business leaders, respectively) the superintendents had also been surveyed about in the prehurricane period. Each of these dependent variables is dichotomous, with a

"1" representing when superintendents collaborated with that particular group.

Independent Variables

Two variables were used in all the models used to test the hypotheses. First, we constructed a variable to represent the size of the shock to the organization. The measure is the number of displaced students absorbed by the district, as reported on the posthurricane survey, divided by the total enrollment prior to the hurricanes and multiplied by 100. This variable, "total evacuees," represents the amount of students absorbed, as a percentage of the regular student body. It was used in particular to test Hypothesis 1 (that the size of a shock, or problem severity, leads to more collaboration).

In the first and all other estimations reported here, we also controlled for the overall size of the school district, because many larger districts have greater administrative capacity than small districts. To control for size, we included the logged enrollment of the district.

To test whether collaboration in response to the influx of evacuees is unrelated to the general level of networking behavior of the top managers during more stable and routine times (Hypothesis 2), we developed from the prehurricane survey a measure of managerial networking prior to the onset of the unanticipated shocks to the school districts. We followed earlier work by Meier and O'Toole (e.g., 2001) and asked respondents to report, on a 6-point scale ranging from daily to never, how often they interacted with each of several external actors. In the prehurricane survey, we asked about interactions with seven external parties: teacher associations, parent groups, local business leaders, other superintendents, federal education officials, state legislators, and the Texas Education Agency. A composite managerial networking scale was created using factor analysis. All four items loaded positively on the first factor, producing an eigenvalue of 1.76; no other factors were statistically significant. Factor scores from this analysis were then used as a measure of managerial networking, with higher scores indicating a greater networking orientation.

Because both surveys asked about interactions with two particular external actors—business leaders/organizations and other superintendents/school districts—we explored Hypotheses 3 and 4 by comparing interactions with each group before and after the hurricane-induced displacement.[3] Descriptive statistics for these variables are displayed in table 6.1.

Table 6.1 Descriptive Statistics

Period and Measure	N	Mean	Min.	Max.
After Katrina				
Total collaboration	508	2.848	0	6
Collaboration with other school districts	509	0.497	0	1
Collaboration with business organizations	509	0.244	0	1
Evacuees as a percentage of previous enrollment	560	0.793	0	7.10
Logged enrollment	560	7.190	3.912	11.969
Before Katrina				
Total networking	405	–0.0005	–1.804	2.827
Networking with other superintendents	420	3.911	2	6
Networking with local business leaders	423	3.783	1	6

METHODS

Because the primary dependent variable—collaboration to assist with the evacuees and their challenges—is ordinal, we used multiple estimators in the analysis. First, the models were run using ordinary least squares (OLS) analysis; then they were estimated as ordered logits; and finally they were analyzed via poisson regression, which is considered more appropriate for this type of dependent variable (Gujarati 2003). Although OLS is not the most appropriate estimator, the results were very similar across the estimators, and the OLS coefficients are most easily interpretable. The models evaluating collaboration with individual nodes were estimated as logistic regressions. Post-estimation diagnostics showed no problematic heteorskedasticity or multicollinearity.

FINDINGS

Our first hypothesis, that managers will engage in higher levels of collaboration when faced with larger organizational shocks, is supported by the analysis. Table 6.2 presents the three different models (OLS, ordered logit, Poisson regression), all of which show that the number of evacuees taken in by the district as a proportion of baseline enrollment is a significant predictor of the extent of total collaboration. Still, although the size of shock (evacuees) is always significant, it is never substantively large. On the basis of the OLS coefficients, a school would have to take on enough evacuees to constitute roughly 3.5 percent of its student population to move the level of collaboration up one unit. The size of the shock helps to shape the extent

Table 6.2 Collaboration in Response to Influx of Displaced Students; Dependent Variable: Extent of Collaboration (0 to 6)

Independent Variable	OLS	Ordered Logit	Poisson
Number of evacuees	0.276	0.287	0.077
	(3.79)[a]	(3.57)	(3.36)
District size	0.477	0.510	0.160
	(9.28)	(8.63)	(9.05)
Constant	−0.850		−0.222
	(2.31)		(1.67)
N	508	508	508
R^2	0.21		
Pseudo R^2		0.06	0.06

[a]The t-scores are included for OLS coefficients. Z-scores are reported for the ordered logits and Poisson estimates.

of collaboration, but it is only part of the explanation. Note, as well, that the sheer size of the district, reflecting the capacity of the organization to engage in various forms of collaborative activity, also contributes to the extent of the result.

For a more complete test of whether the size of the shock is driving collaboration, and also to explore the possible influence of an earlier pattern of managerial networking, we also tested Hypothesis 2, framed as the null hypothesis: that a pattern of managerial networking during normal times does nothing to drive collaborative results when serious problems arise. To examine this relationship, we included in the specification the measure of the superintendent's overall networking score as tapped prior to the hurricanes.[4] If networking were purely a problem-specific response, we would expect that the number of evacuees would significantly predict collaboration but that prior networking would have no effect. The models given in table 6.3 provide evidence to rebut Hypothesis 2—that collaboration during crises is not shaped by prior behavioral patterns developed, or manifested, in more stable periods. The superintendent's overall level of networking prior to the hurricanes is a significant predictor in all the models. Note also that the size of the shock to the organization, as measured by the relative size of the influx of the pool of evacuees, is still a significant predictor of collaboration.[5] In fact, the coefficients for the number of evacuees are relatively stable between tables 6.2 and 6.3. We can conclude that an established general pattern of managerial network-

Table 6.3 Does Noncrisis Networking Predict Collaboration in Crisis Times? Dependent Variable: Extent of Collaboration (0 to 6)

Independent Variable	OLS	Ordered Logit	Poisson
Networking	0.448	0.516	0.156
	(4.08)	(4.27)	(4.00)
Number of evacuees	0.273	0.300	0.077
	(3.14)	(3.13)	(2.76)
District size	0.441	0.474	0.147
	(7.29)	(6.85)	(7.09)
Constant	0.630		−0.148
	(1.44)		(0.94)
N	370	370	370
R^2	0.22		
Pseudo R^2		0.06	0.06

ing is clearly not the only influence on postdisaster collaboration, but also that superintendents with a history of such interaction externally are more likely to engage in higher levels of collaboration in response to the organizational shock.

What explains this relationship? The idea that collaborative relationships would have some element of stability has been discussed in much of the work on interorganizational relations. Researchers often argue that such interunit stability derives from the costs involved in the time-consuming process of establishing the relationship, formalizing processes for shared decision making, and other similar tasks. If this explanation were to be valid, we would expect that superintendents would turn to the *same* external organizations and organizational representatives that are a part of their developed set of relationships when they seek support for handling complicated challenges. We tested for this relationship, as outlined in Hypothesis 3, with the models displayed in table 6.4.

We analyzed whether predisaster interactions between superintendents and two other external nodes—other school district superintendents and also members of the business community—help to explain posthurricane collaboration with other school districts and business organizations, respectively. The idea is to distinguish the influence of a habit or pattern of general interaction externally on the part of top managers, on the one hand, from a history of node-specific interactions and exchanges, on the other. If, over time, networking is driven by stable patterns of interactions

Table 6.4 Are Managers Strategic in Collaboration to Lower Transaction Costs? Dependent Variable: Collaboration with Business Organizations/ Other School Districts

Independent Variable	Business Organizations	Other School Districts
Previous networking with business leaders/other superintendents	0.175 (1.34)	0.120 (1.02)
Number of evacuees	0.341 (2.70)	0.265 (2.32)
District size	0.584 (5.88)	0.192 (2.51)
Constant	–6.679 (7.31)	–2.160 (2.72)
N	383	383
Pseudo R^2	0.15	0.03

in individual relationships, we would expect that superintendents who regularly interact with, for example, business leaders would be more likely to turn to those business leaders and their firms during crisis times. The results presented in table 6.4 do not support this hypothesis. In both the models, more interaction with specific nodes prior to the hurricanes explained none of the variance in collaboration with these nodes after the evacuees had arrived.

We move on to the test of Hypothesis 4. We investigated the possibility that the extent of collaboration with particular external organizations in the wake of disaster is not about building on preexisting relationships but is, rather, partially shaped by managers' general styles of managing outward. To test this hypothesis, we added the general networking measure to the equations from the preceding analysis predicting interaction with the individual nodes. Table 6.5 presents the results, which lend some support to Hypothesis 4. The logit model estimating collaboration with business organizations does not find previous interaction with local business leaders to be a significant predicator of collaboration, but it does show managers' earlier level of overall networking to be related to the likelihood of collaboration with such organizations. In a similar model seeking to predict collaboration with other school districts, prior node-specific interactions are unrelated to collaboration; general networking style has a positive direction, although the relationship to posthurricane collaboration with other school districts is significant only at the .10 level in a two-tailed test.

Table 6.5 Is Collaboration Influenced by Pre-Existing Relationships or Managerial Style?

Independent Variable	Business Organizations	Other School Districts
Composite networking	0.681	0.297
	(3.10)	(1.69)
Previous networking with	−0.126	−0.033
business leaders/ other superintendents	(0.75)	(0.22)
Number of evacuees	0.353	0.282
	(2.73)	(2.43)
District size	0.598	0.163
	(5.89)	(2.04)
Constant	−5.679	−1.375
	(5.85)	(1.49)
N	371	371
Pseudo R^2	0.18	0.04

CONCLUSIONS

The results reported in the preceding section derive from one rather unusual set of circumstances—school districts managing unexpected influxes of high-need students on short notice. Considerable caution needs to be exercised, therefore, before the findings are treated as generalizable to management involving other kinds of natural disasters, or to management challenges of collaboration more generally, because a number of other factors have yet to be explored. In particular, the findings on collaboration here are necessarily focused on the relatively short term; how long such patterns are likely to persist remains an unanswered question. Additionally, the collaboration studied here was largely voluntary; managers chose when to collaborate and with whom they would collaborate. In situations where collaboration might be forced (possibly by the federal government), we may see very different patterns.

For all these reasons, the results of this study constitute a beginning for analysis rather than a real conclusion. The levels of explanation for the extent of collaboration are relatively modest. Further analysis is needed to explore the other factors that contribute to why managers in similar organizations react differently to the same intervention. And how much difference such collaborations make in terms of performance results is a key and thus far unexplored issue. We know that these organizations faced a considerable disruption, but we do not know whether this disruption affected their ability to carry on their core functions. Did the influx of hurricane evacuees affect student outcomes? If so, could increased collaboration help to share the burden of the response and possibly lessen the impact on student outcomes?

Still, a number of the findings from this analysis are interesting and instructive. Organizational capacity clearly makes a difference in the ability to develop collaboration in multiple directions. This finding is unsurprising but also important. The size of the unexpected shock to the organizational system also matters—positively—as a stimulus or prod toward the development of collaboration. Wicked-problem stimuli trigger increased interorganizational collaboration for the school districts dealing with many issues in the wake of major hurricanes. In a net sense, at least, efforts to reach out to partner with others trumps any temptation to hunker down, organizationally and managerially speaking. This finding is encouraging for those interested in whether public management is likely to be responsive to the increased challenges posed by complex issues, even if it suggests that public managers and their organizations may have to do some rather heavy lifting to address their responsibilities.

Most interestingly, the findings given in this chapter demonstrate that public management matters for collaboration. They also provide some evidence regarding how management makes that difference. Controlling for organizational capacity and the size of a shock to an organizational system, a top manager's established style of externally oriented interaction helps to explain the extent of interorganizational collaboration developed after an unexpected disaster. Intriguingly, the node-specific interaction histories seem rather unimportant in this regard, particularly when compared with the general style or habit of managerial networking.

The combination of these findings could speak to the very nature of collaboration and networking. Much of the research on collaboration and networking follows one of two streams. Collaboration is either studied as a structural issue (with the study of a "network"), or the focus is on the more behavioral aspects of collaboration (with the study of the manager's networking activity). Here, we find that collaboration is less a function of stable relationships, and thus structural ties, and more a product of the individual-level decisions of the manager. We need more research on the extent to which interorganizational management is an organizational-level or an individual-level concept, because these differences may affect some of the fundamental assumptions made about how organizations work together.

This finding also suggests that such developed patterns of networking not only contribute in the short term to performance, as earlier research has demonstrated (e.g., Meier and O'Toole 2001, 2003), but also constitute a sort of investment—a social-networking capital, as it were—that can pay dividends on collaboration in the future, and in particular during unexpected crisis periods. In fact, given that administrative systems are typically highly inertial, managerial networking seems to contribute to results in at least three ways: short-term performance improvements, enhancement of the base over time and thus gradual amplification of the impact of networking over time, and also establishment of social-networking capital that can be drawn on in times of need or to help manage significant shocks. All in all, therefore, the contribution of managers to performance and to networked collaboration is a topic that deserves considerably more careful attention both theoretically and empirically. Further, if validated elsewhere, this set of findings carries significant implications for how practicing public managers might spend their time and devote their attention, particularly those operating in systems that are likely to be subjected to sizable and unpredictable shocks from the environment.

An additional finding of interest, implicit in the empirical results reported in this chapter, is that individual-level patterns of behavior (managerial networking) can have organizational consequences (interunit collaboration). Though top managers can be expected to be rather influential in their own organizations, it is nevertheless interesting to see clear relationships between these two levels. Whether the collaborations in question develop from the leadership and direct individual efforts of the managers themselves, or whether others in the organization observe the managerial behavior and are thus stimulated to mimic these externally oriented patterns, or whether perhaps externally oriented managers also invest in building organizational processes and even specialized subunits to help broker the development of more formalized collaboration is an interesting question—but one that cannot be answered with the data at hand.

What can be said is that these organizational systems are stimulated to initiate collaboration when they experience an unexpected and significant wicked-problem shock, and the presence of a manager who chooses to engage in networking during normal times—a truly *collaborative public manager*—also contributes to how these organizations respond. It may be only mildly consoling under the circumstances, given the massive costs borne in the wake of Hurricane Katrina and Hurricane Rita, but it is true nonetheless: In yet another way, public management matters.

NOTES

1. The present chapter explores public management and its links to collaboration. Additional work is under way analyzing the relationship between interorganizational collaboration and performance.

2. Elsewhere (e.g., in O'Toole and Meier 1999) we have referred to these two options in terms of exploiting environmental opportunities or managerial buffering against environmental shocks. In the terms of the formal model we have been working with for the past several years, these are the "M_3" and the "M_4" functions, respectively.

3. The details of the survey questions differed somewhat between prehurricane and posthurricane surveys. In the former case, we asked about the top managers' *interactions with* a range of actors in the environment. In the latter instance, we asked about the *collaborations* between the school district and a range of types of external organizations. The former, therefore, taps individual behavior, while the latter has to do with interorganizational links. The two should be related, but because the items ask for different information, we can expect some attenuation in any connection between the two sets of responses. Nonetheless, the possible link between patterns of managerial behavior and patterns of organizational collaboration is an interesting empirical question.

4. For this and subsequent models, the number of cases is modestly lower. These analyses include only those school districts in which superintendents responded to both surveys.

5. District size also remains significant, as it does in all models reported here.

Part II

HOW PUBLIC MANAGERS COLLABORATE

How do public managers collaborate? The mechanisms of collaboration are as varied as the public managers who do the collaboration. Privatization is one of the managerial tools at the disposal of public managers. Contracting out in whole or in part is another tool. Working side by side with the public is another form of collaboration. Each chapter in part II examines how public managers collaborate through different lenses.

How the tool of privatization is used to navigate complicated networks of service provision that require collaborative public management—both intersectorally with nonprofit organizations, for-profit businesses, and other public agencies, and intergovernmentally with federal, state, and local officials and institutions—is the essence of collaborative public management, and is the subject of chapter 7, by Jeffrey Brudney, Chung-Lae Cho, and Deil Wright. Their work finds that state agency heads are extensively connected through the contracting process with mazes of networks in pursuit of public service delivery. They document that in 1998 and 2004, state agencies contracted for service delivery with other governments, nonprofits, and private firms at rates approximating, respectively, 60, 70, and 80 percent. They develop a summary statistic measuring agency contracting performance based on combinations of two key factors that are part of agency contracting: the cost of delivering services to the public and the quality of the services delivered. They also directly explore the relationship between collaboration and agency contracting and find that state agencies that rated more highly on measures of collaboration are more likely to invest a greater percentage of their budget in contracting.

In chapter 8, David Van Slyke examines the pivotal role of contracting in collaborative public management through a different lens: relational contracting. He finds that contract relationships begin as hierarchically structured transactional arrangements that resemble a dance. The more the parties dance together, the greater the chances that their relationship moves from one party being highly dominant to a more collaborative engagement. Accordingly, public managers require a set of management skills and tools for developing trust and collaboration if relational contracting is to be effective and lead to smart buyer behavior. This contract management human capital, however, is still underdeveloped. Van Slyke's findings have implications for public affairs education in terms of the teaching of public management skills and the tools that are necessary for managing an ever-increasing volume of contractual relationships for which public managers will have responsibility.

In chapter 9, William Waugh asks "How should we best organize for emergency management and homeland security?" He argues that such organizational structure needs to be functional given circumstances. Flexibility—from adaptation to improvisation—is critical. Most important, according to Waugh, more collaborative approaches at the operational and policymaking levels are needed to facilitate disaster response.

In chapter 10, Jay Eungha Ryu and Hal Rainey share their latest research examining five Job Training Partnership Act centers in Texas that provide, in one location, the information and services that individuals need from the complex array of job training, education, and employment programs. Their analysis shows that clients of these one-stop service centers earned about 54 cents more per hour after training than did those who did not have one-stop service. The apparent success of the one-stop service centers shows the value of collaboratively linking together programs and agencies relevant to a public policy challenge.

The importance of implementing collaborative public management in a way that engenders public trust and confidence cannot be overemphasized. Collaborative public programs that are both efficient and effective are a must. The authors in this part offer insights into how public managers collaborate or might collaborate in a way that is both efficient and effective.

Chapter 7

Understanding the Collaborative Public Manager: Exploring Contracting Patterns and Performance for Service Delivery by State Administrative Agencies in 1998 and 2004

Jeffrey L. Brudney, Chung-Lae Cho, and Deil S. Wright

At the outset of the twenty-first century, Kettl (2000, 488) noted the "transformation of governance," arguing that, "in doing the peoples' work, to a large and growing degree, American governments share responsibility with other levels of government, with private companies, and with nonprofit organizations." He further observed that globalization and devolution have layered "new challenges that have strained the capacity of government—and their nongovernmental partners—to deliver high-quality services." Contracting (out) for public services with third parties is one of those "new" challenges that has been evident for a considerable length of time (Mosher 1980; Salamon 1981). Although the popular conception of contracting is one of hierarchy and asymmetric influence, it offers the potential to involve governmental agencies in collaborative and presumptively cooperative and coordinated networks that aim at effective service delivery (Kettl 2003).

Contracting for service delivery may qualify as fitting under the rubric of collaboration, which Fosler (2002, 19) describes as "something less than authoritative coordination and something more than tacit cooperation." In arguing that "collaboration is more pervasive than most [people] think," Kamensky and Burlin (2004, 4) note that the transition to new models of governance "implies collaboration—within agencies, between agencies, between levels of government, and between the public, private, and nonprofit sectors." Elsewhere, Goldsmith and Eggers (2004, 157) cite collaboration as one of an array of skills needed by network managers that encompasses "negotiation, mediation, risk analysis, trust building, . . . and project management." These public managers must "work across sector boundaries and overcome the prickly challenges of governing by network."

In *The New Public Service*, Light (1999, 123) noted that "the government-centered public service is gone for good," and that "what makes the 1990s different is the pace with which governments are turning to private and nonprofit sources." He calls this growing phenomenon "multisectored public service" and observes that "governments at all levels have created an ever-growing shadow of private and nonprofit employees that provide many of the goods and services once delivered in house." Indeed, the bulk of his book addresses the roles and responsibilities that define what it means to be a collaborative public manager. In this chapter we examine these multisectored, interactive, and interdependent arrangements, labeled "intersectoral administration" by Henry (2002), across the fifty American states at two points in time, 1998 and 2004. We believe that working with contracting relationships is a component of collaborative public management.

CONTRACTING AND THE AMERICAN STATES

The states constitute an excellent laboratory for the study of contracting and its relationship with collaboration. Across the states, more than 3,500 executive agencies provide vital services; many of them rely on contracting with other organizations—private, nonprofit, and/or public—to do so. At the same time, state agencies are engaged in a variety of other collaborative activities with these same entities. In this chapter we explore the interconnections between contracting and collaboration among these agencies and organizations.

Contracting

For more than two decades, contracting, as a major subset of privatization (Chi 1993), has been a lightning rod term in the field of public management in the United States and abroad. Whether offered as a set of organizational practices, proposed as a major reform initiative, or advanced as a means of downsizing government, contracting has both galvanized and polarized debates in the public policy–management community (DeHoog

1984; Savas 1982, 1987; Salamon 1989; Rehfuss 1989; Kelman 1990; DeHoog and Salamon 2002; Cooper 2003; Prizzia 2003; Singer 2003).

The scope and content of the literature on contracting are illustrative of the significance of this tool as an instrument of governance. In Salamon's (2002) volume focusing on more than a dozen tools of government, Kelman (2002, 282) observes, "None of the tools of government discussed in this book is more ubiquitous than contracting." Cooper (2003, 11) reinforces the importance of this tool by asserting, "It is difficult to think of any aspect of modern life that is not significantly affected by government contracts." O'Neill (2002, 2) introduces his book *Nonprofit Nation* with the statement that contracting with public agencies is one avenue through which "the nonprofit sector is a major presence in American life."

Missing from most policy/administrative discussions and debates about contracting is a broad-based body of information about the actual use and estimated performance of contracting by a representative cluster of public agencies. Apart from selected surveys at the local (municipal) level, most public administrative experience and research involving contracting are anecdotal, case-specific, or otherwise narrowly focused (Greene 1994, 1996; Siegel 1999). There are notable exceptions, however, including a few at the level of American state governments (Apogee Research Inc. 1992; Chi 1993; Auger 1999; Chi, Arnold, and Perkins 2003; Brudney et al. 2005; Choi et al. 2005; Fernandez 2005). This chapter reports results gathered from large sets of representative agency heads in the American states based on surveys conducted in 1998 and 2004.

The Importance of the States

Granted the controversial and significant character of contracting in the United States and beyond, the question arises: Why focus on contracting among American *state* governmental agencies? The central role of the American states in providing public services is often overlooked both within and outside the borders of the United States. A contemporary text on the American states (Van Horn 2006, 1) begins with the following assertions: "Today, at the beginning of the twenty-first century, state governments are at the cutting edge of political and policy reform. . . . State leaders wield enormous political influence, not only over the destinies of their states, but over the future of the nation. Governors . . . and bureaucrats are responsible for carrying out much of the nation's public business and are setting national agendas too. Increasingly, federal [national] policymakers expect state governments to assume full policy and administrative responsibilities."

It is useful and relevant at the outset to identify two long-term trends that frame the contemporary context for contracting out by state administrative agencies. American state governments have been transformed by two administrative "revolutions" over the past half century (Bowling and Wright 1998a, 1998b). The two indicators of dramatic transformations are (1) state employment and (2) state agency creation.

In 1950, total employment in state governments was slightly less than 1 million. By 2000 state employment totaled 5 million, far exceeding the 2.7 million federal civilian employment. Furthermore, Bohte and Meier (2000) found that changes in state employment explained changes in both local *and* national employment.

Where were (and are) all these new state employees located? They are lodged in the rapidly growing number of existing and new state administrative agencies. In the 1950s, 51 types of agencies were common in most or all of the fifty states (Bowling et al. 2006; Cho and Wright 2007). Each subsequent decade recorded the creation of numerous agencies. By the turn of the century, more than 100 types of agencies were identifiable in the American states.[1] In short, more than 3,500 identifiable and distinct agencies are evident across the fifty states. This extensive and expansive array of agencies is the universe on which we focus our analysis of contracting for service delivery in 1998 and 2004.

In spite of a notable degree of dependence on federal aid funds, state agencies largely stand alone from administrative, bureaucratic, and management standpoints (Cho and Wright 2007). Furthermore, "administrators in state agencies have wide latitude to make vital decisions in important public programs" (Schneider and Jacoby 1996, 240). Administrative discretion extends to the choice of varied implementation tools of which contracting is one of the more substantial and significant (Cooper 2003; Kelman 2002).

Before turning attention to data collection and analysis of state agency contracting, five points merit emphasis. First, state governments and their administrative arms are major and significant players in governing generally and in service delivery in particular. Second, the states are "intermediaries" in the multitiered (but nonhierarchical) system of intergovernmental governance, a setting that places a premium on collaborative connections with other governments as well as the private and nonprofit sectors. Third, not only are state agencies significant providers of public services but their respective agency heads also play crucial roles in deciding which of many tools are selected to produce or deliver those services. Fourth, contracting for services is (and has been) one of the major tools employed. Fifth, and finally, as Bryson, Crosby, and Stone (2006) argue, context, structure, process, and outcomes are all relevant to understanding the design and implementation of cross-sector collaboration(s). Contracting for service delivery by state government agencies meets these and other theoretical and operational considerations for understanding collaboration as pursued by practicing public managers.

SURVEYING STATE AGENCIES: IDENTIFYING CONTRACTING DIMENSIONS

The significance of state government administration has not escaped attention and analysis (Elling 2004; Bowling and Wright 1998a, 1998b; Bowling, Cho, and Wright 2004). A series of nine periodic surveys of state agency directors has been conducted twice each decade starting in 1964 by the American State Administrators Project (ASAP), with the last survey done in 2004 and the next survey set in the field in 2008. These data have enabled scholars to track and monitor trends and variations in both a common core and a shifting array of policy and management issues in state government (Bowling 2006). Despite declining ASAP response rates (from 70 to 30 percent) across the five decades, the number of respondents, varying from 900 to 1,500, has been confirmed as representative of the 3,500 heads of state administrative agencies across the fifty American states (Brudney and Wright 2002; Wright and Cho 2001).

Dimensions of Contracting

The 1998 ASAP survey presented a battery of five questions on significant aspects of state agency contracting for the delivery of services. The 2004 ASAP survey replicated (and extended) these items, so that we have two waves or time periods of contracting information for the state agencies.[2] These items or "dimensions" of contracting consist of

- decision making: decision to use contracting for service delivery;
- diversity: the number of sectors with which the agency contracts;
- density: the percentage of agency budget allocated to contracting;
- directionality: the increase or decrease in contracting over the prior four years; and
- disposition: the service cost and quality effects of contracting.

We employ these data to assess whether those agencies that appear to be more collaborative in other ways engage in more extensive contracting, and whether they achieve better results with respect to service cost and quality ("disposition") through contracting relationships.

This chapter draws on the responses from agency heads in the 1998 and 2004 surveys, whose organizations, numbering about 800 and 600 respectively, were engaged in contracting. The breadth and richness of these data yield important and instructive insights into collaborative public management performance. To our knowledge, few other data sets offer the potential for empirical results on the presence, patterns, and performance of contracting by public administrative agencies.

Contracting for Service Delivery, 1998 and 2004

Table 7.1 presents comparable percentages for each of the five contracting dimensions in 1998 and 2004. The table contains important descriptive information about contracting practices and results across the American states. It is tempting to engage in an extended elaboration and interpretation of the findings displayed in the table. Because collaboration and performance themes are central to this chapter, we bypass an extended discussion and highlight only two prominent findings from these survey results separated by six years.

First, the similarities across the two surveys are remarkable. The divergence in proportions for the dimensions of decision making, diversity, density, and disposition are negligible and insignificant. Roughly two-thirds or more of all state agencies rely on contracting. Contracts with other governments, nonprofits, and private firms are engaged by about 60, 70, and 80 percent, respectively, of the state agencies. Nevertheless, more than half the agencies allocate 10 percent or less of their budgets to contracting. About one-third of the state agencies report increased costs from contacting, but well over half indicate improvement in service quality.

Second, only for directionality do the proportions from the two surveys differ substantially, with the respective percentages for 2004 below those for 1998. By way of context, directionality measures whether over the prior four years service delivery contracting had increased with each of the three collaborating types of entities (other governments, nonprofits, and forprofits). The two other response options were "no change" and "decreased."

The 2004 percentages indicate that in comparison to 1998, contracting increased but at *lower rates*. Still, in 2004 about one-third, two-fifths, and more than half of all state agencies, respectively, reported increased contracting with other governments, nonprofits, and for-profit organizations. The comparable proportions for 1998 were, respectively, half, threefifths, and more than four-fifths. Although contracting for the delivery of services may have peaked across state agencies in 1998, it remained robust in 2004 and continued to increase, albeit at lower rates than the late

Table 7.1 Five Dimensions of Contracting for Service Delivery by State Administrative Agencies, 1998 and 2004 (%)

Dimension of Contracting	1998	2004
Decision making: agency contracts for service delivery (Ns = 1,175 for 1998, 920 for 2004)		
Yes	73	65
No	27	35
Diversity: agencies contracting with sectors (Ns = 850 for 1998, 542 for 2004)		
Other governments	61	58
Nonprofits	71	68
For-profits	83	85
Density: percent of budget allocated by contracts (Ns = 820 for 1998, 590 for 2004)		
10 percent or less	55	61
11–20 percent	15	12
21–40 percent	13	12
Over 40 percent	17	16
Directionality: increase in contracting over last four years		
Other governments (Ns = 457 for 1998, 382 for 2004)	53	32
Nonprofits (Ns = 527 for 1998, 416 for 2004)	61	43
For-profits (Ns = 631 for 1998, 489 for 2004)	83	54
Disposition: cost and quality effects		
Effects on service costs (Ns = 767 for 1998, 589 for 2004)		
Increased	31	35
Decreased	36	28
No Effect	33	37
Effects on service quality (Ns = 780 for 1998, 592 for 2004)		
Improved	52	56
Decreased	10	6
No effect	37	38

Source: Deil S. Wright, American State Administrators Project Survey, Odum Institute for Research in Social Science, University of North Carolina at Chapel Hill.

1990s. To the extent that contracting is related to or a subset of collaboration, the percentages in table 7.1 indicate hypercollaborative public management in state bureaucracies.

Disposition: Cost and Quality Factors in Contract Performance

Economic factors or features in the form of costs have, arguably, dominated much of the research, debate, and interpretations about contracting

(Prizzia 2003). An overemphasis on economic elements has clouded or obscured not only quality-of-service concerns but also issues of accountability (Dicke 2002; Klingner, Nalbandian, and Romzek 2002; Prizzia 2003). We take an initial step in the direction of what Prizzia calls "balancing" by examining cost and quality considerations simultaneously.

In this chapter we concentrate on the disposition dimension of contracting, namely, the assessments provided by the state administrators about the relationship between the cost and quality effects of contracts for agency services delivered by contractors. By combining cost and quality assessments, we identify patterns of contracting performance that serve as a central focus or dependent variable in our analysis. Illustrative of this strategy is table 7.2, which shows that the interconnection between cost and quality factors, as rated by the agency heads, produces three overall categories of contracting performance: enhanced, mixed, and diminished.

Table 7.2 enables us to present, compare, and analyze responses from both ASAP survey years. In a pattern somewhat similar to table 7.1, the

Table 7.2 Disposition Dimension of State Agency Service Contracting: Cost and Quality Performance Assessments, 1998 and 2004

		1998		2004	
Dimension of Service Contracting		N	%	N	%
Performance enhanced					
Cost down, quality up		197	27	117	20
Cost down, quality same		67	9	43	7
Cost stable, quality up		93	13	90	15
	Subtotal	357	49	250	42
Performance mixed					
Cost down, quality down		13	2	6	1
Cost same, quality same		131	18	123	21
Cost up, quality up		99	14	122	21
	Subtotal	243	34	251	43
Performance diminished					
Cost same, quality down		11	1	5	1
Cost up, quality same		75	10	58	10
Cost up, quality down		49	7	24	4
	Subtotal	135	18	87	15
Total		735	100[a]	588	100[a]

[a]Because of rounding, the percentages may not add to 100.

Source: Deil S. Wright, American State Administrators Project Survey, Odum Institute for Research in Social Science, University of North Carolina at Chapel Hill.

percentages for 1998 and 2004 are not dramatically different. There was a modest drop of 7 percentage points, from 49 to 42, in agencies grouped in the enhanced category. In a compensatory fashion, the size of the mixed performance category increased from 34 to 43 percent over the six-year time span. The diminished performance category remained roughly the same, with only a slight drop from 1998 to 2004. The overriding point is that substantial proportions of state agency heads reported that contracting contributed to enhanced service delivery with respect to cost and quality. From two-fifths to nearly half of contracting agencies indicated improvements in costs and/or quality from using contracts to collaborate with third parties in implementing organizational aims.

A variety of factors might explain whether public agencies achieve enhanced, mixed, or diminished performance through contracting, as measured by the effects of the contracting relationship on service costs and quality. Because this question is central to our long-term aims, we anticipate positing a model composed of clusters of variables that would provide a better framework for understanding "what works" in contracting for collaborative service delivery. For our present purpose, however, we are interested in how the propensity of an agency (and its director) toward other forms of collaboration might affect the level of contracting activity as well as the achievement of preferred cost and quality outcomes from this activity. To this end, we develop a measure of contracting performance.[3]

MEASURING CONTRACTING PERFORMANCE

Table 7.2 displayed three broad categories (as well as subcategories) of service delivery performance achieved through agency contracting. Using the subcategories of enhanced, mixed, and diminished performance, we derive a 5-point scale measuring overall contract performance for each agency, which we term the measure of contracting performance (MCP). The MCP assesses contract performance on a scale ranging from +2 (enhanced) through 0 (mixed or neutral) to –2 (diminished). Table 7.3 shows the scoring categories and the proportions of agencies falling into each MCP category for 1998 and 2004.

The top category of greatly enhanced contract performance (which scored +2) encompasses agencies where (perceived) costs were down and quality was up as a result of contracting. This category amounted to 27 and 20 percent of all agencies in 1998 and 2004, respectively. The next group of agencies achieved moderately enhanced contract performance (which scored +1). It consists of agencies where either costs were down and quality was stable or costs were stable and quality was up. This category

Table 7.3 A Metric Measuring Contracting Performance
among American State Administrative Agencies, 1998
and 2004

Measurement of Contracting Performance	1998	2004
Enhanced	%[a]	
Greatly (+2)	27	20
Moderately (+1)	22	22
Neutral (0)	34	43
Diminished		
Moderately (–1)	11	11
Greatly (–2)	7	4
Mean	0.50	0.44
Standard deviation	1.19	1.05
Coefficient of variation	0.42	0.42

[a]Because of rounding, the percentages may not add to 100.

Source: Deil S. Wright, American State Administrators Project Survey,
Odum Institute for Research in Social Science, University of North Carolina at Chapel Hill.

constituted 22 percent of all state agencies engaged in contracting in both
1998 and 2004.

State agencies in the mixed or neutral category of contact performance
received a zero score. These organizations had one of the following three
combinations resulting from contracting: (1) costs down and quality down,
(2) costs same and quality the same, or (3) costs up and quality up. This
category included 34 percent of contracting agencies in 1998 and 43 percent in 2004.

Agencies in the final two categories experienced diminished contract
performance. The moderately diminished group (which scored –1) con-
sisted of 11 percent of contracting agencies in both 1998 and in 2004.
These agencies represented two combinations: (1) costs were stable while
quality declined, or (2) costs increased while quality remained the same.
The final category of greatly diminished contract performance merits a
–2 because reported costs increased as a result of contracting and quality
declined as well. Notably, this group was a small contingent of agencies—
only 7 percent in 1998 and barely 4 percent in 2004.

The mean contract performance scores for 1998 and 2004 are reported
at the bottom of table 7.3. As suggested by the shifting percentages noted
above in the table and confirmed by the two mean scores given in the table,
a modest decline in (perceived) contract performance appears from the

former to the latter period. Though the mean dropped from .50 to .44 between 1998 and 2004, the standard deviation also declined, so that the coefficient of variation (CV) remained the same at .42. In other words, the distribution patterns of performance across the two survey years remained essentially the same.

The value of the MCP is that it represents in a single, summary metric the two central aspects or aims of agency contracting—cost savings and service quality. Focusing on one or the other of these criteria often leads to mistaken notions regarding the overall achievements of contracting. As scholars and practitioners of public administration have long recognized, service delivery options that involve saving money at the expense of quality are false economies. Similarly, concentration on quality alone can likewise exact too high a price. Dicke (2002), for example, notes the complex character of service quality, involving methods of assessment and measurement of effects.

By combining cost and quality dimensions into one useful and easily interpretable metric, the MCP serves as a valuable tool. With a single statistic, we can reasonably summarize and compare the level of contract performance for any group, category, or cluster of state agencies. Negative scores on the metric indicate a net loss to the agency with respect to contracting for service delivery. Scores at or near zero indicate a mixed or neutral performance. Positive scores show a net gain. In the next section, we examine the relationship between the MCP and measures of collaboration.

CONTRACTING AND COLLABORATION

As noted above, the type of contracting discussed in this chapter—traditional "transactional" or formal contracting by government agencies—and collaboration are generally treated as distinct, if not entirely separable in the literature (Agranoff and McGuire 2003a). Formal contracting is often likened to hierarchical, or principal–agent, relationships, whereas collaboration is usually understood as a convergent arrangement among organizations that have similar and congruent goals but are not bound by authority relationships.[4]

Nevertheless, the collaboration literature makes clear the challenges involved in achieving collaboration. At a minimum it involves building trust, avoiding shirking, weathering changes in leadership, coordinating presumably joint activities, and providing monitoring (McGuire 2006; Bryson, Crosby, and Stone 2006). Contracting faces many of the same challenges. The contracting literature demonstrates that ensuring compliance, providing oversight, observing performance, developing trust, and maintaining consistency in the face of change are equally elusive (Cooper 2003). Both types of relationships feature degrees of interorganizational and intersectoral activities.

In this inquiry we explore the empirical relationship between collaboration and contracting by state agencies. More specifically, we address two questions: First, we examine whether agencies that appear to be more collaborative are also more likely to engage in contracting. Our measure of the latter is the percentage of the agency budget allocated to contracting for the delivery of services, or contract "density." This measure as a dependent variable was employed in an extensive examination of state agency contracting (Brudney et al. 2005). Second, we assess whether agencies with higher levels of collaboration appear to achieve better outcomes through contracting as defined by cost-quality improvements assessed by MCP scores. This early and exploratory stage emphasizes the tentative nature of our expectations. We anticipate that state agencies with more collaborative activities will be more interested in pursuing other forms of joint action, such as contracting for the delivery of services. We also speculate that agencies with greater experience in collaboration may prove more adept at achieving beneficial outcomes through contracting (as measured by MCP scores). Third, we consider the possibility that the actions and organizational experience(s) of the agency head are linked to contract density and contract performance.

Bryson, Crosby, and Stone (2006, 44) provide an array of propositions about "cross-sector collaboration that is required to remedy complex public problems." Our empirical approach is compatible with their relational framework. We identify two features (dimensions) of contracting, namely, density (that portion of an agency's budget allocated to contracting) and performance (MCP, based on cost-quality judgments). With these two indicators as dependent variables, we then propose and examine several independent variables intended to measure the extent to which the state agencies (or agency heads) are engaged in collaborative activities.

Data from the 1998 and 2004 ASAP surveys are employed to evaluate the prospective relationships. Although these surveys were not designed primarily to measure collaboration, several promising indicators are available. Contract diversity is the number of sectors (for-profit, nonprofit, and public) with which an agency contracts, from one to all three. Contract diversity can also mean the "publicness" of the contracting relationship, ranging from the most public (contracting with other governments and nonprofit organizations only) to least public (contracting exclusively with business firms). We presume that agencies with more multisectoral relationships and those with greater connections with public institutions rather than exclusively with private firms are more collaborative (Bozeman 1987; Rainey 2003).

Two measures are available in the ASAP surveys as indicators of the collaborative context of state agencies. One is the dependence of the agency on federal aid, measured by the percentage of the agency budget derived from that source. Federal aid is well recognized as requiring interdependent and collaborative activity (Choi et al. 2005). The second is the number of actors involved in policy shifts that affected the agency. The array of actors includes a total of nine types of state, local, and national officials. We might prefer a more direct measurement link to collaboration, but we assume that state agencies more dependent on federal funds and those subject to greater policy shifts in which multiple actors had an influence are more thoroughly enmeshed in collaborative relationships. Bryson, Crosby, and Stone (2006, 46) observe that "cross-sector collaborations are more likely to form in turbulent environments." Federal aid dependency and the number of external actors involved in initiating agency policy change represent promising measures of a turbulent environment (Wright and Cho 2000).

Finally, we explore collaboration of the agency as expressed through the organizational background and contact patterns of the agency head. The organizational mobility of the state administrator is the number of state agencies for which she or he has worked. Contact relationships are measured by the frequency of direct (telephone or face-to-face) contacts between the agency head and other state agencies. Greater agency head experience with other state agencies as well as frequency of contact may be indicative of involvement in collaboration. As Bryson, Stone, and Crosby hypothesized (2006, 52), "Cross-sector collaborations are likely to be more successful . . . [if] built on strong relationships with key political and professional constituencies." (The appendix gives the operational indicators for all the variables.)

Table 7.4 presents the correlations between the measures of collaboration and the percentage of an agency's budget allocated to contracts for the delivery of services for 1998 and 2004. The correlations offer fairly consistent support for the relationships anticipated between the measures of collaboration and agency contracting. In both 1998 and 2004, agencies with higher degrees of collaboration as measured by contract diversity (number of sectors with which contracted) and greater contracting "publicness" (involvement with government and nonprofit entities) allocated more of their budget to contracting. In addition, state agencies with greater dependence on federal aid devoted a larger proportion of their budget to contracting for the delivery of services. Furthermore, those state agencies

Table 7.4 Relationships between Collaboration and
Contract Density, 1998 and 2004 (correlation)

	Contract Density	
Measure of Collaboration	1998	2004
Sector Measure		
Diversity	.257***	.207***
Publicness	−.217***	−.260***
Agency Measures		
Federal aid dependency	.270***	.261***
Agency turbulence	.121***	.100*
Administrator Measures		
Contact frequency	.016	.098*
Organization mobility	.090*	−.018

***$p < .01$; **$p < .05$; *$p < .1$.

in which more actors are involved in bringing about policy shifts reported higher contract density. Finally, the frequency of contact of state agency heads with other agencies was associated with contract density (in 2004), as was the prior job experience of the agency head in multiple state agencies (in 1998). As acknowledged, we would prefer more direct and elaborate measures of agency collaboration. Yet the consistency of support for the expected relationships displayed in table 7.4 is encouraging.

Our second research question asked whether a relationship exists between agency collaboration and contracting performance as measured by improvements in service cost and quality. Accordingly, we examined the correlations between the collaboration indicators and MCP scores across contracting state agencies.

The results fail to reveal statistically significant relationships between the collaboration variables and the MCP. Only the relationship between contract density and MCP achieves statistical significance in the 1998 ASAP survey. This finding indicates that agencies devoting a larger share of their budget to contracting are more likely to achieve better (cost-quality) results; that is, agencies that receive the desired outcomes from contracting are more likely to invest in the approach. Overall, however, the findings show that state agencies engaged in higher levels of collaboration are not more likely to realize cost/quality improvements through contracting. If the MCP, as measured by administrators' cost/quality judgments, approximates contracting "success," then collaborative actors and actions as we have measured them do not predict performance very well.

DISCUSSION AND CONCLUDING OBSERVATIONS

In a recent review of three major volumes on public management titled "Conceptualizing and Measuring Collaborative Networks," Rethemeyer (2005, 117) observed that "public management . . . is network management and network management is about facilitating relationships in order to maintain coproduction among members [of networks]." In a case study of leasing (contracting out) a state park (in Georgia), Van Slyke and Hammonds (2003, 146) emphasized the difference public managers make, observing that "public management capacity actually increased as a result of privatization." We have addressed companion questions of whether agency collaborative activities are associated with the amount of privatization in the form of transactional contracting undertaken as well as the results obtained from this approach with respect to cost and quality.

State executives are, ipso facto, public managers. Their involvement in collaborative networks is not merely optional; it is virtually required for survival. But survival is not their raison d'être. It is therefore no surprise that state agency heads are extensively connected through the contracting process with mazes of networks in pursuit of public service delivery (Wise 1990; Kettl 2002, 2005a; Goldsmith and Eggers 2004; Lynn 2004; Ingraham 2005; Kamensky and Burlin 2004).

The research reported here confirms the extensive engagement through contracting of American state executives in complex collaborative activities. In simple descriptive terms, for both 1998 and 2004, we document that state agencies contracted for service delivery with other governments, nonprofits, and private firms at rates approximating, respectively, 60, 70, and 80 percent. Contracting for the delivery of public services as a major tool for collaboration is examined here not only at the agency level but also across two time periods for several contracting dimensions.

The disposition dimension reflecting the perceived cost and quality effects of contracting provided the basis for developing a summary statistic, the MCP, measuring agency contracting performance. This measure is based on combinations of two resultants key to the success of agency contracting: the cost of delivering services to the public and the quality of the services delivered. This straightforward metric gives a useful indication of overall contracting performance. Positive scores denote net gains in service delivery realized through contracting, negative scores show net losses, and scores at or near zero designate mixed or neutral effects.

In this chapter we directly explored the relationship between agency contracting and other forms of collaboration. As expected, state agencies that rated more highly on measures of collaboration were more likely to invest a greater percentage of their budget in contracting (table 7.4). By contrast, there was no support for confirming a relationship between agency collaboration and the achievement of cost/quality results through contracting. Why? ?

Several factors might account for the apparent absence of more extensive relationships between collaboration and contracting performance. First, as the literature attests, attaining the benefits of contracting is challenging and may be contingent on a variety of critical factors (Brown, Potoski, and Van Slyke 2006). A vast array of literature has addressed this elusive issue for the past two decades without arriving at firm conclusions. From this perspective, it is not surprising that collaboration and the attainment of positive contracting results are not related in the present analysis.

We have examined more ambitious models of the MCP (not reported here) but have yet to develop a satisfactory statistical explanation of this crucial construct. Elsewhere, we have assessed the relationships of MCP scores to both the internal and external dimensions of contracting (Brudney et al. 2006). Our aim was to evaluate whether there are noteworthy intra-dimensional relationships involved in contracting. For three dimensions of contracting, significant positive associations emerged. MCP scores were highest where state agency heads reported (1) more competition among contractees, (2) greater organizational oversight capacity, and (3) increased accountability as well as greater responsiveness to public needs. The analyses presented in this chapter arrive at more mixed results but lead to more far-reaching questions.

A second reason for the lack of relationship between collaboration and contracting performance is that the variables available through the ASAP surveys may not be sufficiently sensitive to the features and nuances of agency collaboration to provide solid tests of expected relationships. Because they canvass the state agency landscape on such a wide array of important topics, the ASAP surveys were limited in the depth information collected on collaboration. For example, the ASAP surveys are unable to provide information on the number of organizations with which a state agency collaborates, which of these relationships may be more (or less) significant or critical to the agency, the level and type of joint activity involved in the collaboration, and the form and purpose of the collaboration. These omissions reveal how challenging it is to assess the possible relationship between agency contracting and collaboration.

Third, our measures of collaboration and contracting are admittedly perceptual. This limitation is particularly relevant to the derivation of the

MCP from executives' judgments about the cost and quality effects of contracting. This approach offers the advantage of providing a complementary method to evaluate the thorny issue of the results obtained by public agencies through contracting. Although it would be very difficult to obtain all the requisite information, MCP scores might be used in combination with more objective measures of contracting performance to provide a more complete assessment.

Despite the absence of objective performance and collaboration measurements in this research, we are confident that state executives can reliably assess the relationships of their agencies with other organizational entities. When questions arise about subjective responses, we adopt the views of Boulding (1959) and other authorities (Weick 1979, 1995, 2001; Pressman 1975; Weidner 1960; Cho and Wright 2004). As Boulding (1959, 120) notes, "We must recognize that the people whose decisions determine policies and actions . . . do not respond to the 'objective' facts of the situation, whatever that may mean, but to their 'image' of the situation. It is what we think the world is like, not really what it is like, that determines our behavior."

In sum, state agency heads are sources of important information and insights about the relationship between contracting and other forms of collaboration for their organizations. As practitioners of the art of collaborative public management, they regularly engage in these practices. Privatization is one of the managerial "tools" at their disposal (Salamon 2002). The essence of collaborative public management is how they use this tool and others available to them as they navigate complicated networks of service provision, both intersectorally with nonprofit organizations, for-profit businesses, and other public agencies, and intergovernmentally with national, state, and local officials and institutions.

Appendix: Description of Contracting and Collaboration Variables

Variable	Variable Measurement	Measurement Category
Contracting measure		
1. Density	Percent of agency budget allocated to contracting	1: 5% or less; 2: 6–10%; 3: 11–20%; 4: 21–30%; 5: 31–40%; 6: over 40%
2. Performance	MCP: combination of cost and quality	–2: Increased cost and decreased quality from contracting through +2: Decreased cost and increased quality (see table 7.3 for full scale and percentage distribution)
Collaboration measure		
Sector collaboration		
1. Diversity	Number of sectors used for contracting	1. One 2. Two 3. Three
2. Publicness	Continuum of types of sectors used for contracting	1: Public (other government only; nonprofit only; other government + non-profit); 2: Mixed (other government+nonprofit + for-profit); 3: Semi-private (other govern-ment + for-profit); 4: Private (for-profit only)
Agency collaboration		
1. Federal aid dependency	Percent of agency budget from federal government	0: none; 1: under 25%; 2: 25–49%; 3: 50–74%; 4: 75% or more
2. Agency turbulence	Number of actors involved in initiating major shifts of agency policy	0–9
Administrator collaboration		
1. Contact frequency	Frequency with other state agencies	0: never; 1: less than monthly; 2: monthly; 3: weekly; 4: daily
2. Organization mobility	Number of other state agencies for whom agency head has worked	0–5

NOTES

This chapter is a revised version of a paper presented at the Syracuse University Maxwell School Conference on Collaborative Public Management, Washington, September 28–30, 2006. We are grateful to Rosemary O'Leary and the anonymous reviewers for excellent comments and suggestions on a draft of the chapter. We thank the Earhart Foundation (Ann Arbor) for supporting this research, as well as the Department of Political Science and the Center for Governmental Services at Auburn University, and the Odum Institute for Research in Social Science at the University of North Carolina at Chapel Hill. We are solely responsible for the contents.

1. The established and new state agencies by decade were as follows: 1950s, 51; 1960s, 13; 1970s, 30; 1980s, 15; and 1990s, 8—a total of 117.

2. For 2004, the ASAP survey obtained data on five additional dimensions of contracting: discretion—the extent of competition among contractees; deliberateness— the degree of agency oversight capability; duty—the extent of agency accountability and responsiveness; divisiveness—the level of controversy surrounding contracting; and determination—the level of public satisfaction with contracted services. All measures are perceptual. We intend to assess all ten dimensions of contracting in the 2008 ASAP survey (in the field as of this writing). In other research authors have grouped the dimensions and analyzed them in two broad categories: internal dimensions focused on agency choice criteria, and external dimensions reaching beyond agency organizational boundaries (see Choi and Wright 2004).

3. It is possible and even promising to further explore the different usage of measuring and knowing what works so far as collaboration characteristics and various indicators of service contract usage and performance. We have broached this strategy elsewhere (Brudney et al. 2006), but it lies beyond our present aim. What should be highlighted, however, is the practitioner-based source(s) for measuring the several contract dimensions, including usage and performance. From one standpoint, the measures of contract usage and performance are "subjective;" i.e., they are based on the *perceptions* of the responding state agency heads. This is in contrast to so-called objective measures of various aspects of contracting because those are designed and applied by presumably detached and/or disinterested observers. For brief discussions of the issues associated with contrasting measurement approaches, see Cho and Wright (2004) and the references cited there.

4. In contrast to our focus on traditional contracting, other chapters in this book deal with "relational contracting." In their IBM monograph, Milward and Provan (2006, 26) describe "relational contracting." They write, "In the real world, hard and fast distinctions tend to blur at certain points. Collaboration and contracting come together in what economists call 'relational contracting,' which is contracting that is based on trust and reciprocity (just like networks) rather than a written contract that specifies what both parties' obligations are in great detail. Relational contracts are typically kept in place as long as they serve the interests of both parties rather than being competitively bid with some frequency. They tend to be used for goods and services where price is less important than quality."

Chapter 8 ✓

Collaboration and Relational Contracting

David M. Van Slyke

In this volume, the role of the collaborative public manager is the central theme. Government contracting is one area in which collaboration is both praised and vilified. Contracting is a pragmatic tool of governance and the most frequently used form of privatization in the United States. It involves government agencies entering into formal relationships with a third party for the production of goods and/or provision of services. Governments at all levels have increasingly used contracting with other governments, nonprofits, and for-profit firms to deliver a wide range of public goods and/ or services. Fundamentally, the argument is that contracting benefits the government because of competition and market forces (Savas 2000). The associated outcomes are cited as lower costs, higher quality, expertise, and innovation. Those opposed to contracting express concern about government's heightened exposure to opportunism, gaps in accountability, and a loss of public management capacity (Sclar 2000).

benefits

concerns

Recent news stories advocating more collaboration in contracting relationships suggest that "top acquisition managers develop [and be encouraged to develop] tight bonds with industry"; that "the process [of contracting] involves close interaction between acquisition officials and contractors, . . . [recognizing] that there's no way to be successful without working together"; and that "the focus [of government contracting officers] should be on creating a long-term relationship between vendors and government officials."[1] Opponents of this approach to contracting suggest that vendors cannot be trusted to execute government's goals without very specific legal contracts and to engage in less than highly specified contractual relationships would be a dereliction of duty and a failure to protect the public's interest. Those critical of a more collaborative approach to contracting suggest that familiarity (close relationships between government officials and vendors) leads to a lack of competition and creates a relationship of government dependence on the winning vendor, which over time can lead to corruption and a loss of accountability.

The public administration literature has tended to treat the topic of contracting in starkly normative and ideological terms, and analysts often draw from a single theoretical framework, such as transaction cost economics or agency theory. A transaction cost approach is often used or at least recommended for deciding whether government should make or buy goods and services based on ease of measurement, observability of service quality, and the asset-specific nature of the product (Tadelis 2002). Similarly, contracts and the manner in which government manages its relationships with vendors have often been framed using agency theory, which in essence provides direction on how a principal (government) can control its relationships with an agent (vendors) in order to reduce opportunistic behavior and achieve goal alignment. Each theory, respectively, requires that a decision be made. First, make the service internal to government or purchase the service through the use of contracts in open markets. And, second, control the agent through the use of incentives, sanctions, and monitoring for purposes of goal alignment or develop more collaborative and trusting arrangements, which may promote alignment but may also result in government being vulnerable to vendor opportunism.

An argument heard in the procurement halls of government and written about in public administration journals is that government managers need to become more trusting and collaborative in their contract relationships with vendors. Yet there are a great many historical reasons beyond the scope of this chapter for why this type of relationship has not formally been the norm among rank-and-file government managers. Scholars have increasingly suggested that an alternative contract management strategy that may promote greater alignment and reduce costs is to develop relationships premised on trust and engagement rather than pursue arm's-length transactional forms that are hierarchical and control oriented. Milward and Provan (2006, 26) state that "collaboration and contracting come together with what they suggest economists call 'relational contracting,' [which] is based on trust and reciprocity rather than a written contract that specifies what both parties' obligations are in great detail." To effectively manage these relationships, they suggest three points that can be associated with relational contracting. The first is that "competitive contracting (often in a thin market with few sellers) is an impediment to collaboration" (Milward and Provan 2006, 12); second, that "collaboration is essential if a client's needs are to be met, . . . since no one organization delivers all of the services a client is likely to need" (p. 12); and third, that "trust is critical for collaboration" (p. 21). For the purposes of examining relational contracting and collaboration, I draw on McGuire's (2006, 1) definition of collaborative public management as "a concept that describes the process of facilitating and operating in multiorganizational arrangements for solving problems that cannot be achieved, or achieved easily, by single organizations."

This new stream of "relational contracting" research frequently juxtaposes the decision as one of whether to use "complete" or "incomplete" contract designs. Though few would suggest the elimination of formal contracts between government and its vendors, the transactional and relational camps recommend differing levels of contractual specificity and detail. In essence, a complete contract signals less trust because of the high degree of specificity and formality in the contract document. An incomplete contract, or a relational contract, suggests more trust as signaled by less contractual specificity and presumably greater flexibility and discretion afforded by government to the vendor. The contract management issue then, and specifically in relational contracting, is viewed as whether to "trust or distrust" the vendor's potential actions, controlling for them through different contract design and governance mechanisms. Embedded deep within these discrete choices are a range of values about, among others, trust and collaboration.

Supporters of a relational approach to contracting contend that relationships are built over time between the purchasing agency and the contracting vendor. This can lead to better coordination on desired product and service outcomes, and over time, better quality and lower costs, including lower contract management costs. Opponents of a relational contracting approach argue that such "relationship-building" activities between government and vendors leads not to the outcomes asserted by supporters of this approach but to favoritism, reduced competition, overreliance on the winning vendor, and diminished public management capacity. This approach is viewed as contrary to the more historical contract management emphasis on contract law. In either case, transactional or relational, public managers exercise discretion in their disposition to trust or not to trust, and this is seen in both the contractual specificity and the degree and quality of involvement the parties have with one another (Van Slyke 2007).

The study of collaboration has received attention from public management scholars largely within the context of networks consisting of multilateral linkages. However, what remains missing is an understanding of the conditions for and processes involved in developing collaborative relational contractual arrangements. This has been the case in the area of government–nonprofit contracts, especially in the social policy field and for social services programs. As Agranoff (2006) notes, there may be more important forms of collaborative management, such as contractual relationships, which need greater explication. In this chapter I focus on understanding the process by which contractual relationships evolve from transactional to relational. This is an important issue because it fundamentally examines contracting, a policy tool that government increasingly uses as a market-based alternative to government provision. The unit of analysis is public managers and their views regarding how contractual relationships change and how that change is evidenced in both the actual contract and the manner in which they manage their vendors. The public managers interviewed for this study are government contract managers in New York State, primarily with responsibility for government contracts at the state and local level with nonprofit organizations for the production and delivery of social services. The data come from extensive interviews conducted with these public managers and nonprofit executive directors. To understand the role that collaboration plays in contractual relationships, it is important to consider how it is developed and evolves over time. This requires looking at the issue of trust. The chapter is organized in the following way. First, the research on government contracting and the context in which it occurs is presented. This includes examining the major findings from studies about the government–nonprofit social services contract environment. Second, the issue of relational or incomplete contracting is presented, drawing on the limited public administration research and the more significant developments from the field of economics and management. Third, the study population and methods are presented. Finally, the findings and management implications are discussed.

BACKGROUND

Collaboration and contracting are not antithetical to one another. Indeed, successful contract relationships often involve some degree of collaboration between the buyer (government) and seller (nonprofits). However, what is less well known is what these collaborative practices are and under what conditions each party enacts them. If the desired outcome is a win–win relationship between the buyer and the seller in terms of reducing risk and uncertainty, then what form does collaboration take, what processes are implemented, and how do the respective actors participate?

Understanding these issues may help the parties work toward and achieve goal alignment.

Contracting

The contracting literature within the field of public administration is well established, and the research to date has focused on any number of important issues. These include the make-or-buy decision, contract design, contract management, contract monitoring, accountability, and the development of public management capacity to ensure that government is a smart buyer of goods and services and is learning from past experiences (Brown, Potoski, and Van Slyke 2006, 2007, forthcoming). The interest in this topic stems from continued government devolution, an expressed (some might say ideological) desire for smaller government, and the pragmatic uses of various privatization tools, such as contracts, vouchers, franchises, and partnerships (Van Slyke 2003). Perhaps not surprisingly, there is growing recognition of the importance and increasing use by government of market-based alternatives and specifically employing contracts with private providers to produce and deliver government services (Kelman 2002). Practically speaking, these reflect the growth of privatization and increasing attention on the contracting enterprise, at least from the perspective of public management scholars.

There are of course proponents and opponents of privatization, each with a litany of reasons for why government should or should not engage markets, using contracts as type of market-based tool. Proponents often argue that markets and the for-profit, nonprofit, and faith-based providers that operate in them are more effective than government because they are closer to clients in terms of proximity; possess stronger incentives to produce higher-quality goods and services because of their nongovernmental forms of ownership; and have oversight mechanisms internal to their operations that focus on reducing costs and enhancing operations through innovation and specialization. Opponents assert that the evidence associated with lower costs, higher quality, and more oversight is both overstated and inaccurate. In fact, they argue, there is ample evidence to suggest that all that ails government production and delivery is not manifestly ameliorated by the use of private contracts (Sclar 2000). The assertion is that instances of fraud, waste, abuse, corruption, and monopoly all can and do occur under contracting because of a lack of governmental oversight, incentives for agents to pursue their own self-interest over the goals of government programs and agencies, a lack of market competition, and asymmetric information issues that primarily stem from service characteristics and thus create difficulties in both measuring and observing the performance of contracted providers.

One of the most important components in the contracting process is the decision about whether government should produce and deliver goods and services or whether it should fund the production and provision of services (Brown and Potoski 2005). Much of this research has focused on writing contract agreements prior to the actual awarding of a contract that specify every component of the relationship that is to take place between the contracting parties. Such contractual specificity, though expensive and often intended to protect risk-averse principals from untrustworthy agents, is a function of several factors that need to be more thoughtfully considered. These include the characteristics of the service, the degree of market competitiveness for the service to be contracted, and the composition and diversity of providers in that market (other governments, for-profit providers, or nonprofit organizations). In addition, prior to writing the contract, public managers need to consider the goals they are trying to achieve through contracting. Inevitably, these are not only programmatic goals but public values, such as fairness or equity, that they would like to see operationalized and implemented. On the issue of values, government has many that it often tries to achieve, including efficiency, effectiveness, service quality, responsiveness, transparency, equality, equity, social justice, and accountability, to name just a few. To achieve all these values would be both difficult and costly, which is why public managers have some difficult decisions to make prior to writing the contract (Brown, Potoski, and Van Slyke 2006).

Public managers will also find that legislative, political, or legal goals have to be met as expressed in the rule of law. For example, government may not only need to deliver a good or service, but any contract awarded must be with a minority-owned (by race/ethnicity, women, veterans, etc.) firm. Therefore, certain "rules of the game" could augment, but are more likely to inhibit, how a contract is written. Recognizing the heterogeneity of client demand and the variability of client needs, government often has to make decisions that provide for those needs. Finally, government has at its disposal certain management tools, procedures, processes, and performance measures that it would like to both track and oversee.

To achieve goal alignment, public managers then are charged with writing a contract that incentivizes a vendor to comply with the terms of the contract as specifically written while also identifying the mechanisms by which the vendor is to be monitored, evaluated, and held accountable. The challenge that remains is one in which a vast range of products and services, those easy to measure and observe and those that are not, are purchased in markets with varying degrees of competition. In each case, contract management is critical to successful contracting (Kettl 1993; Smith and Lipsky 1993; Cooper 2003; Van Slyke 2003). Yet as Kelman (2002) has often noted, contract management is an area in which there has been an underinvestment at all levels of government. This challenge is all the more real because of a dearth in the procurement, acquisition, and contract management capacity of government. Government agencies do not escape responsibility over the quality, fit, and distributional mechanisms of its services provided under contract with private vendors. The reality is that government's responsibilities tend to increase because of contracting as myriad stakeholders internal and external to government have oversight interests for which agencies are held accountable.

Given the challenges that public managers face and the goals they are responsible for achieving when using contracting, the issue of collaboration is all the more important given the benefits it may hold for both parties. Understanding the government–nonprofit social services contracting relationship and its contexts can improve our analysis of how collaboration develops and evolves in these contractual arrangements.

The Government–Nonprofit Social Services Contracting Relationship

The government–nonprofit social service contracting relationship has many different attributes and functions, resulting in part from devolution and various public-sector management reforms directed at achieving lower costs, improved service quality, and a reduced role for government in producing goods and services available in private markets. Social services are complex services for which government may have some expertise. However, government often requires additional expertise, which it must either hire or contract for in order to treat and serve clients. These types of services are prime candidates to be privatized because alternatives to government provision do exist through the use of nonprofits, faith-based organizations, and, increasingly, for-profit firms.[2] Support among policymakers to follow through on historical precedent to uncouple government from providing services that firms in private markets already do or can potentially provide has generally been strong. A number of challenges exist for government when it makes a decision to buy social services using contracts. Four broad categories of challenges have frequently been cited.

First, there is often a lack of competition by geographic market (rural, suburban, and urban) and service type (refugee resettlement, substance abuse and addiction programs). This can create difficulties for public managers seeking to correct for supply-side imperfections (too few market providers, monopsonistic pressures) and limits their use of contract termination and rebidding as a management strategy (DeHoog 1984; Johnston and Romzek 1999; Van Slyke 2003).[3] Second, policy directives, program goals, and implementation requirements are often ambiguously defined and infrequently monitored. This creates conditions of uncertainty that can make it difficult for public managers to evaluate the frequency, consistency, and quality of service delivery among its contractors.[4] The social services attributes described require that public managers use discretion in the implementation of services. This can lead to goal divergence between policy directives and implementation practices, presenting genuine accountability concerns for public managers (Meyers, Riccucci, and Lurie 2001; Riccucci 2005; Sandfort 2000).

Third, ideological motives to contract can also contribute to a lack of administrative capacity in government agencies. Supporters claim that most governmental services can be contracted, while opponents assert that most programs and services are inherently governmental and therefore need to be produced by government agencies and their workers. A predictable result, then, is insufficient contract management capacity. This can have the unintended outcome of limiting the ability of public managers to develop competition, solicit bids, rebid contracts, develop performance measures, and monitor and hold contractors accountable for contract goals, service quality, and client satisfaction. As a result, public managers find they lack the time, resources, training, and support to actively govern the contract responsibilities for which they are responsible (Kelman 2002; Milward and Provan 2000; Van Slyke 2003).[5] Therefore, public managers respond to their own institutional incentives and adopt a risk-averse management style predicated on completing paperwork and reducing uncertainty. As one might expect, these decisions by public managers contribute to a contract governance approach that is not fundamentally directed toward collaboration but encourages transactional efficiencies and goal alignment. And, fourth, contracting relationships between government and nonprofit organizations can have the unintended effect of altering nonprofit governance practices, causing mission drift and the deprofessionalization of staff, and contributing to a position of government funding dependency (Alexander, Nank, and Stivers 1999; Grønbjerg 1993; Kramer 1994; Saidel 1991). Nonprofits' dependency on government funding may at first blush appear to be a benign effect of entering into contractual relationships with government agencies. Yet this outcome does not benefit nonprofits, government agencies, or clients over the long term because of the deleterious effects that dependency has on the effectiveness of third-party governance.

The question, then, is how do public managers manage contracts with nonprofits for programs like social services? Though relational contracting is often noted as consisting of more collaboration and trust, economists approach relational or incomplete contracting differently than public administration scholars. A brief review of the current work on incomplete contracting, also referred to as relational contracting, is presented below. The purpose of this is to frame the context in which government managers may view an evolution in contract management from transactional to relational and the effects of these changes on the dynamics of the contracting relationship.

Incomplete Contracting

Economists have contributed to the work on relational contracting by focusing on different dimensions of contractual specificity. The term "incomplete contract" is used here, but in general it is interchangeable with the concept of relational contracting. Macneil (1978) suggests that relational contracts can be viewed as a "constitution" between the parties— a term quite familiar to public managers whose disciplinary roots are grounded in public law. An incomplete contract is by its very nature lacking rigid specificity because of recognition by the parties that all future contingencies cannot necessarily be foreseen and that any effort to contractually control for unforeseen events imposes costs on both parties that neither has an interest in bearing (Hart and Moore 1999; Tirole 1999). In fact, there is currently no generally accepted definition of a relational contract, but there is agreement on the attributes of such a contract. Williamson's evolved writings (1991, 1996, 2005) suggest that incomplete contracts are a framework of governance that recognizes the need for cooperation and adaptation, both spontaneous and intentional, between the parties ex post contract implementation because of unforeseen contingences, such as transaction costs that neither party may be aware of or can control for unilaterally. Given conditions of contractual uncertainty, the source of value in a contract becomes the continuity of the relationship and repeated transactions over time between the parties. This is a position premised on bilateral responsibility for the achievement of collective action, with neither party acting opportunistically at the expense of the other (Guriev and Kvasov 2005). This is a position held, among others, by Baker, Gibbons, and Murphy (2002, 39), who view relational contracts as "informal agreements sustained by the value of future relationships between firms." Kvaloy and Olsen (2004, 2) assert that "a relational contract relies only on self-enforcement; effort variables are non-verifiable, and the parties honor the contract as long as the present value of honoring exceeds the present value of reneging."

Tirole identifies (1999) three categories of incompleteness: (1) unforeseen contingencies, (2) the costs of writing contracts, and (3) the costs of enforcing contracts. Relational contracts can have both verifiable elements, meaning the terms of the contract that can be measured and enforced in a court of law, and self-enforced elements, those observable elements that are not easily measured and enforced legally but that can be enforced by the principal through the discretion exercised using a range of tools, such as payments or reporting mechanisms, reputation and legitimacy, and contract renewal and termination.

Battigalli and Maggi (2002) highlight some of the costs associated with contract design and completeness. The first is the importance of writing costs and communicating instructions between a principal and agent. They suggest that "the number of events and actions that are potentially relevant is arguably astronomical, so that the cost of writing a complete contract would be very large" (p. 799). They go on to state that "the cost of a contract is not a function of the number of contingencies specified in the contract, but of how hard it is to describe those contingencies in the given language" (p. 801). The more specific your instructions, the more rigid they are, the more time they take to draft or communicate, and thus the more they cost. The greater the rigidity of the contract parameters, the more difficult for the agent to exercise discretion based on their expertise in order to achieve goal alignment.

The focus on discretion inevitably involves issues of quality and rigidity but often fails to recognize exogenous events beyond the principal or agent's control in the external environment. Examples of exogenous events could include policy changes, court interferences, regulatory action, and exit from the market by other vendors. Therefore, if a principal expects that an agent really does have greater expertise, then writing a complete contract may actually constrain the agent's exercise of ability and expertise, unnecessarily restricting their effort and the results to be achieved. Conversely, little to no specificity could present other problems for the principal in terms of agent uniformity in actions taken or the ability to verify results from an agent's action, an issue to be discussed below regarding monitoring and enforcement (Kvaloy and Olsen 2004). Writing contingencies assumes that they are both foreseeable and verifiable. However, such contingencies are a function, deterministically so, of the duration and intensity of the contract (Guriev and Kvasov 2005); the expected frequency of interactions between the principal and agent as they negotiate the goals, processes, and outcomes of the contracted program (Corts and Singh 2004); the developmental nature of the product and its quality; the level of service receptivity and fit with a particular clientele's special needs (Artz and Brush 2000); and, in general, learning to work with one another and how information is exchanged, communication is fostered, and coordination is achieved. Thus a principal may, because of the contingencies described above, also decide not to precisely and rigidly specify all the parameters of a contract as an intentional trust-building technique (Bernheim and Whinston 1998).

Inherent in any contract, complete or incomplete, are the contract management mechanisms by which the principal seeks to align the behavior and actions of the agent through the use of incentives and monitoring. These mechanisms include, among others, incentives and monitoring (Bernheim and Whinston 1998; Levin 2003). However, Fernandez (2005, 23) suggests that "some of the strongest determinants of contracting performance are factors that facilitate adaptive decision making, problem solving, and learning—among them trust, a willingness to work together to identify and solve problems, and reliance on negotiations and other alternative means for resolving disputes." If this is true, the strategic ambiguity associated with monitoring and oversight may be viewed as a trust-building mechanism necessary for collaboration, goal alignment, and lower costs over time in the relationship.

Integral to the incomplete contracting literature is the focus on trust. Though a substantial literature exists on trust formation and trust as the glue of interorganizational relationships (Stoker 1991; Mayer, Davis, and Schoorman 1995; Das and Teng 1998; Jeffries and Reed 2000; Hardin 2002), it is important to note that trust is built through repeated interactions; by instances of cooperation through which trust becomes reinforcing among the parties; and through information exchange and the investment that each party makes in getting to know the others' interests, preferences, motivations and their own organizational governance systems and mechanisms. In many ways, consistency, predictability, transparency, and acknowledging the constraints of both parties is important to the trust-building process—a process based on fairness of procedure and outcome. With an incomplete contract, the expectation is that over time the costs of repeated transactions will decline based on the lack of contractual rigidity and the discretion shared between the parties premised on outcomes that are collectively aligned with each party's interests. One argument is that if the core technology and/or expertise being contracted for is considered to be highly asset specific, difficult to observe and measure, and lacking the ability to be commoditized in alternative markets, then the use of a highly specified contract may do more to promote distrust and moral hazard than the use of an incomplete contract that outlines the general operating parameters of the relationship. Milward and Provan (2006, 21) note that "trust is critical for collaboration . . . in relational contract relationships." And similarly, McGuire (2006, 15) suggests the "important role of the collaborative public manager [is] in building trust."

Relational contracting, then, is not the default outcome for managing a contract relationship but rather is a deliberative decision about contract design and management. Fundamentally, to move to a relational contract requires a philosophical shift on the part of public managers in terms of how contract relationships are to be managed; a shift toward trust, ongoing communication, and collaboration. Such a decision is not without institutional and individual costs, given the risk-averse cultures of public organizations and the lack of incentives for public employees to initiate a contract form whose success is measured by trust and therefore avoidance of moral hazard. Legal analysts are among the first to note that contracts exist because trust does not. This is not to suggest that actual program performance is not measured, but rather that trust is important to the foundation upon which government and vendors agree to the most relevant measures of success.

If trust does exist or is developed, does that lessen the need for highly specified legal instruments to govern the relationships between two parties? Can contract relationships evolve toward less highly specified contracts and more relational forms of contract management over time and because of trust? The concept of trust, therefore, is one of the most vexing issues associated with relational contracts and the work of the collaborative public manager, for whom responsibility is increasingly focused on managing contract relationships with third parties.

METHODOLOGY

To investigate the questions raised in this chapter, a fifteen-question semistructured interview instrument was administered to a purposive sample of public managers and nonprofit executive directors. A multisite, multiprogram sampling stratification strategy is employed. Interviews were conducted in New York, and each took approximately one hour and thirty minutes. The interviews were tape-recorded, transcribed, and coded based on interviewee responses. The data were analyzed using Ethnograph version 5.0.

This sampling strategy was used to specifically examine the extent to which market, political, and contract conditions affect the degree of trust *purpose* and collaboration in government's contract relationships with nonprofit organizations. The counties selected include urban, suburban, and rural counties in New York. The programs selected are from a broad range of social services. This is the case because it is important to investigate the extent to which variation in the degree of task specificity, measurability, observability, market supply, client characteristics, intervention complexity and duration, and political and funding support affect the development of collaboration and relational contracting practices in government's relationships with nonprofit organizations. A second reason for this strategy is that many of these service and market characteristics are in fact antithetical to the conditions often prescribed as advantageous for contracting. Such an approach therefore provides an ideal opportunity to identify conditions under which there is variation in contract management practices and whether collaboration and more relational forms of contract governance develop and evolve because the conditions of social services contracting are frequently contrary to popular prescriptions associated with government's make-or-buy decision.

FINDINGS: TRUST AND COLLABORATION

To date, a strong research stream has developed on how the make-or-buy decisions for services at the opposite ends of the asset-specificity and ease-of-measurement continuum, such as refuse collection and social services, are produced and distributed (Brown and Potoski 2005). However, the manner in which contracts are managed remains an issue of significant concern. In this section, I focus on the manner in which contract relationships develop and the role that trust and collaboration play in that development.

Reasons for Contracting with Nonprofits

There are a host of reasons why public agencies contract with nonprofit organizations to produce and deliver services. One of the first findings from this study has to do with nonprofits being perceived by important stakeholders like elected officials, citizens, and the media as having legitimacy. Approximately 75 percent of the public managers surveyed perceived nonprofit organizations to have higher levels of public trust than their own agencies. For this reason and others, public managers had greater levels of initial trust for, and were more favorably disposed to, nonprofits as opposed to for-profit organizations. The public managers also noted that they contract with nonprofits because of the nonprofits' credibility and to buffer their own agencies from some of the constant performance pressures and media attention associated with being in the "governmental fishbowl." To this issue, public managers provided interesting responses. According to the public managers, if their agencies are providing services, "there is a zero tolerance for anything less than a 100 percent success rate," while others suggested that "nonprofits are not subject to the same media scrutiny as government especially as it relates to failure." Similarly, public managers noted that "when corporations fail, that's development; when we fail, it's a scandal."

Eighty-seven percent of the respondents also noted that government social services agencies seek to contract with nonprofit organizations because of their ability to "think outside the box," and what others referred to as their "creative capability." In thinking outside the box, one deputy commissioner echoed a sentiment consistent with those of the other respondents. On working with nonprofits, he said:

> Nonprofits can bring experience or something to our populations that the government cannot. It's a collaborative relationship with different perspectives. We as a government agency have realized that we cannot work in isolation and therefore need to work in a collaborative spirit with a number of different agencies because we have worked too long in isolation—we can get different perspectives. Government has done it one way for so long that we've lost sight of other and clearer ways that we can do business and they [nonprofits] help to bring that perspective. It's a mutual exchange of experiences and information. Nonprofits have taught me more than I thought possible to learn because I only knew it one way, from one perspective.

The issue of expertise and creativity from nonprofits is salient as a frame of reference and resource for public managers and is therefore viewed by contract managers as an important benefit of collaboration. Public managers recognize the legitimacy of nonprofit organizations and some of the unique strengths they bring as vendors to social services provision (Suchman 1995).

Trust as an Antecedent to Collaboration

Bryson, Crosby, and Stone (2006, 47–48) note that "trusting relationships are often depicted as the essence of collaboration [and] . . . that trust building is an ongoing requirement for successful collaboration." And yet, the work by public administration scholars on relational contracting is relatively straightforward in stating that public managers should engage in relational contracts premised on trust and collaboration. The question then is how to get to that point of trust and beyond to collaboration.

Trust development between parties has cost implications; is affected by time, how power is shared, and the manner is which conflict is managed; and is an outcome based on a range of inputs and activities. There are different types of trust, such as general and particularized trust, though in this section I focus on strategic trust, which is defined as trust that is based on knowledge of and experience with the other party and a mutual expectation of reciprocity (Hardin 2002; Yamagishi and Yamagishi 1994). Trust is a major psychological and social process that underlies developing, maintaining, changing, and discontinuing contracts. As a concept, trust has different meanings and implications across a range of individuals and organizations depending on a party's position of authority, perspective on the contract relationship, and disposition to trust the vendor. Trust involves, as Whitener and others (1998, 513) note, "some level of dependency on the other party so that the outcomes of one individual [actor is] influenced by the actions of another." But trust development is also derived and therefore achieved based on the party's attitudes, values, and beliefs about exchange, reciprocity, resources, and the degree to which they are aligned. This issue of alignment is especially the case for contract relationships.

One of the assumptions about trust in contractual relationships is that the threat of moral hazard is diminished because there are fewer or less intense incentives to exploit asymmetric information for self-interest. Trust is a difficult construct to measure because of problems of endogeneity with other important variables like reputation and especially in the context of collaboration because of the direction of causality and construct validity problems. Notwithstanding those important and difficult methodological and operational issues, the question remains of how trust and collaboration interact with one another in contract relationships. Is trust an antecedent to collaboration? Is collaboration a type of behavior exhibited by two or more parties based on some set of preconditions, such as trust being established? Or is collaboration an outcome of a relationship in which trust develops and evolves over time? These are difficult questions, and they are not addressed in the contracting literature. Here, then, I begin to lay the groundwork for an analysis based on my findings.

Public managers supported the proposition that trust is at the center of contractual relationships and is the single most important criterion for how and under what conditions providers are to be managed. As one manager expressed it, "Trust is outcome based, based on success. You could have a history, but that history is built on success. We're not a very trusting agency."

All the public managers echoed this statement, suggesting that trust evolves based on the other parties' alignment with and achievement of the contract goals. There were some caveats from public managers regarding the degree to which this evolution occurred more or less quickly. One caveat had to do with context. In counties where there was competition—in social services, this is often interpreted to be two or more suppliers—trust development was gradual and evolved over time. In those counties where there was less competition, the development of trust can be seen more as a result of resource interdependency. County social services agencies were dependent on a particular nonprofit, and the nonprofit contractor derived a significant part of its resources from the government contract. The public managers and nonprofit executive directors each described their relationship as one of trust, but premised more on the condition that they need one another, with the county social services managers still feeling as though they possessed hierarchical authority because they are the funder. This relationship of dependency can also be viewed as one of monopsony.

A second caveat is the past experiences of the public managers involved in governing contract relationships. For those managers who had positive relationships with nonprofits, the development of trust was initial and more immediate. In the case of public managers who had mixed experiences, the development was gradual and completely dependent on outcomes. Those outcomes are less specifically about service outcomes as a measure of performance and more often about the degree to which the outcomes are aligned with process activities. Did the nonprofit contractor submit its performance report on time? Did it provide the public manager with timely information when requests were made? Was the contractor clear, consistent, and transparent in its responses to the public manager? Did it adhere to the hierarchical power imbalance, much akin to a traditional principal–agent relationship, without making noise or going around the public manager to more senior agency executives, elected officials, or the media? If the nonprofit did these things, public managers reported a gradual increase in trust and therefore delegated a greater level of discretion to the contractor.

To this point, trust as a unit of analysis has been discussed as a public manager's trust in a particular nonprofit organization. Yet, several other configurations also affect trust. The first is the situation in which a public manager trusts a nonprofit executive director but does not trust his or her organization. I did not find any instances where the nonprofit leader was trusted but the organization was not. The leader was seen as the organization, rightly or wrongly. Then there is the situation in which a nonprofit executive director trusts a public manager but not his or her public agency. I found a number of instances of this relationship. In part this stems from mistrust between executive directors and government agency executives, executive directors and political officials, and agency executives and political officials over commitments to specific programs and client groups. Mistrust was found to be less pronounced between government contract and program managers and nonprofit executive directors. One executive director, echoing a sentiment expressed by half the nonprofit executive directors, summarized his agency's contracting relationship with the Office of Mental Retardation and Developmental Disabilities (OMRDD) in the following manner:

> I have zero trust in OMRDD. My trust in OMRDD is that OMRDD will do what is in the best interests of OMRDD. Period, end of story. In so far as what is best for OMRDD may be in the best interest of our organization and the people we serve I trust that we are most frequently heading in the same direction. Insofar as they're being really good people who understand the overall mission of OMRDD and will carry out that in their daily activities and have good trusting relationships with nonprofits no matter what those agencies are, I have complete confidence that that exists. But when it comes down to a contractual relationship and the best way to put this is that OMRDD will do what is strictly in OMRDD's interest.

In many of the cases, the term "relationship" was an appropriate and accurate characterization of contractual relations between the public agency and the nonprofit service provider. "Relationship" entails being connected and binding participants willingly in mutual accord. Positive contractual relationships were based on each party believing that the other was willing to do what it could to benefit the transacting partner, even if some of the actions were not in its own self-interest. Trust was built one day at a time through communication, conversation, interaction, and the repeated articulation of goals and outcomes. Information exchange and continuous levels of communication were the building blocks for trusting relationships. Neither party approached the contractual relationship at the outset and said that they implicitly trusted the other. Trust, as seen by public managers, was "built on knowing each other's motivations and limitations—certain things public agencies cannot do because they're bound by rules, laws, and regulations."

Clear examples of how trust was demonstrated toward each other were found across the participants. These include nonprofit organizations using their own networks within government and the nonprofit community to advance program funding or policy goals that public managers themselves could not publicly advocate for within their own highly politicized administrative environments but that they supported. Similarly, public managers rewarded nonprofits they trusted by providing information before it became public record on new funding streams, with changes in policy that could affect a nonprofit's revenue base, and by inviting them to participate and present at venues where county social services commissioners were the primary audience. Involving nonprofit providers as stakeholders in decisions, engaging them in identifying need, and showing them respect were all components identified by public managers as necessary for building trust. Nonprofit executive directors described trust as an "attitude" of "what can I do to make this better versus a woe-is-me, this-isn't-right attitude." In this way, nonprofits wanted to be perceived by public managers as part of the solution, not the problem.

What then are the implications of trust for collaboration and relational contracting? As trust between the parties evolved, collaboration was described as each party having confidence in the other that on the major goals of the contract they were aligned with one another. The findings suggest that collaboration evolved in tandem with trust. At the outset of the relationship, contractual compliance mechanisms give rise to cooperation. Nonprofits clearly understand that the road to building trust begins with a willingness to voluntarily cooperate and to actively engage in dialogue and coordination. The duration of this process varied based on a range of contextual factors and the nonprofits' own experiences with government contracting. Trust gave rise to the development of collaboration, which was described as consisting of increasing levels of joint involvement between the parties in developing contract goals, strategies for intervention, performance measures, and appropriate measures for evaluating success.

My analysis suggests that collaboration is operationalized among the parties as consisting of activities and behaviors that are more akin to a partnership. As trust develops and collaboration becomes more institutionalized in the contractual relationship, power is more equally shared, conflict is resolved through dialogue, and each party exhibits more confidence in the other. Each party creates a foundation for making sense of the other's goals, motivations, and preferences and enacted strategies to achieve collaboration rather than mistrust.

With respect to the question of whether trust and collaboration gave way to management practices that may be characterized as relational, the answer is yes. Public managers and nonprofit executive directors each reported that as the relationship evolved over time, there were fewer instances of monitoring, fewer site visits, less frequent formal reporting requirements, and greater discretion afforded the nonprofit contractor. Each party also reported that an evolution from transactional to relational contract management had implications for transaction costs. For public managers, these cost savings are achieved through reduced contract writing costs, less frequent rebidding and letting of contracts, public agencies more effectively using their limited personnel capacity to monitor and review reports from vendors they have less experience with, and reducing conflict through more informal dispute mediation mechanisms. Nonprofit executive directors also noted that trust and collaboration affect the bottom lines of their budgets in positive ways. Their limited personnel and operational capacity can be more effectively used on program and client activities rather than rebidding, reporting, and responding to site visits and audits. This is not to suggest that traditional contract and governance issues were abandoned; rather, they remained in place but were exercised with greater flexibility, discretion, and cooperation. These are evidence of an evolved contractual relationship that is more collaborative than transactional.

The findings reported here suggest and shed light on the issue that contractual relationships evolve and that evolution is dependent on the development of trust. Trust, in this study, is an antecedent to collaboration activities. In turn, collaboration activities over time lead to outcomes in which the parties' interests are aligned with one another and the goals of the contract. When such alignment develops, transaction costs can decline over time as contractual relationships become more trust based and collaborative.

CONCLUSION

Kelman (2005) suggests that public management needs help and requires new theories, hypotheses, and empirical analyses to improve its practice. And he goes on to suggest that while contract design and the degree to which more or less specificity is important in terms of what government signals and agrees to with its vendors before awarding a contract, it is equally important to also invest in contract management capacity after the award. That such investments are built on developing more collaborative and relational approaches to contract governance is an issue of importance for all levels of government that is supported in this study. The findings presented in this chapter suggest that service delivery options with other governments, nonprofits, and for-profit firms can be improved through collaboration.

Professionals in acquisition, procurement, and contract management cite the importance of relationship building as a part of their responsibilities. Government's increasing use of and reliance on contracting requires that contract managers do more than verify that the Ts are crossed and the Is dotted. Public managers are needed who can manage complex contract projects that involve a diverse range of stakeholder relationships and solve difficult contract issues through communication, information exchange, joint involvement in decision making and coordination. Each of these tools can build trust and is necessary to achieve a collaborative relationship. Though there are issues of endogeneity and causality between trust and collaboration, it appears clear that trust and collaboration develop over time and to some extent in tandem with one another.

Relationships can and do evolve and lead to mutual benefits for both parties,[6] but this is a calculated risk as each party exposes itself to some vulnerability that the other will enhance their own self-interest at the expense of goal alignment. Understanding how this evolution takes place is important. Public managers often approach collaboration incrementally, recognizing that trust takes time to develop. Much work continues to be needed on the necessary skills for the collaborative public manager operating in a networked contract environment. This chapter makes a modest contribution to linking these topics and literatures.

NOTES

1. The quotations in order of presentation come from Palmer 2006, Palmer 2005a, and Palmer 2005b. All are available at www.govexec.com and represent just a small sampling of contracting stories with this emphasis.

2. The U.S. General Accounting Office (2002, 3) documented that of the 88 percent of total Temporary Assistance for Needy Families (TANF) funds contracted by state governments, 73 percent were with nonprofit providers.

3. Demand-side imperfections are also a problem, given that some types of social services are monopsonistic in which government agencies are the only buyer of services.

4. Shleifer and Vishny (1998) refer to these types of contracts as incomplete contracts.

5. Milward and Provan (2000) refer to this challenge as governing the hollow state.

6. Just as relationships can evolve, they can also deteriorate. See Brown, Potoski, and Van Slyke (forthcoming).

Chapter 9 ✓

Mechanisms for Collaboration in Emergency Management: ICS, NIMS, and the Problem with Command and Control

William L. Waugh Jr.

The September 2001 attacks on the United States had a profound impact on the profession and practice of emergency management and on the nation's approach to preparing for and responding to catastrophic disasters. Following the attacks, the government single-mindedly focused on the threat of terrorism. State and local emergency managers, however, remained concerned with and responsible for dealing with the more certain risks posed by hurricanes, earthquakes, wildfire, and other familiar hazards. The attacks also brought a fundamental change in the structure and process of emergency management, particularly because the Federal Emergency Management Agency (FEMA) was largely disassembled and moved under the newly created Department of Homeland Security (DHS). Relationships between FEMA and its state and local counterparts changed fundamentally as DHS centralized decision-making processes, funding and training shifted quickly from "all hazards" to terrorism, and policy priorities shifted from comprehensive emergency management (i.e., mitigation, preparedness, response, and recovery) to the prevention of terrorist attacks. Similarly, relationships between emergency management agencies at all levels of government and the nongovernmental organizations on which they depend for support changed as national security concerns reduced the transparency of decision-making processes and the openness to partnerships and other forms of collaboration. Much of the nation's emergency management capacity was excluded from the DHS effort or relegated to dealing with the consequences of terrorism, rather than helping reduce its impact and prevent attacks through the adoption of anti-terrorism measures.

The post–September 11 changes in the national emergency management system, particularly at the federal level, raise questions concerning the roles and levels of responsibility of state and federal governments in our federal system, the coordination of efforts, and the administrative and political processes whereby state officials request federal assistance. As the 2005 Hurricane Katrina disaster demonstrated, there was considerable confusion over roles and responsibilities across the many cities, counties, and states affected and federal agencies involved. The scale of the Katrina disaster and the fact that the National Incident Management System (NIMS) and the National Response Plan were not fully implemented and not fully understood also served to confuse officials and emergency responders at all levels. Leadership was lacking, and cooperation was almost nonexistent. What was needed was a mechanism to encourage collaboration among the local, state, and federal agencies, as well as the hundreds of nongovernmental organizations and thousands of volunteers upon which the nation depends in catastrophic disasters. Collaborative leadership is essential in disasters (Waugh and Streib 2006), and incident management systems necessarily should encourage collaboration. This analysis focuses on NIMS and the Incident Command System (ICS) upon which it is based, in terms of their utility in encouraging collaboration among the many organizations and individuals involved in disaster operations and other emergency management functions.

The DHS apparatus is a closed system, competing with the Department of Justice and Department of Defense for resources while centralizing authority over its constituent agencies and offices and laboratories. Creating a centralized decision-making process has been a priority. The mandates to adopt ICS, the multiagency coordination system (MACS), unified command, and NIMS have centralized federal authority and reduced the participation of nongovernmental and private organizations in disaster planning, training, operations, and other functions. Because terrorism is considered a threat to national security, the federal government is clearly taking the lead in dealing with terrorist events as managed by NIMS. But, under NIMS, the federal government also takes a more central role in dealing with natural and technological disasters. The result was a failure when quick decision making was needed during the Florida hurricanes in 2004 and hurricanes Katrina, Rita, and Wilma in 2005. Indeed, the centralization of decision-making processes was one of the more serious problems during the poor response to Hurricane Katrina, leading to delays in relief to devastated communities and delays in mobilizing national resources to assist state and local emergency management offices.

Critics of ICS and NIMS frequently question whether the incident command structures can facilitate the intergovernmental, multiorganizational, and intersectoral collaboration necessary in large-scale disasters. Collaborative processes are proving more effective than other approaches in local government (e.g., see Agranoff and McGuire 2003a), and the assumption is that they will be more effective in dealing with disasters on a larger scale. After all, the response to a natural disaster is largely ad hoc and involves loosely organized nongovernmental actors; governmental actors; emergent groups, which often become well organized and long lived; and individual volunteers. Control is not an option where practical authority is lacking. Nongovernmental organizations will respond with or ✳ without government approval. Volunteers will come. First responders will self-deploy when needed. Convergence behavior is inevitable.

Integrating the nongovernmental responders into federal, state, and local disaster relief operations is necessary for effective emergency management. This was one of the recommendations in the White House's review of the Katrina response (White House 2006). Integration might facilitate cooptation (see O'Toole and Meier 2004a), but some differences may be difficult to reconcile. Goals differ and distrust is common. Finding common ground is difficult at best. Thus, collaboration requires a new approach to leadership—one that is less dependent upon authority and control and more sensitive to differences in goals and values (Waugh and Streib 2006).

THE COLLABORATIVE EMERGENCY MANAGER

After the command-and-control approach to emergency management proved poorly suited to large-scale disasters in the 1970s and 1980s, emergency managers adopted a collaborative, open approach in the 1990s. This strategy worked much better in coordinating the efforts of public, private, and nonprofit agencies. As standards developed, the profession adopted a comprehensive "all hazards" perspective and began integrating emergency management into the broader functions of government, as well as acquiring the knowledge, skills, and abilities necessary to design, development, implement, manage, and maintain effective programs.

Programs became "all hazard" to provide flexibility and to make the best use of resources. During the "golden age" of FEMA in the 1990s, mitigation of hazards, rather than response to disasters, became the focus. As the mantra went, a dollar spent on mitigation saved four dollars in disaster recovery. Creating "disaster-resistant" and "disaster-resilient" communities became the goal.

The professionalization process in emergency management shares similarities with processes in other fields. Though many emergency managers are drawn from the military, professional emergency managers are expected to be acclimated to a civilian world in which authority is shared and local officials have primary responsibility. All disasters are local, as the saying goes. Moreover, distrust of government authority is such that officials have to cultivate collaborative working relationships with their counterparts in other agencies and in other parts of government, as well as with the general public, to be effective. Developing trust and respect are the first tasks of the professional emergency manager. In short, it is an environment in which interpersonal skill is more important than technical expertise (Drabek 1987), informal relationships outweigh formal authority (Waugh 1993), and leadership means working effectively with diverse networks of governmental and nongovernmental organizations, volunteers, and communities to manage hazards, prepare for disasters, respond appropriately, and recover quickly.

In policy terms, emergency managers are no longer the proverbial "cavalry" riding in to save communities from imminent disaster. Rather, they provide support for those trying to mitigate, prepare for, respond to, and/or recover from disaster. In operational terms, emergency managers are not first responders. Instead, they are risk managers and facilitators of response and recovery. The term "first responder" has been adopted by many, however, because federal grants are available to first responders (e.g., firefighters, police officers, and emergency medical personnel) but not to second and third responders (e.g., emergency managers and hospital emergency personnel).

At the local level, emergency managers might have broader responsibilities, depending upon their relationship to emergency response agencies, but the role has generally been defined as coordination and integration rather than operations (Waugh 1993). Those emergency managers housed in fire or police departments tend to focus more on the response mode. But, more and more, emergency managers are focusing on assisting emergency responders and providing overall coordination and integration support. The emergency management agency's emergency operations center (EOC), as distinct from response agency EOCs and incident command posts, is the vehicle for collaboration. It provides communication links and brings together representatives of the response agencies to share information and to coordinate efforts.

The most obvious artifact of the cultural change wrought by the creation of DHS was the clothing. Emergency managers were those in polo shirts and casual slacks, dressed to staff EOCs for days and to gather information at disaster scenes. The blue jeans, turnouts (i.e., firefighter gear), and uniforms of first responders became less and less common. However, September 11 and the creation of DHS and its state and local counterparts changed all that. The most obvious sign of change was the invasion of suits—the dark suits and dark ties worn by the new managers and executives overseeing emergency operations—and uniforms. The "suits"—that is, law enforcement and national security officials—came dressed for the office rather than the EOC or disaster scene. They were removed from the perspective of the emergency responder and the emergency manager. More important, they were removed from the culture of improvisation, adaptation, and flexibility that had come to characterize emergency management for the past two decades. The suits were more interested in standard operating procedures, unity of command, narrow spans of control, task specialization, divisions of labor, and the other attributes of classic bureaucracy. Of course, the fire services, police, emergency medical services, and emergency managers had had standard operating procedures and clearly defined lines of authority, but most had learned that circumstances often required adjustments in procedures to assure effective responses.

The suits also brought a focus on prevention—namely, preventing terrorist attacks—and an ignorance of the broader functions of emergency management. As a result, there was little investment in programs to reduce the impact of terrorist attacks, to prepare first and second responders to deal with terrorist disasters that cannot be prevented, and to recover from devastating attacks quickly. Attention to hurricanes, earthquakes, and other natural and technological disasters became a low priority. The national security officials also focused on counterterrorism programs (e.g., apprehending known and suspected terrorists) rather than antiterrorism programs (e.g., securing facilities and other potential targets). The myopic view of the "war on terrorism" left emergency responders and emergency managers to fend for themselves with mandates to prepare for chemical, biological, and radiological attacks, but without the resources to do so. Weapons of mass destruction became "the mother" of all risks. The competition for resources among the counterterrorism agencies also had its effect in terms of priorities on technologies to detect chemical, biological, and radiological agents and the security of civil aviation—rather than responder training, securing nonaviation sites, and community preparedness. The dominance of "gun-toters" within DHS translated into programmatic priorities, budget alloca-tions, and human resource allocations. FEMA was only a very small part of DHS—roughly 5,000 employees in a department of 170,000—and was taxed to support law enforcement and national security programs. The result of that taxation and the lack of attention to nonterrorist hazards by DHS was the very poor federal response to the Katrina hurricane and flood, as well as poor federal responses to the 2004 hurricanes and Hurricanes Rita and Wilma after Katrina (Waugh 2006).

Thus far, rebuilding FEMA and the nation's capacity to deal with cata-strophic disasters of all sorts has been a slow, contentious process. FEMA and DHS have experienced brain drain as experienced administrators have retired or moved to the private sector or other public agencies. A remark-able aspect of the disaster response effort was the number of new people hired to manage operations. Inexperienced FEMA personnel, who were re-placements for those who have left, are one of the problems inhibiting the recovery effort along the Gulf Coast as well (e.g., see Hsu 2006; Marino 2006).

This is the context within which collaboration is expected to happen in emergency management and DHS. The collaborative nature of emer-gency management is well documented (Waugh 2003; Wachtendorf 2004; Waugh and Streib 2006; Patton 2007), and the need for collaboration in DHS is generally accepted (Wise 2002; Waugh and Sylves 2002). The national emergency management system includes nongovernmental organizations, ranging from faith-based disaster relief organizations to private firms that specialize in debris removal, the delivery of critical ma-terials, fire and flood damage clean-up, and managing response operations and recovery processes (to mention but a few), as well as public agencies. Professional associations of engineers do building and infrastructure dam-age assessments, social scientists do impact assessments of social and psychological effects and provide interventions as needed, and professional emergency managers often do assessments of capabilities to manage re-sponse and recovery efforts. In short, disaster management is not just a governmental function. Indeed, nongovernmental organizations will re-spond whether asked or involved in the "official" operation or not. The title of California's manual on using volunteers is *They Will Come* (Office of Emergency Services 2001) and, in fact, they will come. Tens of thou-sands of volunteers were used in the World Trade Center response. Doz-ens of volunteer organizations emerged during the hours, days, and weeks that followed the attacks.

The question of whether DHS can learn to collaborate was addressed in a recent "Point/Counterpoint" commentary in *Homeland Protection*

Professional magazine (Bannon 2006). The new department, according to Charles Wise, was simply too new to have established the strong working relationships that are necessary in major disasters. He suggested that as it matures, DHS will get better at adaptive management, responding to the unexpected. Bill Jenkins of the Government Accountability Office, conversely, expressed the view that "creating a culture of adaptability" will be a problem because the Washington bureaucracy is not, by nature, adaptable. However, Wise argues that organizations can be both hierarchical and adaptive, but he notes that the high turnover in personnel presents a challenge to establishing collaboration because relationships have to be continually rebuilt. Given that DHS was created specifically to deal with the threat of terrorism, its lack of attention to natural hazards and its lack of skill in collaborating with local authorities is understandable, albeit shortsighted and lamentable. Both agreed that establishing strong working relationships among federal, state, and local officials is essential.

To that end, FEMA has created a new Federal Incident Response Support Team program that will deploy FEMA personnel to locations when disaster is imminent to act as liaison between local and federal officials. Teams are currently located at the FEMA regional offices in Atlanta and Chicago for quick deployment. Each team will bring communications equipment to assist in linking local and state and federal operations (Wright and Randle 2006) and, thus, are expected to provide the responsiveness to local needs that was lacking in the Katrina response. The teams might also help rebuild the relationships that were established by FEMA regional office personnel in the Witt years.

The necessity of developing long-term, close working relationships among the agencies responsible for responding to natural and unnatural disasters has been noted since the creation of DHS. FEMA had worked hard to develop and maintain those relationships during the Witt years, but they were not maintained by DHS. Indeed, the need to create networks for each of the essential emergency management functions was pointed out as essential for dealing with terrorist incidences. The emergency management system was built from the bottom up with local responders as the foundation (Waugh 2000; Powers 2003). Local officials had ultimate legal and political responsibility for dealing with hazards and disasters.

COLLABORATION, IMPROVISATION, AND INCIDENT MANAGEMENT SYSTEMS

Ad hoc responses are most common as emergency management agencies and nongovernmental organizations mobilize to deal with disaster. Michael

Scardaville (2003) of the Heritage Foundation argues that no jurisdiction can have a completely adequate response plan for a large-scale terrorist incident and that response is most often characterized by ad hoc efforts, major uncertainties, and conflicting priorities. A centralized, command-and-control system, thus, is not possible, because no single incident commander would be able to monitor everything and respond effectively. Therefore, he suggests a "multiuse culture" like FEMA or the U.S. Coast Guard is most effective, and DHS should rely on a "network of high-level regional offices" rather than trying to direct operations from Washington. This model was not implemented, and the slow response to Katrina was in large measure caused by overly centralized decision-making processes. Allocations of resources, mobilization of personnel, and other critical decisions were made in Washington—often well after needs were apparent to officials closer to the Gulf Coast and after conditions had become desperate for those in the storm's path (Waugh 2006).

The capacity to improvise, as well as adapt to changing circumstances, is also critical. Wachtendorf's (2004, 30–32) study of the September 11 response summarizes the improvisation literature and concludes that the capacity to be creative is essential in catastrophic disasters. In lesser disasters, *reproductive improvisation* can rebuild damaged or lost capacities and *adaptive improvisation* can lead to organizational and operational innovation to address unanticipated circumstances. *Creative improvisation* is necessary to adjust the organization, decision-making processes, and priorities to new demands. Wachtendorf concludes that "creative improvisation occurs when an organization or collectivity of organizations, determines that a structure, activity, resource, or task element is needed in order to respond to an event, but where no prior plan or model exists, resulting in the enactment of novel strategies under time constraints to produce that element. Creative improvisation [was] . . . possible because the [organization] was able to accurately read and integrate the cues of constituent organizations and members were able to draw upon repertoires of both specialized and shared knowledge to produce novel arrangements." A shared vision of the objectives is critical, and organizations need strong sense-making skills to understand and respond to new demands, as well as to address the needs of constituent organizations. In other words, a participatory, open decision-making process is necessary.

Therefore, given the nature of disaster responses and the role of emergency management within the nation's DHS apparatus, the organization of emergency management and DHS programs is critical. Following September 11, a series of Executive Orders and Homeland Security Presidential Directives (HSPDs) created structures to oversee programs and to deal with specific kinds of threats (e.g., to critical infrastructure). HSPD 5 in February 2003 dealt with the management of domestic incidents and required state and local compliance with the provisions of NIMS. NIMS Guidance was issued in March 2004, and the use of NIMS was mandated when the National Response Plan (NRP) was adopted in April 2005. NIMS was in the implementation stage, and the NRP was very new and not widely understood by many federal, state, and local officials when Katrina came ashore a few months later (Waugh 2006). NIMS remains a central feature of the new National Response Framework that is slated to supersede the NRP in 2007 or 2008.

The NIMS Incident Management organization is outlined in table 9.1. The foundation is ICS, and there is acknowledgment that coordination is necessary as events get larger. The expectation is that a MACS organization will be established to coordinate larger-scale responses. As incidents get larger and more jurisdictions are involved, a unified command should be implemented. In theory, the mechanisms for coordination and, perhaps, collaboration should be in place. This analysis explores the degree to which they really are. The figures that follow illustrate the ICS organization, the unified command organization, the MACS organization, and the regional, state, and national NIMS organizations.

Now, local and state responders are required to adopt ICS and to be compliant with NIMS to qualify for federal funds and to receive federal disaster assistance. The implementation of ICS has not been without critics, but NIMS has drawn far more criticism. Critics have tried to draw attention to the shortcomings of such hierarchical, command-focused systems, the problem of command when no one has (or many have) legal and political authority, and the resources and response capacities that are not accommodated by closed administrative systems. The ICS and NIMS structures are not flexible, adaptive, or creative enough to deal with major disasters of any sort, and many components of the national emergency management system will not be conversant with ICS or compliant with NIMS when officials attempt to direct disaster operations. Also, ICS and NIMS are designed for emergency response operations and not for mitigation, preparedness, and recovery operations.

INCIDENT MANAGEMENT SYSTEMS

ICS is a sacred cow among fire service personnel. However, because it does not fit current management and decision-making theory, it has received a great deal of academic attention and criticism. ICS is based upon a traditional military command structure, that is, the classic Weberian

Table 9.1 National Incident Management System

Incident Command System	Multiagency Coordination System	Unified Command
Commander directs operations at disaster scene from Incident Command Post.	Agency or government representatives coordinate resources and support operations. Often regional coordination.	Provides mechanism for multiple jurisdictions to coordinate support. Emergency operations center supports collaborative decision processes.
Area Command links incident commands to coordinate operations.		

bureaucratic model. Though ICS has some elements of management by objectives and the development and communication of objectives is a central tenet, it is essentially a command-and-control system. Generally, the effectiveness of ICS in the fire ground and as a tool for responding in a disciplined manner to structural fires and wildfires is not questioned. Indeed, these are the very purposes for which it was developed. Milward and Provan (2006) argue that such fires are relatively routine for firefighters and a bureaucratic approach works well for them because they share common values and a common language. Buck, Trainor, and Aguirre (2006) come to essentially the same conclusion, citing the importance of the fire community's shared values (figure 9.1).

ICS was originally created in the early 1970s to coordinate wildfire responses in California. Coordination problems became evident when large wildfires required the involvement of many fire departments and other emergency response agencies and when firefighting operations extended across jurisdictional boundaries. The system was designed by the FIRE-SCOPE project (Firefighting Resources of Southern California Organized for Potential Emergencies, changed to Firefighting Resources of California Organized for Potential Emergencies in 1987; see www.firescope.org), which was chartered by Congress in 1972 to assist the U.S. Forest Service in helping Southern California fire agencies. Training for ICS and MACS began in 1977, and it was successfully applied to wildfire responses in 1978. FEMA developed a similar ICS system in the 1980s. The system evolved from the old Civil Defense system under the Department of Defense (hence the frequent reference to the military nature of ICS) (Kerr 2004). The use of ICS is also mandated by federal law for responses to hazardous materials accidents and, thus, has become a familiar tool for the U.S. Environmental Protection Agency and its state counterparts.

Over the past thirty years, ICS has been widely adopted for wildfire and structural fire responses in the United States, but there are still some differences in ICS structures and processes that can affect joint operations. The brand of ICS practiced depended upon where it was taught, and increasing numbers of firefighters learned it at the National Fire Academy in Emmitsburg, Maryland. ICS was used during the responses to the Murrah Federal Building bombing in Oklahoma City, the World Trade Center bombing in 1993, and the World Trade Center and Pentagon attacks in 2001. A recent study of the use of ICS in the response to the Murrah Federal Building bombing concluded that ICS was very effective (Cook 2006). Alethia Cook interviewed those involved in the response, particularly those from the Oklahoma City Fire Department who managed the search-and-rescue operation, and the consensus was that ICS worked

Figure 9.1 Incident Command System Organization

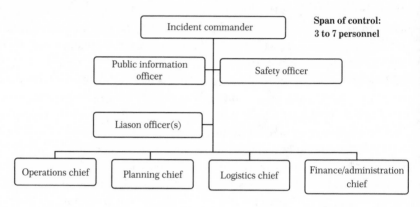

The incident commander's
"command" and "general" staff:

for them and was effective in managing the incident. Though issues arose concerning jurisdiction over those responses, emergency operational plans or decisions made immediately following the events facilitated the implementation of ICS.

However, jurisdictional conflicts, the involvement of large numbers of nongovernmental response-and-recovery organizations, and even the involvement of a large number of government agencies that cannot share authority may complicate or even preclude the use of ICS to organize and manage an emergency response. In some local governments, authority is shared among two or more officials and emergency plans may not resolve the issue. In essence, no one official may have jurisdiction over an emergency response, and emergency response officials may not have the authority to turn resources over to someone else. So-called turf issues are frequently cited as obstacles to effective disaster responses, but officials are accountable for resources and may not be legally able to transfer responsibility—particularly to someone from another jurisdiction. Thus, accountability systems may trump command systems.

In wildfire cases, it is common for several fire departments to respond to large wildfires, and ICS facilitates the integration of resources and the development of a single plan of action. In essence, ICS involves the identification of an incident commander, who is responsible for determining priorities (objectives) and directing the emergency response. In theory, the first responder to arrive at the scene is the commander, and responsibility shifts to more senior responders as more units or departments join the effort. The commander is supported by a command staff (information officer, liaison officer, safety officer, and others as needed), and the organization is divided into sections for finance/administration, logistics, operations, and planning (e.g., see Irwin 1989). The DHS NIMS manual describes the "typical" incident command structure as having the four sections or components, but it suggests that more components may be needed, such as intelligence/information gathering (DHS 2004). In the fire services, low- to high-technology devices (from blackboards to laptops) are available to facilitate communication so that the incident commander can turn over command to another and have records of decisions made, resources deployed, and so on, to provide a comprehensive situational map for the new commander. It is taken as a matter of faith in the fire services that ICS assures the necessary unity of command for a disciplined response. In practice, however, there are some differences in ICS training and, therefore, the functions may vary from agency to agency. Moreover, some fire departments do not use ICS (figure 9.2).

A MACS organization is adopted when more jurisdictions become involved. The MACS structure utilizes the EOC as a locus of coordination. The MAC group consists of agency representatives and is responsible for establishing priorities, allocating resources, integrating communications systems, sharing information, coordinating decisions, and developing geographic strategies and contingency plans. There may also be local area, operational area, regional, geographic area, and statewide MACS to coordinate efforts, as well as a national, multiagency coordinating group (FIRESCOPE 2006).

The size and membership of MACS groups can vary. EOCs typically include representatives from nongovernmental organizations, but that frequently means that only the American Red Cross and perhaps the Salvation Army have regular places in the room because local emergency management agencies rely heavily on their resources. Other disaster relief

Figure 9.2 Multiagency Coordination System Organization

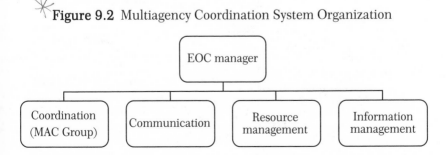

organizations may be represented by the Red Cross. Private-sector organizations, such as power companies, may or may not have a similar presence.

As events become even larger, a unified command organization is adopted. In a unified command group decision, processes are expected to guide action. In theory, no single person or agency is in charge under unified command; representatives of the autonomous participant organizations make decisions by consensus. But in practice, not all agency representatives understand the concept of consensus. In fact, theories may differ as to the existence of a leader. The most common notion is likely that, if no one is in charge, "I am in charge." As the saying goes, one should "lead, follow, or get out of the way" (figure 9.3).

The NIMS organization has more layers, from regional to state to federal levels, to support disaster operations. Figure 9.4 shows the area command structures. The State of California has already developed its own regional coordination and support structures, and there is some question as to how these organizations will function—mostly whether they are collaborative or directive bodies.

CONCLUSION

The requirement to adopt NIMS has raised questions about the structure of emergency response and emergency management agencies. A debate on that very topic took place during the fall of 2004 on the International Association of Emergency Managers (IAEM) listserv, which is made up of mostly local emergency managers. Many local EOCs, for example, are organized around emergency support functions (ESFs), as suggested by

Figure 9.3 Unified Command

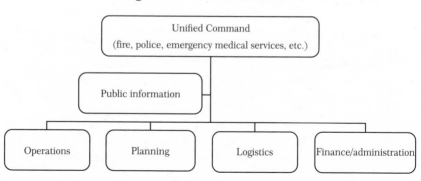

Figure 9.4 Incident Management under the Area Command
Organization of the National Incident Management System

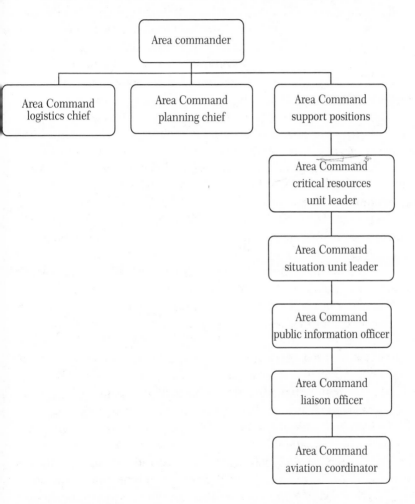

Note: The Area Command becomes the Unified Area Command when an incident becomes
multijurisdictional. It operates under the same basic principles as the Incident Command
System.

the Federal Response Plan and the NRP. (The NRP was revised to recognize ESFs after outcries from the emergency management community.) The debate was renewed in the summer of 2006 as emergency managers, emergency responders, consultants, trainers, and others were implementing ICS/NIMS to satisfy the federal mandate. The responses varied from complete support for ICS as a scalable incident management tool that should be taught to everyone who might be involved in a disaster response (or any other management situation for some) to qualified support from those who question its utility in large events involving multiple jurisdictions and nongovernmental organizations. There was also some qualified opposition by those who do not feel that ICS is appropriate outside the fire ground. In many respects, the discussion appeared similar to discussions a decade ago of total quality management, which had developed an almost cultlike following. ICS, according to most, is a management tool that should be adapted as needed to circumstances. Indeed, Craig Fugate (2006), director of the State of Florida's Division of Emergency Management, complained of "ICS zealots" who insist on trying to fit circumstances to the technique. Clearly, as the saying goes, "If all you have is a hammer, everything looks like a nail." One of those involved in the IAEM listserv debate, in fact, mentioned an incident in which the incident commander set up an ICS structure with only five people involved in the incident and all involved in the operational side of the response. Clearly, personnel may fill more than one ICS staff and command role.

What is the problem with ICS? Perhaps the most frequent focus of management criticism is its highly centralized, hierarchical, "command-and-control" systems; thus, the classic critique of the Weberian model. Such systems, by their very nature, are inflexible, slow, and cumbersome and would be much less adaptable in task environments characterized by uncertainty and rapid change. Certainly the federal response to Hurricane Katrina was plagued by centralized decision-making processes that failed to address problems along the coast. Officials contended that the problem was a lack of "situational awareness" because of poor (or nonexistent) communication between Washington and state and local officials, not to mention among the agencies involved in the search-and-rescue and other operations. But that is precisely the problem with centralized processes: Decisions cannot be made by officials onsite. Instead, information has to be communicated to decision makers far removed from the disaster scene so that they can make decisions and communicate them back downward. In short, the problem was not too little leadership from Washington; rather, it was too much reliance on direction from Washington. It was not a problem common in federal disaster operations conducted through FEMA regional offices prior to the agency's absorption into DHS. Regional office officials had close working relationships with their state and local counterparts prior to the creation of DHS, but they were eroded both by changes of policy under DHS and by the retirements of many FEMA employees who had cultivated the relationships (Waugh 2006).

There have also been criticisms of ICS in operations involving military personnel, work in the public health context, and among organizations that rely heavily on volunteers. Reports following the deployment of military personnel to deal with wildfires in Colorado in the 1990s concluded that the personnel had some problems dealing with the pace of decision making and action. The wildfire response did not fit the "battle rhythm" in which military personnel typically operate. Public health officials have expressed concern that the single incident commander model violated their notions of consensus building in public health emergencies. Decentralized decision making is the norm when expertise may be scattered among many units of the public health community or among individual medical specialists. No one doctor or official may have the expertise to make decisions. Indeed, nonmedical personnel may also have difficulty finding arriving at a consensus. Finally, there are cultural problems when nonhierarchical organizations, such as volunteer organizations, have to interact with highly hierarchical ones. The most common conflicts are among police and military units and civilian agencies. In disaster operations, critical functions are carried out by ad hoc or emergent organizations that have little inclination either to answer to commanders or to develop their own commanders (Waugh 2002, 2003). And some people simply abhor bureaucracy and will not cooperate. That perspective has been expressed by volunteer organization members (see Waugh and Streib 2006).

Clearly, ICS works in smaller, noncatastrophic events. ICS works when the responders are part of a community with a shared language, shared objectives, and a shared vision of how operations should work. ICS works in firefighting. The fire community understands the system, and the tasks are largely routine, even if there is some uncertainty in dealing with structural fires and wildlfires (e.g., see Milward and Provan 2006). But ICS and NIMS may not work in catastrophic events when there is not a shared vision and they become difficult to maintain when the response involves intergovernmental, intersectoral, and volunteer participants (see Buck, Trainor, and Aguirre 2006). "ICS zealots" may be a problem even in smaller events when they do not understand the need to adapt, to improvise, and to learn. Indeed, the personality and training of the incident commander may be the critical variable. By contrast, Randy Hansen (2006), a Seattle

Fire Department battalion chief, has argued that those experienced with ICS can "flex" the organization to make it more flexible and inclusive, but this may not be useful for all phases of emergency management. Adequate training and experience are necessary for ICS to work, and that is a significant problem when many agencies do not use ICS and those that do may not use it often, even to maintain a trained cadre.

Questions do need to be answered to assure that the nation is ready for another September 11 or Katrina-type disaster. First, at what point, in terms of the size of the operation, does the centralized decision making become problematic? Second, does ICS work in all contexts, from the fire services to medical institutions? Third, if not NIMS, then what? Management theory does suggest particular organizational structures and processes if the need is for them to be highly adaptable and innovative, able to coordinate multi-organizational operations, able to communicate effectively and quickly within and among organizations, and able to cultivate and manage networks so that they can be focused on common goals. In general, theory suggests that such organizations be flat, nonhierarchical or minimally so, and not overly compartmentalized (specialized as to task). Communication, coordination, and collaboration become more difficult as the differentiation of the organization increases. They should avoid compartmentalization because it inhibits communication and coordination.

Speeches following Hurricane Katrina frequently mentioned the need for "nimble" organizations. However, these calls were usually followed by prescriptions for greater centralization of decision making in Washington (i.e., less nimble structures). How can first, second, and third responders be taught to see NIMS as a tool rather than a rule? They need to understand how to adapt, improvise, and work in a world where authority is shared, resources are scattered, and tasks require the participation of many disciplines. Community participation in disaster operations is critical. Capacity building and "disaster resilience"—the ability to recover quickly and to deal more effectively with future disasters—is cultivated when communities and their residents have a role in disaster response and recovery (Comfort 1999).

How should we organize emergency management and homeland security? Donald Kettl argues that the organization is less important than the leadership (2005b). Goldsmith and Eggers (2004), conversely, offer alternative models for managing networks. Though they describe disaster management as utilizing an ad hoc model, their "civic switchboard" model may be more appropriate (Goldsmith and Eggers 2004, 69–71). In this switchboard model, government agencies provide a broad perspective and serve to connect the players. In the case of nongovernmental disaster relief organizations, many are connected via the National Volunteer Organizations Active in Disaster (NVOAD), which is mentioned in the NRP. Some states also utilize their state VOADs to organize nongovernmental participants. Anticipating volunteers, receiving and training them, inventorying and certifying capabilities, and fitting them into the disaster operation is a complex switchboard-like function. Communities use community emergency response teams because they are organized and trained to fill predetermined roles, usually assisting fire and police departments. Organizing spontaneous volunteers and integrating emergent groups into disaster operations are much more problematic in the chaos of disaster—even when personnel are trained to do so and commanders and policymakers are willing to accept their assistance. Milward and Provan (2006, 15) warn that ICS may be used against "unknown unknowns"—problems that are neither understood nor predictable. It may also be used in circumstances that require wide participation by nongovernmental organizations that do not understand how it works and may well react negatively to any attempt to impose authority.

There are several implications for emergency management leadership. Organizational structure needs to be functional given the circumstances. Flexibility—from adaptation to improvisation—is critical. Leaders need to be able to "flex" the organization, as Chief Hansen called it. However, the bigger issues may be whether NIMS is based upon assumptions that do not hold in a federal system of shared authority and shared responsibilities. Direction from state capitals and/or Washington did not work during the Katrina disaster. More collaborative approaches at the operational and policymaking levels would greatly facilitate the disaster response, as well as the mitigation, preparedness, and recovery processes.

Chapter 10

Collaborative Public Management and Organizational Design: One-Stop Shopping Structures in Employment and Training Programs

Jay Eungha Ryu and Hal G. Rainey

The present study indicates success in the "one-stop service" approach to the decades-old quest for providing integrated service for clients of the many different employment training programs that governments provide. Sometimes earnest advocates tout the desirability of a particular procedure or approach, such as collaboration (or, similarly, teamwork or participative management) without adequate attention to designing structures and processes to support the procedure. Sometimes existing structures, such as "stovepiped" hierarchies, will negate the potential benefits of a desirable approach, such as collaboration or teamwork, if not reformed. The weak yet apparent success of one-stop service centers for employment and training programs shows the potential value of linking together efforts and agencies relevant to a public policy challenge, in collaborative fashion. Public managers can consider this form of design for implementation in a variety of policy areas, and public managers can enhance their skills for working with these kinds of designs.

These centers provide, in one location, the information and services that individuals need from the complex array of job training, education, and employment programs. The centers are designed to support collaborative public management by bringing together services and information from different agencies and programs, which in effect work together to serve the program participant. The implementation of these centers in five Texas districts provides an opportunity to compare them with settings lacking such centers and to use those others as counterfactuals. The one-stop centers can be regarded as an example of improving public service delivery by moving away from hierarchical, centralized organizational forms and toward more flexible, "customer-oriented" forms (Ewalt 2004, 49; Brudney, Hebert, and Wright 1999; Hennessey 1998; Kearney, Feldman, and Scavo 2000). Later, the Workforce Investment Act (WIA) mandated the adoption of such centers nationwide, eliminating chances for such comparisons. This analysis will show that clients of one-stop service centers for employment and training in Texas earned about 54 cents more per hour after training than did those who did not have one-stop service. In reflecting on the organizational design implications of the one-stop centers, the analysis also contributes to the growing literature on the influence of organizational and managerial factors on program performance and policy effectiveness (e.g., Boyne and Walker 2005; Meier and O'Toole 2003).[1]

THE STATUS OF TEXAS ONE-STOP INITIATIVES UNDER JTPA PROGRAMS

Although the WIA mandated one-stop shopping structures for all states in 1998, thirty-three states had implemented or experimented with the structures for their job training programs as of 1997 (D'Amico et al. 2001; Barnow and King 2003; Kogan et al. 1997, A-2). We use program data from the one-stop pilot centers in Texas because WIA's mandate for the full implementation of one-stop structures makes it virtually impossible to obtain counterfactual examples to evaluate the impact of one-stop initiatives after the 1998 WIA mandate. Though the WIA was passed several years after the collection of the data we analyze, its specifications about the one-stop designs are very similar to those for the Texas one-stop centers. The WIA's mandate to implement the design nationally underscores the importance of evaluating its use in Texas.

In Texas, the one-stop concept came into focus as part of the state's efforts to upgrade its workforce. A state Senate committee had analyzed problems in the state's workforce development programs, focusing on such shortcomings as a lack of responsiveness to businesses and to program clients, and excessive fragmentation from the client's viewpoint. Similarly, participants in a forum sponsored by the State Job Training Coordinating Council identified needs and objectives for the new system that included, among others, the coordination of statewide systems and initiatives; partnerships among business, government, and education; and the need to reduce competitive bureaucratic practices, enhance information sharing, and adopt an integrated service delivery approach. Developments such as these brought attention to the one-stop design as a way of achieving collaboration among the many diverse entities and programs involved in workforce development (State of Texas 1994, part two, section I).

In 1993, Texas enacted the Workforce Competitiveness Act, which created the Texas Council on Workforce and Economic Competitiveness (State of Texas 1994, part two, section I). This council was the result of collaborative efforts to address declining labor productivity in Texas. The council had responsibility for developing an integrated local workforce development system, called one-stop career centers, drawing on statewide local inputs, including five pilot sites that had already implemented one-stop efforts between 1990 and 1993 (State of Texas 1994, part two). This experimentation with the one-stop approach in the five districts prior to the Workforce Competitiveness Act suggests that the one-stop initiative also includes characteristics of what Ewalt (2004) calls bottom-up integration, because the Texas system reflects preexisting local discretionary experiences.

The council subsequently developed a plan to phase in implementation of the one-stop designs across a three-year period. The act also authorized the council to provide oversight to achieve consistency among the one-stop designs by ensuring similar procedures and common standards to achieve "universality" rather than "random examples of differing levels of coordination and integration" (State of Texas 1994, part two, section III). The state government was to provide policy direction and strategic planning for the one-stop initiative. A categorization of alternatives, such as Ewalt's (2004) described above, would probably characterize the Texas one-stop initiatives as a top-down, system-oriented mandate from the legislature. These combined top-down (i.e., enhanced immediacy) and bottom-up (i.e., flexibility) features of the program design phase first led us to expect that the Texas Local Workforce Development Areas (LWDAs) with one-stop centers would be more effective than those under the traditional service delivery system.

Statewide administration in Texas provides another reason to hypothesize that the one-stop centers would be effective. The Texas Employment Commission (TEC) served as the fiscal agent and administrator for the one-stop pilot projects. TEC had to lead cooperative efforts between several state agencies. Two interagency staff teams housed in TEC were responsible for providing technical assistance to the one-stop pilot programs and integrated information systems design (State of Texas 1994, part two, section III). The literature on the coordination of public programs often emphasizes coordination through informal agreements and interactions among agencies with shared needs and interests (Jennings and Ewalt

1998), but researchers also emphasize the importance of stability over time and reasonable degrees of central influence over a network (Milward and Provan 2000). The Texas system of administrative coordination around and in the one-stop structures has distinctive features, even as compared with other states' one-stop systems, in that it combines participation, informal agreements, and interaction, with more central authority that enhances stability and consistency throughout the system. The administrative authority of the state backed and supported the coordination of the multiple programs and agencies, which in turn should have enhanced the integrated customer service objectives of the Texas one-stop system.

In addition to coordinated and integrated services for customers, customers could obtain specialized services through a case manager who served as their primary contact, assessed their skill level for more specialized services, and reassessed training needs as needed (State of Texas 1994, part two, section III; for case management, see Hill 2006). Program design for collaborative management, administrative authority to support such a design, and case management for customers were expected to enhance the performance of the one-stop structures.

DATA AND METHODOLOGY

We analyzed whether program participants in the five pilot areas had earnings outcomes higher than those for the remaining LWDAs. We controlled for the characteristics of individual participants, as well as the social and demographic characteristics of the LWDAs. Because data for these purposes were not available on all programs, we focused on two Job Training Partnership Act (JTPA) programs, Title II-A adult and Title II-C youth programs, from the 1994 JTPA. We used the Standardized Program Information Report (SPIR), the reporting system with which the U.S. Department of Labor collects data on JTPA programs for the fifty states (Upjohn Institute 1994). We analyzed hourly wages at program termination and at follow-up (thirteenth week after termination) for Title II-A adult participants and hard-to-serve individuals and hourly wages at follow-up for Title II-C participants. The appendix describes the variables used in our models. Although employability is very frequently used to measure job training program performance, we could not conduct multilevel logistic analyses of employability because there is too little variation in the employment variables. SPIR contains information on 44,396 participants in JTPA programs in Texas during program year, 1994.

Because program participants in the Texas JTPA training programs are nested under twenty-nine LWDAs and higher-level variables are disaggregated into lower-level variables, the present study adopted a two-level hierarchical linear modeling approach to analyzing the earnings outcomes of JTPA participants, which accounted for contextual variables at the LWDA level as well as clientele characteristics (Heinrich and Lynn 2000, 81; Hox 1995, 1–7; Steenbergen and Jones 2002). The participant records and the characteristics of LWDAs come from the 1994 SPIR data.

RESEARCH FINDINGS

The results of statistical analyses partially support our expectations. The evidence indicates that the collaborative structures of service delivery in the Texas one-stop centers improve program outcomes measured in terms of the hourly wages of program participants.

The Impact of One-Stop Initiatives on Earnings Outcomes

As table 10.1 shows, one-stop structures generally do not outperform those without such structures. But controlling for various factors indicates the opposite. Our findings partially support the expectations that one-stop structures providing coordinated access to multiple services should lead to better employment and earnings outcomes (see tables 10.2 and 10.3). For the Title II-A program, clients of LWDAs with one-stop pilot initiatives in Texas during program year 1994 had a mean hourly wage at follow-up (i.e., the thirteenth week after program termination) about 54 cents higher than the clients of LWDAs without such service delivery designs ($p = .0570$). The participants in the one-stop structures were generally less advantaged, according to our mean comparisons. They had lower

Table 10.1 Comparison of Outcomes of Title II-A and Title II-C Programs between One-Stop LWDAs and Non-One-Stop LWDAs

	Title II-A		Title II-C	
Outcome	One-Stop (n = 941)	Non-One-Stop (n = 7,525)	One-Stop (n = 660)	Non-One-Stop (n = 5,164)
Hourly wage at termination	6.296[a]	6.97	5.15	5.4
Hourly wage at follow-up	6.84[a]	7.23	N.A.	N.A.

Note: LWDA = Local Workforce Development Area. N.A. - not available.

[a]The difference between the two groups is significant at $p < .01$. The sample number for hourly wage at follow-up is less than that for termination due to some missing values.

Table 10.2 Regression Results for Title II-A Programs

	Hourly Wage at Termination		Hourly Wage at Follow-Up	
Variable	Coefficient	Significance	Coefficient	Significance
Intercept	5.1685	.0007	5.6104	.0002
	Level I Variables			
Demographics				
Age	.0153	.0090	−.0031	.7420
Female	−.7035	<.0001	−.5058	.0043
Black	−.3744	.0002	−.7885	<.0001
Hispanic	−.4080	.0001	−.7254	<.0001
Indian or Alaskan	−.3188	.5448	−.6634	.4750
Asian	−.5490	.1579	−1.4468	.0189
Participant potentials				
Received supportive services	.1537	.0017	.2179	.0079
Highest school grade completed	.1227	<.0001	.1575	<.0001
Employed	.3421	<.0001	.1697	.1740
Prewage	.0804	<.0001	.1226	<.0001
Barriers to employment				
Hard-to-serve individuals	−.1208	.0233	−.0853	.3645
Welfare recipient	.1331	.3471	−.2537	.2971
Single head of household	.1388	.0980	.2265	.1092
Reading skills below 7th-grade level	−.1694	.1455	−.0248	.9026

JOBS program participant	-.0618	.7475	.0771	.8290
Limited English proficiency	.0761	.6986	.2336	.4740
Lack work history	-.1357	.1840	-.1398	.4337
Long-term AFDC recipient	-.2567	.2034	-.2492	.4724
Substance abuse	-.1608	.6242	-.4560	.5037
Training services				
Basic skills training	-.4368	.0003	-.3457	.0950
Occupational skills training	1.1785	<.0001	1.1138	<.0001
On-the-job training	-.0559	.6773	-.0107	.9634
Work experience	-.2638	.2257	-.7972	.0289
Weeks of training	.0126	<.0001	.0125	.0014
Level II Variables				
Average annual earnings	-.0007	.9910	.0331	.5445
Earning growth	.0079	.8564	-.0421	.2691
Employment	.0013	.9565	-.0064	.7761
Unemployment rate	-.0585	.0746	-.0587	.0470
Population density	.2496	.2969	.1322	.5037
Employee/resident worker ratio	-.0057	.5414	-.0128	.1213
One-stop structure	.3734	.2179	.5369	.0570
Number of observations used	3,734		2,252	
-2 residual log likelihood	16,208.8		11,034.7	

Table 10.3 Regression Results for Title II-C and Title II-A (Hard-to-Serve) Programs

Variable	Hourly Wage at Termination (Title II-C)		Hourly Wage at Termination (Title II-A, Hard to Serve)	
	Coefficient	Significance	Coefficient	Significance
Intercept	.6615	.5583	5.0635	.0138
	Level I Variables			
Demographics				
Age	.1706	<.0001	.0222	.0416
Female	-.3298	<.0001	-1.0925	.0059
Black	-.3652	.0042	-.0028	.9899
Hispanic	-.3739	.0012	-.3911	.1909
Indian or Alaskan	-.7103	.4276	-1.7992	.2512
Asian	-.0129	.9839	.1182	.9453
Participant potentials				
Received supportive services	.1080	.0665	.1157	.4567
Highest school grade completed	.1558	<.0001	.0694	.1713
Employed	.1712	.0317	.7480	.0219
Prewage	.0603	.0117		
Barriers to employment				
Hard-to-serve individuals	-.1345	.0263		
Welfare recipient	.0853	.6077	.6411	.0282
Single head of household	-.0356	.7702	-.1486	.6167
Reading skills below 7th-grade level	-.1033	.3499	-.1941	.3433

Variable				
JOBS program participant	.0891	.7341	−.0757	.7676
Limited English proficiency	.1644	.6413	.2672	.5487
Homeless			−.1906	.6072
Lack work history	−.0825	.3196	−.2113	.2577
Long-term AFDC recipient	−.3274	.1945	−.3154	.1786
Substance abuse	−.4935	.3425	.0877	.8211
Training services				
Basic skills training	−.3175	.0085	.3517	.1925
Occupational skills training	.5004	<.0001	.9711	.0001
On-the-job training	−.2947	.1125	.4949	.0723
Work experience	−.2812	.0202	−.0485	.9281
Weeks of training	.0092	.0002	−.0027	.7265
Level II Variables				
Average annual earnings	−.0081	.8616	.1010	.3162
Earning growth	−.0007	.9818	.1263	.0695
Employment	−.0235	.1990	−.0257	.5160
Unemployment rate	−.0494	.0402		
Poverty			−.0772	.0044
Population density	.0763	.6524	−.2174	.4923
Employee/resident worker ratio	.0098	.1702	−.0052	.7502
One-stop structure	−.0818	.7069	.8270	.0607
Number of observations used	2,210		386	
−2 residual log likelihood	8,889.4		1,496.8	

pretraining wages on average, and they were mostly lower on other indicators of potential for success. Because the variable *prewage* is such a strong predictor, one would have expected that the one-stop participants would have lower *prewage*, so that when one controls for *prewage*, they should show even more progress. This is what we have found. When we did not include *prewage*, the effect of one-stop structures was just 47 cents.

If the program participant works forty hours a week for fifty weeks in a year, the 54 cents per hour becomes about a $1,080 advantage in annual earnings. This appears to be a practically significant advantage for a low-income person. In addition, as shown in table 10.1, the average hourly wage at follow-up for the Title II-A program is $7.23. Thus, one-stop structures help increase hourly wage at follow-up as much as about 7.5 percent. Jennings and Ewalt (1998) found that administrative consolidation increased weekly earnings at follow-up by 4.2 percent. Our finding with the Texas one-stop centers suggests a higher increase in earnings outcomes. One-stop structures, however, did not increase the hourly wage at termination for the Title II-A and II-C programs.

In the literature on welfare-related job training programs, researchers continue to seek evidence about whether welfare-related programs have differential impacts for hard-to-serve individuals (e.g., Hill 2004, 99–100). To contribute to this research, we tested whether one-stop structures have distinctive effects on hard-to-serve individuals, and table 10.3 shows the results for the hard-to-serve participants in the Title II-A program. We identified 1,135 individuals who are categorized as hard-to-serve participants. After removing the individuals for whom values were missing for other independent variables, 386 observations were available for the regression model. We could not include *prewage*, however, because the sample number was further reduced to 145. Thus, the sample number for each LWDA is about four or five, too small for reliable inferential statistics. As the result shows, clients of LWDAs with one-stop structures have a higher mean hourly wage at termination of about 83 cents ($p = .0607$). Our findings suggest that one-stop structures help hard-to-serve individuals. Hard-to-serve individuals should benefit from the better-integrated services and guidance that one-stop structures provide. The Texas one-stop system specifically emphasized helping customers with employment barriers, such as limited English proficiency and technological illiteracy. These individuals should have had more trouble with self-directed searches and should benefit from a program design that provides additional interaction with staff/counselors (Holcomb and Barnow 2004). The Texas one-stop system emphasized provisions for job-training centers to coordinate with other systems in the community "to further the employment and independence goals of people with multiple barriers to employ-ment" (State of Texas 1994, part two, section III). Our evidence suggests that these enhancements in service coordination for hard-to-serve indi-viduals explain why our findings indicate more positive effects than some studies of other types of job-training programs have found.

Independent Variables

Especially when public services are delivered under networked, multilat-eral yet still hierarchical organizational structures, constellations of program characteristics need to be taken into account (Bloom, Hill, and Riccio 2003; Hill and Lynn 2004). We controlled for three clusters of control factors: clientele characteristics, environmental factors for LWDAs, and organiza-tional structures (Heinrich and Lynn 2000). The values of most independent variables used in our regression models differed across LWDAs with and without one-stop structures for Title II-A and II-C programs.

Clientele characteristics include demographic indices, indicators of an individual's economic disadvantage, indicators of a program participant's potential, and the types of programs in which individual trainees partici-pated. The effects of the clientele characteristics are mostly in the direc-tion one would expect based on the literature. As program participants got older, hourly wages at termination for Title II-A and II-C programs increased, with high levels of statistical significance for these statistics. Heinrich (2000) also reports higher earnings outcomes for older adult participants in the JTPA Title II-A program. Barnow (2000), however, shows that the earnings of adults older than fifty-five years, measured ten months after random assignment into JTPA programs, were much lower than those of younger participants. These seeming differences in findings appear to result from the way the age variable is categorized, with hourly wages increasing with age of participant, although not for the oldest categories of participant (fifty-five and above). As table 10.2 indicates, however, for the present data the age of program participants did not have a significant relation to the hourly wage of the Title II-A participants at follow-up.

Some previous studies, which focused on impact analysis without taking into account program implementation structures, reported that female participants had higher earnings outcomes (Dickinson, Johnson, and West 1987; Bloom et al. 1996). Recent studies with more control variables show that females have lower earnings outcomes (Heinrich 2000; Barnow 2000). Our results are in line with these latter studies; female participants' hourly wages at termination and follow-up for Title II-A and II-C programs were significantly less than those of male participants (all at $p < .01$). The results in tables 10.2 and 10.3 are also consistent with previous findings that program effects for the traditionally disadvantaged groups—such as blacks, Hispanics, Indians or Alaskans, and Asians—are lower than for whites (Heinrich 2000; Barnow 2000).

The program structures of JTPA have been reformed frequently, especially during the 1990s, in ways aimed at preventing "cream skimming," or selecting the most-promising clients and leaving out less-promising ones. The evidence indicates, however, that local job training centers still tend to select enrollees with characteristics (e.g., better education and crime records) most likely to lead to higher employment and earnings outcomes, instead of training less-promising individuals who might benefit the most from such training activities (Courty and Marschke 2003; Barnow and Smith 2004; Heinrich 2000, 2004). Thus, program participants with the highest potential for achieving the program goals might show higher earnings outcomes. The regressions in tables 10.2 and 10.3 control for indicators of potential such as *received supportive services*, *highest school grade completed*, *employed*, and *prewage*. These variables show positive relations with earnings outcomes, mostly with strong statistical significance.

One issue closely related to cream skimming concerns program participants with barriers to employment, often termed "hard-to-serve" individuals. They tend to have lower earnings outcomes. We included the variable *hard-to-serve individuals*, which we constructed using the SPIR data description, and we included additional indices of barriers to employment (Hill 2004, 95–121). As expected, the results show that for the Title II-A and II-C programs, most of the variables measuring such barriers to employment have negative relations with earnings outcomes, with high levels of statistical significance. The unexpected positive sign of *single head of household* might measure stronger efforts of single heads of household to make earnings for their entire family.

Previous findings also suggest that the type of training influences earnings and employability outcomes. In general, more work-related training—such as on-the-job training, job search assistance, and vocational training—enhance employability and earnings outcomes more than basic or remedial education (Bloom et al. 1996; Heinrich 2000; Bloom, Hill, and Riccio 2003, 567). Our findings show consistency with previous research for certain training variables. Tables 10.2 and 10.3 show that occupational skills training has a strong positive relation with hourly wage at termination, but basic skills training has a negative relationship with wage at termination. Previous research has not included *work experience* in the analysis, but our results, indicating that work experience relates negatively with hourly wage at termination, suggests the value of taking this variable into account.

Finally, we included various measures of environmental economic factors (the Level II variables in tables 10.2 and 10.3) for LWDAs from the SPIR economic data set. The availability of jobs in local job delivery areas is critical for improved employability, job retention rate, and earnings outcomes (Bloom, Hill, and Riccio 2003; Barnow 2000; Heinrich 2000; Ewalt 2004, 49–70). Consistent with previous research, the results given in tables 10.2 and 10.3 show that *unemployment rate* relates significantly and negatively to earnings outcomes.

DISCUSSION

One factor missing in our model pertains to the management and employee capacity in the LWDAs. Researchers are paying increasing attention to the roles managers play in implementing public services, and they are concluding that those roles make significant differences in program outcomes (e.g., Meier, O'Toole, and Nicholson-Crotty 2004; Meier and O'Toole 2003). In job-training programs, the evidence indicates that such managerial factors as emphasis on quick job entry, emphasis on personalized service, the level of cooperation between the staff and supervisor, and the quality of performance management all significantly improve outcomes (Bloom, Hill, and Riccio 2003; Heinrich and Lynn 2000). In all four models in tables 10.2 and 10.3, the variance components for LWDAs (Level II variance) are statistically highly significant even after controlling for economic indices and the one-stop status of LWDAs. This indicates that significant amounts of variance remain unexplained by the inclusion of Level II variables in our regression models. We expect management factors would play strong roles in accounting for this unexplained variance. Otherwise, our results generally support other findings in research on the performance of public programs and service delivery, including the important influences of clientele characteristics, organizational structures, and environmental factors.

The unexplained variance reflects our inability to test very directly the influence of specific managerial behaviors, caseworker behaviors, and program procedures. In addition, the data set does not enable us to firmly rule out certain alternative explanations based on self-selection and potential confounding factors, although we can make a case against such interpretations. The five LWDAs with one-stop designs were experimenting with them prior to the WIA, and before the Texas legislation designated them as pilot sites. What if the five sites differed from the other LWDAs on some uncontrolled factor that influenced earnings outcomes? Could the five have more innovative and effective management that led to the experimentation with one-stop shopping but that also led to the superior earnings outcomes? Could they have received special infusions of resources in support of the experimentation?

Little evidence supports such interpretations. Telephone interviews with Texas officials and other documentation (State of Texas 1994) give no indication that the five one-stop LWDAs were considered special or superior in performance or in human capital. In addition, Texas officials applied for a federal grant to support the one-stop pilot centers with the five LWDAs after the implementation of the one-stop initiatives. Therefore, this grant could not present the confounding factor of additional resources for the one-stop LWDAs. In addition, our numerous control variables rule out many possible confounding effects of differences between the one-stop LWDAs and the others. As mentioned above, we also performed t-tests of the differences on all the control variables in our analysis, between the one-stop LWDAs and the others. The t-tests indicated numerous statistically significant differences, indicating a mixture of advantages and disadvantages for the five one-stop LWDAs but, if anything, an overall disadvantage. For example, African American participants had lower earnings outcomes than whites, and the five LWDAs had fewer African American participants. Conversely, Hispanic participants also had lower earnings outcomes, and the five had more Hispanics. The one-stop LWDAs had fewer substance abusers but also fewer employed and high school graduates, and their areas had higher levels of unemployment and poverty.

Overall, the differences indicated both advantages and disadvantages for the two types of LWDAs, but that the five one-stop LWDAs had a larger number of more significant disadvantages. This is consistent with the weaker earnings outcomes for those five, reported in table 10.1, prior to the introduction of the control variables. The evidence supports the conclusion that the five one-stop LWDAs were not at an overwhelming disadvantage, but that they were operating under less advantageous conditions and overcoming those disadvantages in the sense of having higher earnings outcomes. As suggested above, the differences in clientele characteristics weigh heavily against an interpretation of more "creaming" in the one-stop LWDAs. These patterns of evidence make it hard to sustain interpretations alternative to the conclusion that the one-stop designs contributed to the better earnings outcomes in LWDAs using those designs.

CONCLUSION

There have been many calls for reforming public programs and service delivery through redesign and reengineering, more emphasis on customer service, and more collaborative approaches, and there have been many actual initiatives to implement such reforms. Opportunities are fairly rare, however, to analyze evidence on whether such improvement initiatives relate to quantifiable performance and outcome measures. The one-stop career centers implemented in five LWDAs in Texas during 1994 provide such an opportunity that allows comparing them with the other LWDAs as counterfactuals. The present analysis contrasts with previous research on one-stop initiatives by analyzing objective outcome data rather than investigating the overall structures and conditions of various one-stop programs nationwide. As suggested at the beginning of the chapter, we need to consider organizational and program designs that facilitate collaborative public management. Developing knowledge of such designs and their implementation is an essential element of collaborative public management. Collaborative public managers, and the research to support them, can continue to develop knowledge of the skills to establish such designs that involve sharing information and services among programs and organizations, and the skills, attitudes, and behaviors conducive to working effectively with them.

The findings here generally reaffirm previous research that found that organizational structures, clientele characteristics, and environmental factors do make important differences in improving program outcomes. To this stream of research, this study adds evidence that the more collaborative, integrated, customer-focused one-stop delivery system in the JTPA training programs results in higher earnings outcomes. One-stop centers are designed to provide program participants with comprehensive and well-coordinated information on job availability, job skills that employers want, and custom-tailored training and education programs. The new organizational structures also provide employers with opportunities to induce program participants to obtain job skills they need the most. This customer-oriented service delivery was further enhanced by the formally mandated and centralized coordination of related welfare and training programs and agencies. The coordination is aimed at reducing duplication and redundancy in similar job-related public programs in Texas and at achieving consistency in the programs. The evidence here indicates that local service delivery areas with the collaborative, customer-oriented one-stop structures increased the hourly wage at follow-up for adult participants by as much as 54 cents; they had similar positive effects on the wage at termination for hard-to-serve adult individuals. The pilot nature of the one-stop initiative in Texas during program year 1994 suggests that full implementation of one-stop initiatives under JTPA structures in Texas and other states might have an even stronger influence on earnings outcomes than is indicated by the present analysis.

Appendix: Variable Descriptions and Means for Title II-A and Title II-C Programs (Means are reported in parentheses. The first mean is for Title II-A programs and the second mean is for Title II-C programs).

Variable	Description
Hourly wage at termination	Hourly wage of a program terminee when the terminee entered full or part-time unsubsidized employment upon program termination (6.89; 5.37)
Hourly wage at follow-up	Hourly wage of a program terminee at follow-up (13th week after program termination) (7.18; N.A.)
Demographics	
Age	Age in years (31.8; 18.6)
Female	1 for female and 0 for male (.67; .59)
Black	1 for African Americans and 0 for others (.24; .21)
Hispanic	1 for Hispanic and 0 for others (.39; .57)
Indian or Alaskan	1 if a participant is American Indian or Alaskan Native (Not Hispanic) and 0 for others (.003; .002)
Asian	1 if a participant is Asian or Pacific Islander (Not Hispanic) and 0 for others (.01; .004)
Participant potentials	
Received supportive services	The sum of dummy indicators showing if a participant received support services on transportation, health care, family care, housing or rental assistance, counseling, needs-based/related payments, and others (.45; .39)
Highest school grade completed	18 scale values ranging from no school grade to PhD or equivalent (11.6; 10.6)
Employed	1 if a participant was employed during the 7 consecutive days prior to application and 0 for others (.22; .19)
Prewage	Hourly wage paid to the participant during the 26 weeks prior to application (5.56; 4.74)
Barriers to employment	
Hard-to-serve individuals	The sum of indices for hard-to-serve individuals pursuant to the SPIR data format (basic skill deficient, school dropouts, cash welfare recipient, offenders, individuals with a disability, homeless individuals, and SDA established category) (2.08; 1.79)
Welfare recipient	1 if a participant received welfare services including AFDC (Aid to Families with Dependent Children), GA (General Assistance), and RCA (Refugee Cash Assistance) (.24; .18)
Single head of household	1 for single head of household and 0 for others (.26; .09)
Reading skills below 7th-grade level	1 if a participant's assessed reading skills are below 7th-grade level and 0 for others (.14; .20)

JOBS program participant	1 for JOBS program participant and 0 for others (.11; .04)
Limited English proficiency	1 for limited-English language proficiency and 0 for others (.08; .05)
Lack work history	1 if a participant has not worked for the same employer for longer than three consecutive months in the two years prior to application and 0 for others (.29; .61)
Long-term AFDC recipient	1 for a participant listed on the AFDC grant who has received cash payments under AFDC for any 36 or more of the 60 months prior to application and 0 for others (.10; .06)
Substance abuse	1 for a participant who abused alcohol or other drugs, as defined by the Governor and 0 for others (.02; .006)
Training services	
Basic skills training	1 if a participant received instruction normally conducted in an institutional classroom or one-on-one tutorial setting and 0 for others (.2; .58)
Occupational skills training	1 if a participant received instruction conducted in an institutional or worksite setting designed to provide individuals special skills and 0 for others (.68; .45)
On-the-job-training	1 if a participant received training in the public or private sector which is given to an individual while s/he is engaged in productive work and 0 for others (.17; .05)
Work experience	1 if a participant received work experience/entry employment experience/private internships and 0 for others (.04; .22)
Weeks of training	The number of weeks of training for a participant (33.1; 30)
Level II Variables	
Average annual earnings	Average annual earnings in retail and wholesale trade in a Service Delivery Area (SDA) in 1994 (in thousands) (17.1; 17.6)
Earning growth	Three-year real growth rate of annual earnings in retail and wholesale trade, 1991 to 1994 in a SDA (.14; −.1)
Employment	Percent of employment in manufacturing, agriculture and mining in a SDA in 1994 (17.8; 17.2)
Unemployment rate	Unemployment rate in a SDA in 1994 (7.7; 8.2)
Population density	Population density in a SDA in 1990 (in thousands, maximum of 7.0) (.67; .91)
Employee/resident worker ratio	The ratio of employee to resident worker in 1990 (99.1; 101.6)
One-stop structure	1 if a SDA implemented one-stop structures for JTPA programs and 0 for others (.11; .11)

NOTE

1. Upon request, a review of this literature on organizational and managerial influences on program and policy performance is available from the authors. The authors will also gladly provide an extensively footnoted version of this chapter, with notes concerning the nature of the five local pilot areas, the Texas agencies involved, the characteristics of the one-stop centers, and numerous details and justifications about the dataset, the analytical methods, the concepts and variables, and other details. These notes were eliminated due to space constraints, but the authors welcome interested readers' queries and requests for these notes.

Part III

HOW AND WHY PUBLIC MANAGERS GET OTHERS TO COLLABORATE

The chapters in part III push our thinking about public managers getting others to collaborate. In chapter 11, Robert Alexander and Rosemary O'Leary study collaborative management behavior prompted by external stimuli to a relatively new federal agency, the U.S. Institute for Environmental Conflict Resolution (USIECR). They examine the intersection of collaboration, legitimacy seeking, and organizational culture. Government organizations traditionally are characterized by a lack of competition. But in the case of the USIECR, competition and competitors are the two major variables affecting the evolution of this new organization. They also find that a statutory mandate requiring funding beyond direct appropriation encourages collaborative behavior in an effort to overcome competition in the early evolution of a public agency. Finally, they hypothesize that an organization with a mission to facilitate the use of alternative dispute resolution processes will adopt a collaborative culture approach in reacting to institutional pressures and in managing resource and political dependencies.

In chapter 12, Kirk Emerson contributes to the discussion of collaborative environmental management based on her work as director of the USIECR. She describes two examples of work focused on the synthesis between practice and performance in the field of environmental conflict resolution. The first type involves a collaborative effort to synthesize antecedent conditions, process dynamics, and outcomes into an operating model for evaluating environmental conflict resolution programs. The second type addresses the necessary demands for both principled engagement and effective performance as expressed in a recent federal environmental conflict resolution policy statement. These are both interesting examples of collaborative action in their own right, where facilitated discussion among diverse, often-conflicting interests and jurisdictions yielded constructive outcomes. Her chapter makes the connection between theory and practice in a vivid and concrete way.

The implications of the growth of collaborative public management for public policy, public management, and public affairs education are examined by Paul Posner in chapter 13. He argues that the emergence of third-party governance as the dominant strategy for achieving public objectives has tested the skills and knowledge of public administrators with new challenges in policy development and implementation. Moreover, the new environment for public programs is more complex and uncertain and less predictable and controllable than ever before. Posner outlines his vision of a master of public administration curriculum to address these changes and complexities.

These three chapters bring together cutting-edge research on collaboration, cutting-edge collaboration practice, and cutting-edge pedagogy for collaboration.

Chapter 11

Collaborative Approaches to Public Organization Start-Ups

Robert Alexander and Rosemary O'Leary

On February 11, 1998, Congress passed PL 105-156, the Environmental Policy and Conflict Resolution Act, creating the U.S. Institute for Environmental Conflict Resolution (USIECR), a new federal organization housed in the Morris K. Udall Foundation and mandated to assist federal agencies involved in environmental conflicts.[1] Though the emergence of a new program in the federal government is nothing new, the USIECR faced a statutory requirement not seen in many other organizations: to work closely with regionally based professionals in delivering its services. Kirk Emerson, then a member of the research faculty at the University of Arizona's Udall Center, was tapped as the first USIECR director. Emerson, with the leadership team of the Udall Foundation, immediately faced many questions.

How do you start up a new public organization? How, on such a limited budget, do you fulfill this geographic requirement? How does such a mandate play into all other internal and external forces affecting organizational evolution in these formative years? This chapter puts the reader in the shoes of Emerson and the leadership team to enable the reader to understand how one public organization successfully became institutionalized as a collaborative organization, while working under many constraints.

Fortunately, we were able to track the leadership team members as they "grew" with the USIECR from birth to adolescence. We were given wide access to Udall Foundation board representatives, USIECR staff members, congressional personnel, and USIECR advisers, who were involved with the creation of the agency from the very beginning. We were given wide access to meetings, archival data, and agency communications. But most important, we were given wide access to the leadership team.

First, we review the literature on the birth and evolution of organizations, the institutional nature of the public-sector organizational environment, and strategic management. Next, we present the propositions that guided the research and explain the methodology. Third, we present the results of initial analysis, focusing on both the external and internal factors that influenced the evolution of the USIECR. Finally, we close with lessons learned for public management, paying particular attention to collaborative strategy in the public sector.

THE BIRTH AND EARLY EVOLUTION OF AN ORGANIZATION

Most theories on organizational emergence largely center on private-sector organizations and examine cost-minimizing, profit-maximizing entrepreneurial arrangements in resource-competitive environments (Aldrich 2001; Aldrich and Martinez 2001; Zucker 1989). Organizational birth occurs within an existing population of organizations that is dense (Hannan and Freeman 1977) and where the resource environment is rich and conducive to innovation and competition (Carroll 1984).

The period immediately after the initial emergence of an organization is a time of rapid evolution of boundary setting and the development of routines and norms (Aldrich 2001). These early processes are highly subject to forces present in the organizational environment, such as stakeholder demands, resource availability, and legal requirements (Scott 2003). How embedded the organization is in a competitive market environment also has an impact (Aldrich 2001). The role of key stakeholders changes over time depending upon the stage of organizational life cycle, along with the level of dependency of the organization on others (Jawahar and McLaughlin 2001). Legitimacy is seen as an essential factor in driving these evolutionary processes, the lack of which creates a "liability of newness" against the organization in its search to obtain the resources necessary for survival (Stinchcombe 1965). External forces are not alone, however, in influencing the direction of young organizations. Individual entrepreneurs and leaders interact with the organizational environment to shape the emergence and adoption of norms (Aldrich and Martinez 2001; Boin and Christensen 2004; Finnemore and Sikkink 1998).

A direct application of these theories to public organizations may only produce partial explanations due to differences in the public-sector organizational environment. First, birth processes in the public sector are distinct from those in the private sector. Rather than entrepreneurial emergence in a resource-competitive environment, the creation mechanism for a public agency occurs through political processes.

After emergence, public-sector organizations differ in composition and arrangement of their institutional, resource, and stakeholder environments (Frumkin and Galaskiewicz 2004). Stakeholders include elected officials, service clients, and the general public. Performance measures extend beyond the financial bottom line. Authority mechanisms trend toward the hierarchal and political. Expectations of accountability include the public interest; a wide range of public laws place legal constraints on personnel management and other agency actions (Van Slyke and Alexander 2006; Nutt 1999; Rainey 2003; Rainey and Bozeman 2000).

Only a few scholars have empirically examined how these differences may affect public organization evolutionary processes (e.g., see Ritti and Silver 1986). Boin (2004) asserts that it is the relatively more important role of the political and institutional environment that delineates the differences, leading to the notion that public organizations *institutionalize* more than they seek survival in a competitive market environment.

In this conceptualization of organizational survival, institutionalization occurs when an agency has assumed a certain level of "taken-for-grantedness," or legitimacy. Briefly, legitimacy describes how organizations seek to establish congruence between social norms and values of the status quo and the social values associated with the activities of the organization (Ritti and Silver 1986 ; Suchman 1995; Zucker 1989) to enhance organizational survival and decrease Stinchombe's (1965) "liability of newness" (Aldrich and Fiol 1994; Singh, Tucker, and Meinhard 1991; Suchman 1995). Obtaining legitimacy subsequently secures a level of political and financial resources, assuring perpetuation of organizational activity. It is not only important, therefore, to examine legitimacy from the perspectives of how organizations create activities and structures to seek legitimacy but also to determine how external forces in turn shape these strategies (Ashforth and Gibbs 1990; Hybels 1995; Oliver 1997; Walker, Thomas, and Zelditch 1986).

STRATEGIC MANAGEMENT

Leaders engage in strategic management of their internal resources and their external environments (Nutt and Backoff 1993). Because legitimacy is an important resource for agencies seeking institutionalization, legitimacy-seeking strategies likely prevail in public agency leadership in the early stages. These strategies include adapting and conforming to prevailing definitions; communicating to alter the definition of legitimacy so that the definition conforms to the reality of the organization; and communicating so that they are identified with highly legitimized symbols, values, and institutions (Dowling and Pfeffer 1975). Leaders select such *actor-based* strategies to identify, understand, and manage key stakeholders. Conversely, *agency-based* strategies focus upon the organization's capacities and its place in its environment. Overall, leaders practice adaptive management, which maximizes organizational learning and the development of planning systems (Nutt and Backoff 1993).

A UNIQUE SET OF CIRCUMSTANCES

From the outset, the USIECR leadership team faced a unique set of constraints and capacities within which to select and develop norms for institutionalization. First, the USIECR was to be a program embedded within a separate independent agency in a location outside Washington. Second, funding was to be based on both fees for services and more traditional appropriated funding. Third, language in its enacting legislation required regionally based services, suggesting a close relationship with environmental conflict resolution (ECR) professionals in the private sector.

We wanted to know how these factors would have an impact on the actor and agency-based strategies selected by the USIECR's leadership during its birth and emergence. Three propositions guided our study:

- *Proposition 1: The USIECR's early strategic management will include agency-based strategies that are reactive in nature and include frequent occurrences of learning.* New organizations face a high learning curve in the influence of their organizational environments. As such, the leaders of these organizations are likely to be agency focused and will likely exhibit strategies of adaptive management where organizational learning is high.
- *Proposition 2: The USIECR's prebirth strategic management will target key political and budgetary stakeholders. Its postemergence strategic management will target potential clients and promoters of professional norms in the ECR field.* Due to the institutional context of public organizations, the diminished role of market forces in early evolutionary processes, and the goal ambiguity derived from multiple, conflicting stakeholders, we expect public managers to exhibit a high prevalence of legitimacy-seeking strategies from key stakeholders in pursuit of agency institutionalization.
- *Proposition 3: Institutional and cultural variables of mission, statute, and professional experiences will encourage collaborative man-*

agement strategies to be used in the USIECR's early strategic man-agement. Due to the USIECR's very small size at birth, we expect its strategic management processes in the initial phases of its institutionalization to be susceptible to specific cultural and institutional influences, such as mission and staff professional backgrounds.

SOURCES OF DATA AND METHODS

Due to the nature of capturing evolutionary processes in a rich data environment and the challenges of gaining access to sufficient data sources, the research design of this study is in the form of a single case study. The data derive from fifty-two semistructured interviews collected in two phases. An initial round of seven interviews occurred in 2002, followed by a more detailed interview protocol applied to fifty-two subjects in 2005. One follow-up interview occurred with a key manager in 2007. Those interviewed included the USIECR and Udall Foundation staff, Udall Foundation board members, members of the congressional staffs of the elected officials involved with USIECR legislation, USIECR federal agency clients, USIECR advisory committee members, consultants, professional mediators and facilitators, and academics who study conflict resolution. The program director, Kirk Emerson, was interviewed formally four times and again informally on seven occasions. We verified and supplemented interview analyses through the examination of archival records, newspapers, newsletters, and government documents, including testimony, budget records, enacting legislation, and Udall Foundation board meeting notes. Further, we participated in three USIECR conferences, a board meeting, and an advisory meeting.

The interview subjects were grouped into seven stakeholder groups, as suggested by theory (table 11.1). Interview protocols were developed for each stakeholder group, which captured information about the external and internal forces affecting strategic decision making and organizational evolution from 1996 to 2007. Each protocol contained the same core of questions, with additional ones tailored to each group. Interviewees who were members of more than one group were interviewed according to their primary association with the USIECR. Generally, interviewees were asked when they first became aware of the USIECR and what their expectations were. They were asked what the USIECR's greatest challenges have been and what innovations it has developed or promoted. They were questioned about whether they considered it a developed, credible agency and, if so, at what point they felt that happened. In all the interviews, we listened for evidence of external and internal forces shaping the USIECR's evolution.

Table 11.1 Interview Subjects

Category	Quantity	Agency/Organization
Academic	5	University of Michigan Indiana University University of Virginia
Federal advisory committee member	4	U.S. Forest Service Council of Environmental Quality Nonprofit stakeholder Attorney
Practitioner	10	Private/nonprofit environmental conflict resolution firms
Staff	6	U.S. Institute for Environmental Conflict Resolution Udall Foundation
Agency	10	U.S. Environmental Protection Agency U.S. Department of the Interior Federal Energy Regulatory Commission Federal Highway Administration
Board	3	Udall Foundation Board
Congress	2	U.S. House staff U.S. Senate staff

We coded all data in the NVivo qualitative analysis software package for environmental and internal forces, as well as for strategic decisions and evolutionary change. Secondary analysis by two separate researchers triangulated the frequency and distribution of how often these forces were mentioned in interviews. These were compared with observations and documents to verify validity. "Chains of evidence" (Yin 2003) were established, and the credibility/logic of explanations was analyzed. A set of interview participants reviewed conclusions to check assumptions and interpretations.

As such, any conclusions to be drawn from this study remain relevant primarily to the experience of Emerson and the USIECR. However, we think that our observations and analysis greatly inform the dialogue about strategic management in the early institutionalizing processes of public agencies.

RESULTS

This first phase of our research requires an understanding of the organizational context in which strategic decisions were made during the first seven years of the USIECR's existence. This is best described in two parts: those influencing forces that were outside the organization, and those forces shaping the decision-making environment from within.[2] We paid particular attention to the development of organizational structures and the rapid institutionalization of work processes and external relationships.

Various references to the strategic management approach of the USIECR's leadership team are woven throughout these two analyses. The approach includes the reaction to and anticipation of the internal and external forces, both perceived and unknown.

External Forces Influencing the USIECR's Evolution

Stakeholders mentioned seventeen major external forces that influenced the USIECR's early evolution and institutionalization. Of these seventeen forces, the top four pertain to *actors* in the USIECR environment, while most of the rest were *institutional* and *cultural* forces (figure 11.1). Lumping together clients and customers, here we discuss the top six forces mentioned in our interviews.

Figure 11.1 Major External Forces Influencing the Evolution of the U.S. Institute for Enviornmental Conflict Resolution, 1998–2005

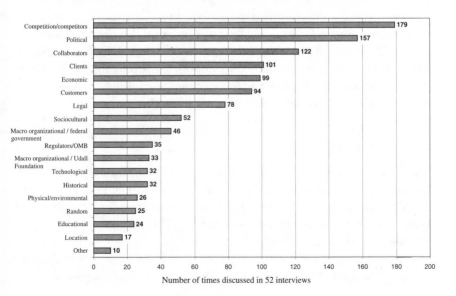

Number of times discussed in 52 interviews

Competition and Competitors

Insiders, agency personnel, and ECR professionals mentioned "competition" and "competitors" as forces in the USIECR environment 179 times in 52 interviews. Insiders—including the leadership team, USIECR program managers, congressional staff, federal agency staff, and foundation board members—perceived competition for limited financial resources. Driving much of this discussion was the statutory language leading to the belief within the Office of Management and Budget (OMB) from 1998 to 2006 that the USIECR would become entirely self-sufficient, based upon client fees. Insiders also felt that an early sense of competition with other federal entities that were promoting ECR was inherent as the USIECR searched for its unique niche. This was especially the case when finding a niche was of paramount importance for organizational survival.

Field practitioners and agency personnel mentioned competition in the context of history. For example, several field practitioners pointed out, "We were here first." They expressed concern that their expertise, experience, and prior successes in the field were not adequately appreciated and acknowledged by the "new kids on the block." Members of agencies providing ECR services for several decades expressed a desire to have the USIECR show greater recognition for what they do and what they have to offer.

Actions taken by the USIECR leadership team corroborate the importance of this external force. Even before the legislation passed establishing the USIECR, experienced practitioners and agency personnel were approached collaboratively to help guide statutory language development. Subsequent outreach was made for most program development, including USIECR staff hiring, the development of the USIECR's Roster of Neutrals (i.e., its roster of trained mediators), planning for the National Environmental Conflict Resolution Conference, and the National Environmental Conflict Resolution Advisory Committee.

Political Factors

The second external factor mentioned most often in interviews as influencing the evolution of the USIECR was "politics" or political influences. In this context, the 157 discussions almost always revolved around Congress, the USIECR's enabling legislation, and OMB. These were most prevalent in interviews with insiders.

A large portion of the points made by interviewees here could apply to nearly all federal programs: the need for congressional support, the imperative not to exceed the mandates of the enabling legislation, and the challenges in dealing with a sometimes unsupportive OMB early in the organization's existence. Discussion about the USIECR becoming entirely fee based was unique to it and a difficult prospect. Most federal agencies did not have the money to pay full fees to the USIECR for its services, and, in some cases, it needed to show independence from agency funding. However, some OMB staff thought that the USIECR would become a fee-based agency after its first five years and that congressional support for it would be phased out. If this were not to become a reality, the USIECR's survival might be jeopardized at reauthorization.

Collaborators

Interviewees mentioned "collaboration" 122 times. This factor was discussed most often by interviewees who were the USIECR's clients and customers, its advisory committee members, members of private dispute resolution firms, and ECR field professionals. Starting up a new federal ECR program was challenging, and the USIECR leadership team had an enormous need for information during this period. The team found it extremely useful to identify certain stakeholders as collaborators. The leadership team incorporated the advice of external stakeholders into many of its initial decisions, such as on those concerning statutory language and staff hiring, as well as on potential members of the roster of trained mediators and the National Environmental Conflict Resolution Advisory Committee.

Viewing collaborators as a shaping force external to the USIECR differs from viewing collaboration as a strategy in response to internal and external factors. We discuss this latter idea further on in the chapter.

Clients and Customers

The fourth major external factor affecting the USIECR's evolution was "clients" and "customers." This was expected, given the emphasis on fee-based services. The "insiders," Emerson, other USIECR staff, and Udall Foundation Board members, were the interviewees who most often expressed a concern about obtaining clients and customers.

This focus on clients and customers differs from that of the typical public organization because it was most often coupled with statements about competition, economics, and education. Specifically, the USIECR and Udall Foundation staff expressed great pressure to continually educate politicians, OMB, and the public about the need for and format of their services. Adding to this challenge, the USIECR also felt it had to develop a culture of neutrality to gain and retain legitimacy as a broker of ECR services. This made the search for clients and customers more sensitive. The public as "client" was mentioned by insiders only symbolically and was discussed in terms of maintaining mission focus.

Economics

Interviewees felt that economic forces also played a strong role the USIECR's evolution during its first five years. These forces were mentioned ninety-nine times and pertained to the need for funds to run the USIECR. In particular, agency clients and peers, such as Environmental Protection Agency personnel and those associated with private dispute resolution firms, wondered aloud what the future held for the organization in terms of congressional budgetary support, even though they themselves considered the USIECR "established."

As mentioned above, the interviews showed that an awareness of economic forces was apparent in any discussion about clients, political forces, and potential competition. Again, the key tension was perceived to be between the need to market and "sell" services and the need to produce services to gain legitimacy in the eyes of budget gatekeepers.

Legal Factors

Major stakeholders discussed legal factors and forces seventy-eight times in their interviews. Most of the comments concerned the need for the USIECR to comply with its enabling legislation and other laws. Not surprisingly, the ten lawyers interviewed mentioned this factor as the strongest force in the USIECR's environment. These comments also included a discussion of political factors and, to a lesser degree, factors that concerned being a part of the federal government system.

Interviewees mainly discussed legal factors that apply to all federal programs, including the importance of the empowering and constraining aspects of the law and the desire not to exceed the mandates of enabling legislation. Unique to the USIECR, however, is that it is housed within the Udall Foundation, an independent federal agency, established to continue the conservation legacy of Representative Morris K. Udall (D-AZ) through education and training. Second, the USIECR is a networked organization that pays out an estimated 70 percent of its combined appropriation and project revenues to the contracted ECR professional mediators on its roster. It is unusual for such a small federal program to have such financial complexity.

Internal Factors Influencing the Evolution of the USIECR

The internal factors that moderated the USIECR's evolution included fixed internal organizational qualities present at the outset and dynamic organizational traits that derive from these original qualities. Others were the evolving leadership and staff behaviors that interacted with each other and with the external forces described above to produce structural and procedural decisions.

The fixed qualities of location, size, and agency mission influenced the evolution of organizational culture and personnel characteristics. These, in conjunction with external forces, yielded leadership and staff strategic behaviors that included boundary-spanning and buffering actions. Of these actions, the most significant were those involving collaborative management.

Fixed Qualities

Organizations are aggregations of social relations unified by a common purpose. Accordingly, with the USIECR, several key qualities present at the outset established a baseline upon which its more dynamic characteristics rapidly developed and evolved. Its location in Tucson, its small size, and the authorizing language of its founding statute came together with its individual leaders' traits, social networks, professional backgrounds, and personalities. These greatly affected its mission enactment, organizational culture, work processes, program development, and strategic behaviors.

Size and Location

Its small size and its location within the Udall Foundation in Tucson immediately defined the USIECR. Its program staff stressed in interviews that the small size yielded a more horizontal organizational structure where staff members had more opportunity to engage in organizational-level decision making. At the same time, early work processes governed by rules and regulations for federal agencies were much more difficult to develop, due to the distance from Washington, the staff's lack of direct federal agency experience, and the necessity for a few staff members to handle a multiplicity of regulation compliance activities.

Fifteen external stakeholders familiar with the federal agency system discussed the USIECR's small size as both a liability and an advantage. The liability aspects included the challenge of pursuing their mandate with so few resources and personnel and the difficulty of maintaining legitimacy with OMB and Congress when the USIECR barely registered on the federal "radar screen." At the same time, these interviewees pointed out the advantage of operating unnoticed in political climates not traditionally supportive of their work.

Clients also said that the distance from Washington enabled the USIECR to craft an image of being different from the traditional Washington culture of federal agencies. It was able to maintain its identity as neutral in its dealings with agency clients. At the same time, distance also made it more difficult to establish and maintain relationships.

Finally, the leadership team all noted that it was not an easy task to start an organization within another agency where programs and missions differed significantly. Internal procedures and protocols already formed at the Udall Foundation had to be adjusted and adapted to the USIECR's needs.

Founding Statute and Publicness

Twelve of fourteen insiders mentioned that the statutory language establishing the USIECR was an internal factor, particularly as it pertained to the staff members' enactment of their mission and purpose. These insiders included the USIECR program staff and leadership and Udall Foundation board members. Ellen Wheeler, the Udall Foundation's chief operating officer, explains: "The core for us was certainly our statute and it still is. I mean, that's sort of the Bible. You have to go back to that all the time."

A key provision of the statutory language required that USIECR services be proximate to the conflicts with which they became involved. This eventually became addressed through development of the USIECR's Roster of Neutrals.

Dynamic Qualities

The evolving organizational qualities of personnel characteristics and internal culture affected strategic management behaviors as well. Decisions made at the organizational level reflected the personalities of staff in addition to the values developed within their work culture.

Personnel Characteristics

Two distinct hiring periods occurred during the USIECR's first seven years. In the first, program staff were hired with the intent that they would provide direct mediation services and come on board with professional expertise in direct mediation. However, when the decision was made to establish a roster of private sector-mediators who would be contracted to mediate USIECR-managed conflicts, it quickly became apparent that program staff needed to function more as project managers. A second wave of program staff hiring within the second year infused the USIECR with a majority of its existing senior program staff, who, as a team, brought together experience with environmental issues, law, and conflict resolution. External stakeholders perceived these professional characteristics and skills as greatly influencing the work environment in which the USIECR's processes and programs developed.

Twelve interviewees perceived the culture of USIECR staff as being initially "academic" and not in line with the approach taken by more established federal ECR professionals. In addition, the USIECR did not have any senior-level staff with significant federal agency experience. Though this attribute allowed innovation, it also yielded initial legitimacy challenges when the USIECR tried to work collaboratively with other federal agencies.

Organizational Culture

Culture is for the group what character and personality are for the individual. The challenge of depicting an evolutionary conception of organizational culture lies in understanding how multiple perspectives, in this case interviewees, talk about and around this important construct. The idea of "culture" shapes stakeholders' perceptions and influences individuals' behaviors. As suggested above, perceptions of the USIECR's organizational culture by external stakeholders were described variously as "academic," "productive," "collaborative," and "constraining."

Internally, USIECR staff perceived an organizational culture of commitment to high-quality performance so much that finding an appropriate balance between work and personal life posed challenges. Two staff members likened their experience to being part of an entrepreneurial start-up in the private sector, where passion and commitment fuel much of the productivity. Observations made at the Environmental Conflict Resolution Conference and the Udall Foundation Board meeting reflected this feeling of pride and commitment in the work that was being done. Individual staff members also seemed to use the small size of the USIECR as a starting point for this pride, as if to say, "Look what we can do with what we have."

The strongest aspect of the USIECR's culture recognized by all interviewees is the value of neutrality. Part of this value derives from the professional experience of internal staff in the field of ECR and the nature of the mediation and facilitation work mandated in the USIECR legislation. The neutrality value also stems from strategic action on behalf of USIECR leadership to instill an organizational norm that would quickly generate legitimacy across a wide range of stakeholders. Dave Emerson at the Department of the Interior explains: "Well, I think it's critical to their success because if they are not seen as a neutral, then . . . they would be viewed as pro-federal agencies. . . . If you are viewed as proagency by the other interested parties in a conflict, then they are not going to want to use you. So, they can only accomplish their mission and survive if they are considered neutral."

STRATEGIC BEHAVIORS

The data derived from our interviews, government records, and archival materials indicate that fixed and dynamic factors interacted with external forces and the organizational context of the public sector to influence both boundary-buffering and boundary-spanning, or collaborative, behaviors on behalf of the USIECR leadership team.

Boundary-Buffering Behaviors

Boundary-buffering behaviors served to protect the USIECR's internal characteristics—such as its organizational culture, work processes, and programs—from external threats, while maintaining its legitimacy and identity. The cultivation of neutrality as an organizational norm is a key example. By law, as federal employees, USIECR program staff cannot engage in the direct lobbying of Congress. This reality became all the more important as the USIECR sought legitimacy based upon its reputation as an unbiased provider of mediation services. As a result, the USIECR leadership team actively isolated program staff from contact with political gatekeepers.

Another example of boundary-buffering behavior lies in the early tension between experienced ECR professionals in both the public and private sectors and USIECR programs. The fact that these professionals felt that they were not given enough credit as the USIECR produced its first programming is evidence that it was moving quickly to carve out its niche and establish boundaries.

Boundary-Spanning Behaviors

Boundary-spanning behaviors involve crossing organizational lines to couple with external stakeholders in order to manage limited resources and build legitimacy. Collaboration dominates this set of behaviors when conceptualized as the sharing of power and resources (e.g., information, money, clients, and authority) between entities to achieve common goals (Bryson, Crosby, and Stone 2006). The USIECR experience provides many examples of the use of collaboration to manage external forces and internal factors acting upon the organization in its early years.

Initial collaborative efforts involved building relationships with existing professionals whereby the USIECR leaders received information and the consulting professionals obtained access to USIECR program design. These individuals were invited to contribute to the enacting statute language, to planning the National Environmental Conflict Resolution Conference, and even to hiring initial USIECR staff. Engaging individuals from key agencies and organizations in this way also moderated perceptions of competition. Interviewees providing critical commentary on USIECR actions, nevertheless, maintained respect for the intent and professionalism of USIECR staff members.

The Roster of Neutrals enabled a great deal of outreach to the private practitioner community, which was performed in a manner consistent with previous outreach—openly sharing the authority of program development with those with more experience building rosters to present their ideas and concerns. USIECR staff anticipated correctly that those contacted would then be the first professionals to apply for membership on the roster or at least would spread the word that it was to be a high-quality program.

Client interactions were also approached collaboratively. Each contract or interagency agreement established with a federal agency provided for flexibility, within which the USIECR and the agency could develop new exchanges not previously considered. Elena Gonzalez, a dispute resolution specialist at the Department of the Interior, explains: "This office works very closely [with the USIECR] in a lot of respects. We share a lot of information, resources in terms of if we are working on something and developing it, training or anything that we are doing, we keep them appraised so that if there are opportunities to coordinate, to share information, for them to attend something that we are doing, or to come and speak, present a briefing, or what have you, and we try to do the same . . . to keep up with the things that they are working on." In addition, Emerson spear-headed the formation of Environmental Conflict Resolution Roundtables with representatives from other federal agencies to exchange information about agencies' practices and innovations.

Another major example of collaboration was the development and implementation of the National Environmental Conflict Resolution Advisory Committee (NECRAC). This project provided the means to recruit otherwise unengaged stakeholders from multiple domains as USIECR advocates. NECRAC also produced a report that has been used as a tangible product describing the USIECR's relevance to national environmental policy and that has been widely circulated and presented to key stakeholders. Evidence of the collaborative symbolism behind this report was obvious at the 2005 Environmental Conflict Resolution Conference.

CONCLUSION

A range of institutional constraints and organizational capacities, reflecting much of what we expected, shaped the strategic management behaviors adopted by the USIECR leadership team. We predicted that the USIECR's early strategic management would include agency-based strategies that would be reactive in nature and include frequent occurrences of learning, and it did. We predicted that the USIECR's early strategic management would center on legitimacy seeking, including strategies targeting key political and budgetary stakeholders, and it did. We predicted that the institutional and cultural variables of mission, statute, and professional experiences would encourage the USIECR's leaders to use collaborative management strategies in its early institutionalizing processes, and they did.

Given the growing emphasis on collaborative approaches to public management (Agranoff 2005; Berry and Brower 2005; Kickert, Klijn, and Koppenjan 1997b; O'Toole and Meier 2004b; Page 2003; Provan and Milward 2001), we were most surprised by the prevalence of perceived competition in the earliest phases of the USIECR's development. When we conceptualize that public organizations primarily institutionalize as they evolve, we do not immediately consider that competition plays a primary role. Yet at the same time, competitors for resources and political support were also perceived as collaborators, suggesting that the USIECR's leaders recognized the importance of relationship building with key stakeholders to maximize legitimacy in the pursuit of institutionalization. Future research on the birth and emergence of public agencies must focus on the role such stakeholders play in the evolution of collaborative agencies.

NOTES

1. ECR consists of an assorted set of techniques, processes, and roles that enable parties in a dispute to reach agreement, usually with the help of one or more third-party neutrals (see O'Leary and Bingham 2003).

2. As noted by prior theorists, the notion of organizational boundaries, and thus internal and external, serves an analytical role but results from individual perspectives of the beholder, limiting transferability to broader conclusions (Pfeffer and Salanick 1978; Scott 2003; Weick 1995.) Therefore, it is important to note that we as researchers enact "internal" and "external" of the USIECR based upon analysis of interview data in response to such questions as "Who do you think are important people or groups of people from whom the USIECR has needed to cultivate support?" and "Who does the USIECR serve?" and "Who participates in program and project development decisions?" and not based upon direct questioning of what is internal and external.

Chapter 12

Synthesizing Practice and Performance in the Field of Environmental Conflict Resolution

Kirk Emerson

Lisa Bingham and Rosemary O'Leary, in their conclusion to the December 2006 special issue on collaborative public management of the *Public Administration Review* (*PAR*), describe the "parallel play" occurring in the research on collaboration by scholars of public administration and management and by researchers studying conflict resolution. They suggest that a synthesis across these disciplinary lines is missing, as demonstrated by the articles in the *PAR* special issue (Bingham and O'Leary 2006, 161–65).

I agree with this conclusion from the dual perspective of a public manager and a conflict resolution practitioner. This "parallel play" is not only occurring in research; it is occurring on the ground in practice as well. For example, public managers are exploring cooperative networks and partnerships with stakeholders, but when challenges arise, they may not be familiar with or skilled in interest-based negotiation, let alone multiparty negotiation. Unfortunately, most public managers may still consider it a sign of management failure to bring in a mediator or facilitator. Instead, such a move might be an indicator of progressive management, of anticipating conflict and identifying when third-party assistance can assist with remedial or preventive conflict management.

Likewise, public policy mediators or public engagement facilitators may not be fully versed in the "wicked" nature of a particular policy problem they are being asked to mediate. They may be unfamiliar with the arcane regulatory constraints involved or, for that matter, the extent of political influence being brought to bear behind the scenes. The issue may get framed too narrowly or a proposed process not fit some administrative requirement or time frame. The focus of the intervention might remain on a dispute to be resolved instead of a new institutional arrangement to be designed.

That said, an increasing number of public managers and conflict resolution practitioners are synthesizing the principles and practice of collaborative public management and conflict resolution. They are conducting collaborative processes and building collaborative organizations and networks in local, state, tribal, and federal government as well as in the private and nonprofit sectors.

Two exemplars of this cross-fertilization are the Policy Consensus Initiative, led by executive director Christine Carlson, and the Collaborative Action and Dispute Resolution (CADR) Office of the U.S. Department of the Interior, directed by Elena Gonzalez. The Policy Consensus Initiative operates as a nonprofit organization promoting collaboration and conflict resolution among state agencies and elected officials. CADR is a federal program advancing collaborative public management and conflict resolution throughout the Department of the Interior. In both cases, Carlson and Gonzalez lead by example and from perspectives that integrate their experience as managers with explicit conceptual frameworks for collaborative leadership and conflict resolution. These and other integrators, such as many of those mentioned in the special issue of *PAR*, have found that "missing synthesis" in their practice.

In this chapter, I describe two examples of work focused on the synthesis between practice and performance in the field of environmental conflict resolution (ECR). The first example involves a collaborative effort to synthesize antecedent conditions, process dynamics, and outcomes into an operating model to evaluate ECR programs. The second example addresses the necessary demands for both principled engagement in ECR and effective ECR performance as expressed in a recent federal ECR policy statement.

These are both interesting examples of collaborative action in their own right, where facilitated discussion among diverse, often-conflicting interests and jurisdictions yielded constructive outcomes. The emphasis of this discussion, however, is on the effort to make explicit the synthesis between practice and performance. Before launching into these illustrations, a brief description of ECR is in order.

ENVIRONMENTAL CONFLICT RESOLUTION

ECR encompasses a range of tools, techniques, and processes by which diverse parties are assisted in reaching agreements or resolving disputes concerning environmental, natural resources, and public land issues. Depending on the level of conflict among the parties and the degree of agreement required, facilitators or mediators work with the parties to improve communication, clarify interests, build trust, break through impasses, and fashion solutions that most effectively address the interests represented. ECR and public policy dispute resolution in general draw on the principles and practices of interest-based negotiation and mutual-gains bargaining to optimize outcomes based on increased information sharing and mutual understanding.

ECR is best understood as a mechanism to assist diverse parties to gain an understanding of their respective interests and to work together to craft outcomes that address those interests in effective and implementable ways. ECR takes many forms and can be applied in many settings, but in the context of federal decision making, it enables interested parties (including state, tribal, and local governments; affected communities; and citizens) to engage more effectively in the decision-making process. Interested parties are no longer merely commentators on a federal proposal but also act as partners in defining federal plans, programs, and projects (National Environmental Conflict Resolution Advisory Committee 2005, 12).

ECR can be used in a variety of settings: during policy development and planning processes (considered "upstream" applications); in the context of siting, licensing, and rulemaking; and in administrative appeals and litigation ("downstream" applications). Generally, ECR processes involve several parties and multiple issues. Frequently more than one government agency is involved, often at more than one level (federal, state, tribal, or local). These issues are matters of public interest and require consideration of those at the table as well as public engagement. ECR processes require compliance not only with the pertinent substantive laws and regulations but also with procedural requirements, such as the Federal Advisory Committee Act of 1972 (PL 92-463) and open meeting laws.

The field of ECR emerged in the late 1960s when the first environmental mediations occurred (Dukes 2004) and has matured alongside the broader conflict resolution or alternative dispute resolution (ADR) profession. The ECR field has been bolstered by developments in national and state environmental policy and regulation that created more opportunities for both citizen engagement and legal standing to object to public agency decisions (chief among them, the National Environmental Policy Act of 1970, PL 91-190). The ECR field has also been supported and shaped by state and federal laws encouraging the use of alternative dispute resolution (e.g., the Administrative Dispute Resolution Act of 1996,

PL 104-320; the Regulatory Negotiations Act of 1996, PL 102-354; and the Alternative Dispute Resolution Act of 998, PL 105-315). It has also cross-pollinated with the field of public participation, particularly where complex and controversial public issues are at stake.

In 1998, the Environmental Policy and Conflict Resolution Act (PL 105-156) established the U.S. Institute for Environmental Conflict Resolution (USIECR) within the Morris K. Udall Foundation, an independent federal agency. Its mission is to assist parties in resolving federal environmental, natural resources, and public land disputes through mediation, training, and other appropriate means.

The USIECR's work typifies the breadth of ECR activity at the federal level. ECR has been employed to

- mediate a timber sale by the Bureau of Land Management in Oregon where plaintiffs had sued for stronger protection of old-growth forests;
- negotiate a new rulemaking for specific national parks or natural protected areas on off-road vehicle use, protection of endangered species, and even off-leash pet rules;
- mediate a bistate collaborative environmental review process to both protect a historic lift bridge and accommodate growing transportation needs with a new highway bridge between Minnesota and Wisconsin;
- convene a community dialogue to address how to mitigate the noise impact of an Air Force base on adjacent residential neighborhoods;
- manage interagency negotiations at the technical level, for example, in selecting and calibrating a hydrologic model to use on a restoration project in the Everglades; or at the regulatory level, between the National Park Service and Federal Aviation Administration to reach agreement on how to address the long-standing battles over restoring natural quiet in the Grand Canyon;
- manage multistate and multitribe deliberations over restoration of endangered species populations in the Missouri River Basin, or for sage grouse habitat conservation, or desert tortoise protection in the Southwest; and
- assist a congressional committee by assessing the potential for parties to negotiate a national policy proposal on disposition of e-waste.

As the use of ECR has grown at the federal, state, and local levels, more public managers are gaining familiarity with these processes, as initiators or sponsors, as parties, and increasingly as facilitators themselves.

Not only is ECR being institutionalized through new programs, practitioner rosters, and administrative infrastructure, but public managers also are building their own negotiation and conflict management skills and are beginning to integrate ECR approaches into their own management repertoires for dealing with challenging environmental conflicts.

SYNTHESIZING AN OPERATING MODEL FOR ENVIRONMENTAL CONFLICT RESOLUTION

In the late 1990s, as the USIECR was being launched, the study of ECR focused primarily on the role and actions of mediators, based primarily on individual or small-N case studies (Emerson et al. 2003). University researchers and "pracademics" dominated the literature, which was primarily descriptive and normative. In fact, some previous efforts to engage researchers and practitioners in the empirical study of environmental mediation or dispute resolution, as it was primarily referred to then, had generated some discomfort, if not discord, between the two communities (Bingham, Birkhoff, and Stone 1997).

In 1996 a controversial study by the RAND Corporation compared court-referred ADR to litigation based primarily on settlement rates and time to settlement (Kakalik et al. 1998). Although the RAND study did not consider multiparty environmental ADR, the potential for misinterpretation or extrapolation of its findings was of concern to many in the public policy dispute resolution field (Hensler 2000).

For example, the use of settlement rates or time to settlement might be an appropriate performance measure for court-related ADR cases, but should it be the cardinal measure for evaluating complex, multiparty environmental disputes that were being negotiated over a lengthy environmental review process? The deliberative processes required in mediating public policy conflicts incorporate principles such as fairness, inclusive representation, and autonomy. Progress might be better measured along several dimensions, and outcomes might also include process accomplishments (e.g., perceived fair treatment) and improvements in relationships.

By the late 1990s, court-based ADR programs were maturing and evaluation studies were under way. Few executive branch programs at the state or federal level had been evaluated at that point. An extensive evaluation of the U.S. Postal Service's ambitious workplace program, Redress, had just gotten under way (Bingham 1997).

At that time, there were several robust state-based public policy programs, many of them the original state programs jump-started with grants from the National Institute for Dispute Resolution (1987) in the later

1980s. These programs provided ADR services and training for multiparty dispute resolution in several public policy arenas, although primarily in the environmental arena (including energy, transportation, and land use).

At the federal level, the U.S. Environmental Protection Agency (EPA) was the primary sponsor of federal environmental dispute resolution. Since the late 1980s, EPA had administered a contract that supported $2 million to 3 million a year in third-party assistance. The focus at that time for most of the other federal ADR programs, including the federal Interagency ADR Working Group led by the U.S. Department of Justice, was on workplace and procurement applications.

Not only were long-standing state programs interested in making a case for continued funding based on evaluating their track records, but new federal programs like those developing at the U.S. Department of the Interior and the Federal Energy Regulatory Commission, as well as the USIECR, were also seeking to demonstrate success and build internal and external support. A part of the federal programs' interest in evaluation was also being driven by the growing emphasis on performance measurement by the President's Office of Management and Budget (OMB) in accordance with the passage of the Government Performance and Results Act of 1993 (PL 103-62).

Thus, a mutual interest in program evaluation arose among public policy dispute resolution program administrators at the state and federal levels. This interest coalesced in a collaborative partnership initiated by the USIECR and the Policy Consensus Initiative. This partnership grew from 1999 through 2006 to include the Oregon Dispute Resolution Commission, the Oregon Department of Justice, the Massachusetts Office of Dispute Resolution, EPA's Conflict Prevention and Resolution Center, the U.S. Department of the Interior's Office of Collaborative Action and Dispute Resolution, the Federal Energy Regulatory Commission's Dispute Resolution Services, the Florida Conflict Resolution Consortium, the Maryland Mediation and Conflict Resolution Office, the Ohio Commission on Dispute Resolution and Conflict Management, the Federal Highway Administration's Office of Project Development and Environmental Review, and the Inventory Monitoring Institute of the U.S. Department of Agriculture's Forest Service (Emerson and Carlson 2003).

The Indiana Conflict Resolution Institute was also supportive of this effort from the outset and cosponsored a conference in Washington in 2001 at Syracuse University's Greenberg House, which led to the publication of *The Promise and Performance of Environmental Conflict Resolution* (O'Leary and Bingham 2003). The William and Flora Hewlett Foundation provided the USIECR with additional core support to lead the interagency ECR evaluation studies that grew out of this partnership. Several evaluation consultants also assisted this effort over the years.[1]

The central challenge of this evaluation work was to articulate and measure the key program interventions made by public agencies or their agents and the expected outcomes and benefits derived from those public investments. This required considerable conceptual and methodological work on the part of the interagency evaluation team. No systematic model had been constructed at the program level that specified what public agencies actually did and what outcomes they hoped to achieve through their efforts. In the rubric of program evaluation experts, there was no explicit "program theory" or "logic model" that mapped inputs to outcomes.

This challenge forced the evaluation team to think simultaneously about best practices and underlying principles, how these were translated into measurable actions they could carry out or influence, and what specific outcomes they should be accountable for having affected or achieved. Numerous general claims about the value and benefits of public policy dispute resolution and environmental mediation in particular had been made over the past two decades of work in the field—some empirically based, others based in mediation practice theory, and others perhaps more aspirational. Best practices for engaging public agencies and stakeholders in individual cases existed, but not at the program level (Society of Professionals in Dispute Resolution 1997).

What claims of performance should a public agency make for which they would be held accountable? What means and strategies were they confident would generate those performance outcomes? These were the questions with which the members of the interagency evaluation team struggled, initially within their own agency staff and then collaboratively within the interagency team.

Fortunately, and rather remarkably, the evaluation team discovered that beneath the experiences of operating independently in different state and federal agencies, there was indeed a commonly held program theory. The very process of trying to articulate that program theory in an operating model helped hone and validate it.

The evaluation framework given in figure 12.1 provides the most recently refined version of the ECR program theory or operating model that was generated by the evaluation team. Though some participating agencies have slightly different elaborations of this model, this has become the basic model currently being tested with a multiagency data set (Orr, Emerson, and Keyes 2008). Each process condition, process dynamic, outcome (at the end of the process and longer term), and impact has been operationalized and can be measured through postagreement surveys of

Figure 12.1 Environmental Conflict Resolution Evaluation Framework, U.S. Institute for Environmental Conflict Resolution

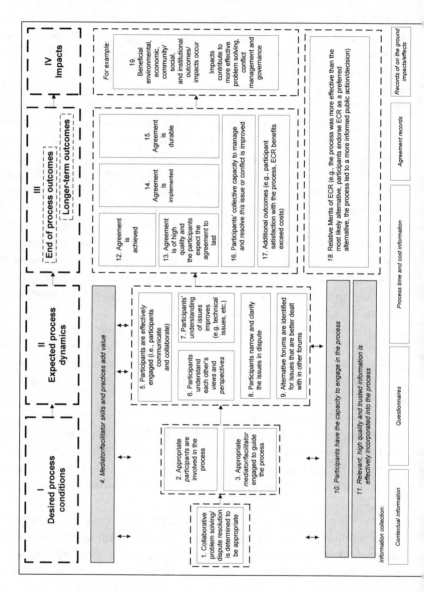

participants and ECR practitioners. The USIECR received clearance from OMB under the Paperwork Reduction Act to collect this information for its own cases as well as for those of other federal agencies. EPA has adopted the measures as well to evaluate its cases and is collecting that information directly, and the U.S. Department of the Interior has also adopted the framework and measurements.

A further cross check on this conceptual framework was performed through an extensive literature review of empirical research conducted by Julie MacFarlane and Bernie Mayer in 2004 (U.S. Institute for Environmental Conflict Resolution 2006). The literature review reassured the evaluation team that they had not left any significant variables out of the model—that is, any factors and conditions over which program managers would have some control. It was not the intent of this model to explain fully the predicted outcomes but rather to determine the extent to which specified conditions and factors that they could influence or support would contribute to optimizing those outcomes.

Another significant testing of this evaluation framework came from engaging with other researchers, practitioners, and program managers in the ECR field. Several conference sessions and workshops were conducted over a two-year period to refine the model through broader input from the field. Building agreement within the ECR community was an essential ingredient for this overall evaluation process to succeed in the future, as evaluation measures and performance analysis become institutionalized into agency procedures. Preliminary analysis of a data set of fifty-two cases also confirms the general workings of this model (Orr et al. 2008).

Don Kettl has referred to the importance of turning performance measures into performance management (Kettl 2005b, 23). Working through this synthesis of conditions, factors, process dynamics, outcomes, and effects into an articulated program theory has helped the public managers on the evaluation team become more explicit about what services they are delivering and why. Demonstrating outcomes is just one benefit of this effort. Of particular importance, the case-based evaluation data can provide timely feedback to the parties, the third-party mediator, and the program managers themselves. The evaluation team has made it possible to start institutionalizing one of the hallmarks of ECR and the public policy dispute resolution field: reflective practice.

SYNTHESIZING PRACTICE AND PERFORMANCE IN POLICY

Collaborative public management and alternative/appropriate conflict resolution both require a greater emphasis on "process," not in the bureaucratic sense of more procedural red tape but in terms of assuring that certain principles of engagement among parties are respected and consistently enacted. Fundamentally, public deliberation and collaborative decision making depend on establishing (and often, first restoring) and maintaining trust among the participating individuals and the institutions they represent. Consistent compliance with such principles by all participants (especially by public agencies) in large part makes this possible (Leach and Sabatier 2005).

Behind this trust-building process orientation can be found important normative claims to the legitimacy of democratic governance, including such values as adequate representation, inclusiveness, transparency, and procedural fairness. Collaborative public management and conflict resolution are in and of themselves "good" according to this view and should become standard operating-procedure, a worthy end in itself to which public managers should aspire.

There is another perspective, of course, that emphasizes the instrumental value of collaborative public management and conflict resolution as they contribute to preventing bad things from happening, overcoming inertia or obstructions, and leading to better outcomes. Through this lens, one uses these processes strategically, when the risks of continuing business as usual are low or plummeting, and the process has been deemed worth the investment. Here, performance is the key—the agreement reached, the decision made, the crisis averted. And the hallmarks of performance are efficiency and effectiveness compared with alternative management practices.

I have overdrawn these two perspectives (but not much) to introduce a second arena in need of greater synthesis from both the practice and research communities. Is collaborative public management a means to an end or an end in itself? Are conflict resolution skills essential to a new (and better) management philosophy or are they simply tools for improved public decision making? And must we choose between the ostensibly competing call for the use of basic collaborative principles and democratic deliberation, on the one hand, and the demand for effective and efficient management performance, on the other?

This distinction between the normative and the instrumental use of collaboration plays out in many ways. It shows up in what public managers expect of conflict resolution processes or how public managers demonstrate program performance or justify their budget requests to support, for example, extensive stakeholder involvement. It is manifest in how mediators approach multiparty negotiations, prepare their project work plans, or describe their particular style and philosophy of mediation.

The source of this perceived tension may well be what Thomson and Perry (2006) point to as competing political traditions that both claim patrimony to collaboration in public administration. The roots of collaboration are buried deep in American life and public administration. When placed within the context of an American public ethos, collaboration can be understood as a process that is rooted in two competing political traditions: classic liberalism and civic republicanism. On one hand, classic liberalism, with its emphasis on private interest, views collaboration as a process that aggregates private preferences into collective choices through self-interested bargaining. Organizations enter into collaborative agreements to achieve their own goals, negotiating among competing interests and brokering coalitions among competing value systems, expectations, and self-interested motivations. On the other hand, civic republicanism, with its emphasis on a commitment to something larger than the individual (whether that be a neighborhood or the state), views collaboration as an integrative process that treats differences as the basis for deliberation in order to assist at "mutual understanding, a collective will, trust and sympathy [and the] implementation of shared preferences" (March and Olsen 1989, 126).

I find this analysis of the dualist roots of collaboration both convincing and useful in understanding the tension between collaborative practice and performance as we see it on the ground and in the literature. It also suggests that though the roots may vary, together they simply strengthen the justification for collaborative public management and conflict resolution as both ends and means.

I would argue we need to make these dual perspectives more explicit in practice and through research for at least two reasons. First, both perspectives can lead to setting high bars for accomplishment—engage fully and fairly all affected and interested parties, on the one hand, or perform faster, cheaper, and better than the alternative management approach, on the other hand. Can we do both? Must we do both? If not, where should the balance be? In addition, like the evaluation model previously discussed, these perspectives are inextricably linked. If we push too far on the deliberative values side, we risk managing process for process's sake. Claims of "process fatigue" set in. If we push too far on the performance and efficiency side, we risk jeopardizing the trust-building principles of engagement that make collaborative public management and conflict resolution effective.

Lest one think this is simply a conceptual dilemma, let me illustrate one effort that has brought both sides of the collaboration equation together in a recent national policy statement. On November 28, 2005, Joshua

Bolten, then the director of OMB, and James Connaughton, chairman of the President's Council on Environmental Quality (CEQ), issued a joint ECR policy statement. This statement directs agencies to increase the effective use of ECR and their institutional capacity for collaborative problem solving. It includes a definition of ECR and sets forth "Basic Principles for Agency Engagement in Environmental Conflict Resolution and Collaborative Problem Solving." It also includes a compilation of mechanisms and strategies that may be used to achieve the stated policy objectives.[2]

This policy direction developed from a request in August 2003 by Chairman Connaughton to the USIECR to work with senior staff of key federal departments and agencies to develop basic ECR principles and recommended guidance on ECR. Over the next two years, the USIECR worked collaboratively with representatives of the Departments of Agriculture, Army, Commerce, Defense, Energy, Homeland Security, Interior, Justice, Navy, Transportation; OMB; EPA; the Federal Energy Regulatory Commission; and CEQ to develop basic principles and draft guidance.

A federal agency survey informed these interagency discussions, providing useful information on existing department resources, challenges, and creative approaches for reducing environmental conflicts and improving environmental decision making. CEQ then took the staff recommendations and together with OMB formulated the final policy guidance.

The memorandum requires annual reporting by departments and agencies to OMB and CEQ on progress made each year, periodic leadership meetings, and quarterly interdepartmental senior staff meetings to be facilitated by the USIECR.

This joint memorandum presents an explicit policy commitment to furthering the effective use of ECR and collaborative problem solving throughout the federal government. It also represents a dual commitment to the principles of collaborative practice and to the need to demonstrate performance.

The basic principles for agency engagement were the product of several months of interagency discussion and negotiation. However, they also "draw on over thirty years of collective experience and research on interest-based negotiation, consensus building, collaborative management, and environmental mediation and conflict resolution. These principles provide guidance for preventing and reducing environmental conflicts as well as for "producing more effective and enduring environmental decisions," as stated in section 1 (c) of the OMB-CEQ ECR Policy. The memorandum directs federal agencies to "ensure their effective use of ECR and other forms of collaborative problem solving consistent with the 'Basic Principles of Environmental Conflict Resolution and Collaborative Problem

Solving,' as stated in section 4(a) of the OMB-CEQ ECR Joint Memorandum on Environmental Conflict Resolution (November 28, 2005)":

Informed Commitment
Confirm willingness and availability of appropriate agency leadership and staff at all levels to commit to principles of engagement; ensure commitment to participate in good faith with open mindset to new perspectives

Balanced, Voluntary Representation
Ensure balanced, voluntary inclusion of affected/concerned interests; all parties should be willing and able to participate and select their own representatives

Group Autonomy
Engage with all participants in developing and governing process; including choice of consensus-based decision rules; seek assistance as needed from impartial facilitator/mediator selected by and accountable to all parties

Informed Process
Seek agreement on how to share, test and apply relevant information (scientific, cultural, technical, etc.) among participants; ensure relevant information is accessible and understandable by all participants

Accountability
Participate in process directly, fully, and in good faith; be accountable to the process, all participants and the public

Openness
Ensure all participants and public are fully informed in a timely manner of the purpose and objectives of process; communicate agency authorities, requirements and constraints; uphold confidentiality rules and agreements as required for particular proceedings

Timeliness
Ensure timely decisions and outcomes

Implementation
Ensure decisions are implementable; parties should commit to identify roles and responsibilities necessary to implement agreement;

parties should agree in advance on the consequences of a party being unable to provide necessary resources or implement agreement; ensure parties will take steps to implement and obtain resources necessary to agreement

These principles are consistent with the best practice guidance on public policy dispute resolution developed for federal agencies by the conflict resolution profession (Society of Professionals in Dispute Resolution 1987). Recently, the Environment and Public Policy Section of the Association for Conflict Resolution endorsed them and the ECR policy in letters of support to OMB and CEQ and to its professional membership.

Unsurprisingly, these principles bear a striking resemblance to those called out by researchers on collaborative management and deliberative democracy. For example, Bill Leach's democratic merits of collaborative governance—inclusiveness, representativeness, impartiality, transparency, deliberativeness, lawfulness, and empowerment—can be easily cross-walked with the eight basic principles above (Leach 2006). Likewise, Archon Fung's dimensions of participation that bounded his democracy cube—legitimacy, justice, and effectiveness—are manifest in the eight principles of engagement in ECR and collaborative problem solving (Fung 2006).

These principles are now on record as federal policy, having coalesced from best practices long understood by ECR practitioners, theoretical constructs validated through research, and foundational understandings of senior federal public managers. As such, they can directly shape expectations of future collaborative action and conflict resolution both inside and outside government. They can be used by public managers as they consider the appropriateness of engaging in such processes. They can be upheld by nongovernmental parties to test the government's commitment to following such processes. They can provide a touchstone for negotiating consensus protocols and holding parties to good faith negotiation.

But are they enough? Federal policymakers did not think so. Principled engagement was only part of the equation. The need to demonstrate outcomes and improved performance had to be addressed as well. A problem in environmental governance had been articulated in section 1(a) of the OMB-CEQ ECR Memorandum, and ECR was presented as one way to effectively deal with the challenges of

- protracted and costly environmental litigation;
- unnecessarily lengthy project and resource planning processes;
- costly delays in implementing needed environmental protection measures;

- forgone public and private investments when decisions are not timely or are appealed;
- lower-quality outcomes and lost opportunities when environmental plans and decisions are not informed by all available information and perspectives; and
- deep-seated antagonism and hostility repeatedly reinforced between stakeholders by unattended conflicts.

The interest in accountability and performance is apparent simply from the joint issuance from OMB and CEQ. Though CEQ is the administration's lead environmental policy adviser, OMB is the federal budget overseer. Furthermore, it was understood that departments and agencies would be more likely to increase their use of ECR if they could demonstrate for themselves and report to OMB and CEQ the effectiveness of these processes within their own domains, particularly with respect to cost savings.

The specific performance guidance in the OMB-CEQ memo is stated in section 4(b) of the OMB-CEQ ECR Memorandum: "Given possible savings in improved outcomes and reduced costs of administrative appeals and litigation, agency leadership should recognize and support needed upfront investments in collaborative processes and conflict resolution and demonstrate those savings in performance and accountability measures to maintain a budget neutral environment."

In addition, section 5(a)(4) of the memorandum offers a set of mechanisms and strategies for increasing the effective use of ECR through improving internal capacity. This includes recommendations to focus on accountable performance and achievement through

- periodic progress reports,
- issuing guidance on expected outcomes and resources,
- conducting program evaluation,
- conducting ECR case and project evaluation, and
- responding appropriately to evaluation results to improve the appropriate use of ECR.

No specific performance measures were set forth in the ECR policy. The requirements for the first annual reports from agencies sought general baseline information and encouraged agencies to consider how they might use ECR in the future. An informal interagency discussion group has been meeting to consider if and what to recommend to OMB and CEQ with respect to specific performance metrics that would be useful for all agencies to collect and report on. Their recommendations will be informed by the findings from the first annual reports on fiscal year 2006 activities. Meanwhile, each agency has designated an ECR point of contact at the deputy assistant secretary level. They meet and share information at quarterly ECR forums convened by the USIECR.

Whether the balance struck between ECR principles and performance in the ECR memorandum is the right balance will depend in large part on how federal agencies choose to respond to the policy direction of the ECR memo. For those agencies with long-standing programs in place, this ECR policy provides opportunities to reinforce the value of their work, expand the use of ECR internally, and share their expertise and leadership with other agencies. For those agencies with very few environmental conflicts, the policy requirements may appear unnecessary or burdensome. For those agencies facing environmental controversies and in need of new approaches to ongoing or rising challenges, this policy guidance may prove useful and timely.

CONCLUSION

Applying conflict resolution skills and processes can be viewed as practicing collaboration in the breach—that is, under the most trying of circumstances. Public managers who have been involved in working to reach agreement among diverse, contending interests are learning valuable lessons and skills that can be applied in myriad other and even less challenging settings.

Alternative dispute resolution processes have been institutionalized in many areas of public management, particularly for workplace and procurement conflicts. Despite its longevity, ECR is just beginning to be institutionalized within public agencies. The linkages between practice and performance are becoming better articulated in evaluation frameworks and policy guidance at the federal level.

Surely, the demands on collaborative public management to demonstrate effective practice and generate valued outcomes will be similar to those on ECR as managing through collaborative action becomes more widespread and is subjected to greater scrutiny. In anticipation of these demands, public managers and researchers would do well to focus on the "missing synthesis" that would integrate some of the lessons learned from ECR and the conflict resolution field in general with the developing experience in collaborative public management. The two illustrations in this chapter underscore the importance of making more explicit the linkages between the underlying principles of best practice and performance of ECR and, by extension, of collaborative public management.

NOTES

The views expressed in this chapter are solely those of the author and do not reflect the official position of the U.S. Institute for Environmental Conflict Resolution or of the Morris K. Udall Foundation.

1. The consultants on this evaluation project included David Fairman of the Consensus Building Institute; Bernie Mayer of CDR; Julie MacFarlane and Tomas Miller of the National Research Center, Inc.; Kathy McKnight and Lee Sechrest of Public Interest Research Services, Inc.; and Andy Rowe of GHK International.

2. The OMB-CEQ ECR Policy Memorandum and other background material can be found at http://ecr.gov/ecrpolicy/index.html. The policy memorandum defines ECR as follows: "Under this policy, Environmental Conflict Resolution (ECR) is defined as third-party assisted conflict resolution and collaborative problem solving in the context of environmental, public lands, or natural resources issues or conflicts, including matters related to energy, transportation, and land use. The term 'ECR' encompasses a range of assisted negotiation processes and applications. These processes directly engage affected interests and agency decision makers in conflict resolution and collaborative problem solving. Multi-issue, multi-party environmental disputes or controversies often take place in high conflict and low trust settings, where the assistance of impartial facilitators or mediators can be instrumental to reaching agreement and resolution. Such disputes range broadly from administrative adjudicatory disputes, to civil judicial disputes, policy/rule disputes, intra- and interagency disputes, as well as disputes with non-federal persons/entities. ECR processes can be applied during a policy development or planning process, or in the context of rulemaking, administrative decision making, enforcement, or litigation and can include conflicts between federal, state, local, tribal, public interest organizations, citizens groups and business and industry where a federal agency has ultimate responsibility for decision-making. While ECR refers specifically to collaborative processes aided by third-party neutrals, there is a broad array of partnerships, cooperative arrangements, and unassisted negotiations that federal agencies enter into with non-federal entities to manage and implement agency programs and activities. The Basic Principles for Agency Engagement in Environmental Conflict Resolution and Collaborative Problem Solving presented in Attachment A and this policy apply generally to ECR and collaborative problem solving. This policy recognizes the importance and value of the appropriate use of all types of ADR and collaborative problem solving" (section 2, OMB-CEQ ECR Memorandum).

Chapter 13

A Public Administration Education for the Third-Party Governance Era: Reclaiming Leadership of the Field

Paul L. Posner

The publication of this volume reflects a historic shift in the practice of public administration. Public administrators have been pressed to, in effect, create new models of public action that differ markedly from the organizational and bureaucratic models that have characterized traditional public administration. Governments at all levels have been called upon in the past half century to expand their roles in the social and economic life of the nation. These roles go well beyond their own capacities, resources, and legitimacy. Accordingly, policymakers and agencies have adopted a wide range of tools that distribute responsibility and authority for financing and results across a variety of independent third parties, including state and local governments, nonprofits, and private companies. To leverage the participation and compliance of these sovereign "partners," the modern government program now relies on indirect governance tools, such as grants, contracts, credit, insurance, and regulations. The model of a hierarchical organization that controls the policy formulation, financing, and implementation of programs has largely been cast aside in the last half century of governmental change. Various forms of collaboration across governmental and sectoral boundaries increasingly define the practice of public administration.

The emergence of third-party governance as a primary strategy for achieving public objectives has tested the skills and knowledge of public administrators with new challenges in policy development and implementation. The new environment for public programs is more complex and uncertain—and less predictable and controllable—than ever before. Future practitioners will sorely need improved guidance and training, which can best be provided in our schools of public administration. These programs will have to offer curricula to help students understand the increasingly challenging public management environment they are encountering in the many sectors where public administration is, in fact, practiced.

THE EMERGENCE OF THIRD-PARTY GOVERNMENT

The public sector at all levels in our system has increasingly come to rely on a wide and diverse range of third parties to develop, design, and implement public programs. As Lester Salamon (2002) has noted, most of the federal budget is devoted to funding programs and operations featuring a critical role for third parties—states, local governments, private contractors, nonprofits, and other entities. Indeed, it is difficult to find many major federal mission areas that do not rely heavily on third parties for program delivery and even goal definition. Even the function of defending the nation's borders has become a matter dependent on other actors beyond the Pentagon, whether it be defense contractors, local fire departments, or other first responders, which have become the line of first defense in the event of a terrorist attack.

Similar trends are present at the state and local levels as well. Contracting accounts for nearly 20 percent of state budgets (Bartle and Korisec 2000). At the local level, leaders are realizing how reliant they are on other sectors to meet public goals and expectations. For instance, protecting the critical infrastructure in cities from a variety of human-made or natural threats often calls for collaborations with private owners of such assets as rail yards, port facilities, and chemical plants (Kamarck 2004). Mayors and other local leaders find themselves increasingly reaching for a wide range of financing and governance tools—tax credits, leasing arrangements, and regulatory controls—to engage these networks in new partnerships and alliances.

As the performance movement gains influence across all levels of government, the focus on outcomes lends itself to multisectoral, third-party governance strategies. Whether it is achieving environmental, public health, or transportation goals, achieving these broader societal objectives requires cooperation and resources that are difficult to contain or capture within conventional governmental boundaries. Thus, restoring the Chesapeake Bay has prompted the establishment of a multistate commission, which is supported by an executive council and committees comprising representatives from surrounding states, more than ten federal agencies, regional planning organizations, environmental nonprofit groups, academic institutions, and citizens' groups.[1]

Traditional government hierarchical organizations obviously still remain relevant, but their ability to achieve their missions is being tested as they must find ways to achieve their goals in the shadow of networks. As the boundaries between organizations increasingly blur, even traditional agencies have had to become more open, interactive, and "conductive" to develop the capacity to function in networked environments with other sectors and organizations. Networks, too, have been challenged to achieve the advantages of collaboration, while leveraging the authority, expertise, and resources of hierarchies. As Agranoff (2007) suggests, networks themselves rarely have independent authority and resources; rather, they must work to leverage, activate, integrate, and facilitate the contributions of independent organizations, both public and private.

PRACTITIONERS NEED HELP

Third-party governance provides important advantages to public managers at all levels. Third parties can help to enhance the legitimacy of government, share the costs, provide critical skills and authority not available to governments, and help adapt programs to unique local conditions and needs. However, this emerging approach to governance also complicates the projection of public goals and raises unique accountability challenges. A greater range of actors is invited and empowered to share in the process of determining program goals and delivery, with far less certain results than might be obtained through traditional hierarchies. The disconnects between smart policy proposals hatched inside government and the results achieved years later are greater, particularly if we fail to understand this more demanding and complex public management environment. O'Toole (2000) succinctly sums up the problems facing public officials by noting that third-party networks offer more opportunities for free riding and free wheeling. It may be no coincidence that the period of growing public-sector reliance on third parties coincided with a broad, sweeping indictment of the capacity of government to deliver on those expectations.

Achieving accountability in these relationships is particularly challenging. Though promoting accountability for complex government programs is rarely straightforward, the issues and dilemmas are even more daunting for programs relying on networks using third-party tools. Agencies that deliver services directly with their own employees have certain accountability advantages; transactions are internalized within hierarchies that are more cohesive and responsive to central leadership (Lehman 1989). Obvious challenges are presented when government must use independent actors it does not fully control to achieve its goals, especially because, as Don Kettl (1988b) has noted, transferring *who* does the work does *not* relieve the federal government of the responsibility for performance.

The greater complexity faced by public administrators is depicted in figure 13.1. The traditional world of direct government provision was able to focus on the right dimension of the figure, because the management environment of the government agency was the principal factor responsible for determining the results of government programs. The agency itself, whether the Forest Service or the Department of Veterans Affairs, controlled the funding, the rules, and the employees responsible for achieving the goals of these organizations. However, in the world of third-party governance, the management of agencies is but one of several important factors influencing results. As figure 13.1 indicates, achieving goals in third-party environments requires a concentration on the selection and design of the tool, as well as on the nature of the third-party network used to implement the program. In many respects, these dimensions have a greater bearing on the results of such programs as Medicaid and even homeland security than do

Figure 13.1. The Three Faces of Governance

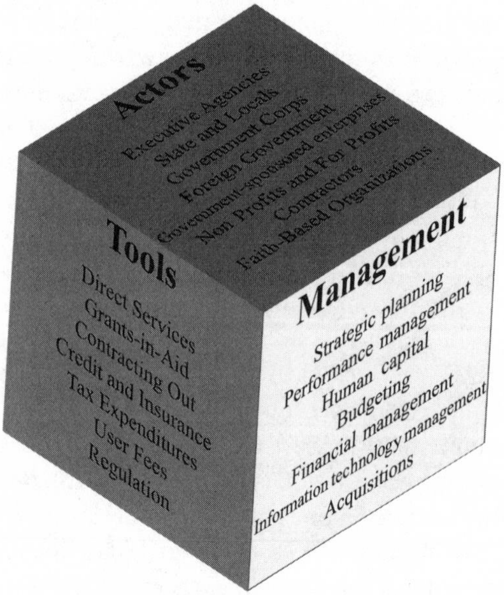

Source: U.S. Government Accountability Office

the internal workings of the federal agencies themselves. Even agencies commonly thought of as relying on traditional hierarchies, such as the Internal Revenue Service (IRS), have become increasingly dependent on third parties to achieve their goals. The IRS, for instance, has recently contracted out the collection of a portion of delinquent tax debt and it fundamentally depends on other sectors, such as employers and banks, to accurately report on wages, interest, and other items of taxpayer income or deductions.

Moreover, as these third-party tools become more indirect, their design and management become more complex and variable. The shift from bureaucracies, with their focus on command and control, to contracting arguably calls for greater sophistication in negotiating and bargaining with increasingly diverse and less-well-understood for-profit and nonprofit organizations in the private sector (Cooper 2003). However, for other tools, the opportunity to influence program implementation through face-to-face interaction with third-party providers shrinks. Tax expenditures, for example, are not managed in the traditional sense, except in the rather infrequent cases when the IRS examines the claim in an audit. Instead of transactional reviews, the most important leverage that public managers have over these kinds of tools is in the choice and design of the tool at the outset. Relatively obscure features of policy design, such as risk sharing for loan guarantees and matching funds for grants, will have an important bearing on the kind of management involvement that banks or state and local governments will have in these programs. The eligibility formulas used for tax expenditures become an important determinant of how to target this government subsidy to various kinds of claimants. Each tool has its own political economy—with packages of incentives, sanctions, and third-party opportunities—that will substantially sway the program's outcome.

INTERFACING THIRD-PARTY TOOLS AND NETWORKS

Public policy analysts and managers increasingly need to understand third-party tools and how they interact with various implementation settings. This emerging and elusive skill set will be needed to broker intelligent interventions to address complex problems. Among the other important requisites for designing effective programs, then, are the understanding of the differential properties of various tools and the design options available in tailoring them to specific circumstances. However, knowledge of the implementation networks likely to be engaged in program implementation is of equal or greater importance.

The networks with which public agencies work have become increasingly diverse and less traditional as third-party tools have become ever more indirect. Thus, government agencies have become reliant not just on other public agencies but also on such actors as banks, insurance companies, and private developers to become latter-day "street level" bureaucrats responsible for the delivery of such programs as guaranteed student loans, flood insurance, and low-income housing.

This calls for a level of understanding of complex networks that is often elusive to public officials and full of misconceptions. Federal grant programs are typically delivered through long implementation chains that are often difficult to understand, let alone influence. For example, child care block grants provided to states are often subsequently subgranted to counties. The counties, in turn, often contract directly with private providers for actual services, as well as issue vouchers directly to families to purchase child care services (Posner et al. 2000). Accountability can become diffused and confused in such an environment, which really constitutes fourth- or fifth-party governance. Moreover, a rich environment of collateral tools and programs at federal, state, local, and nongovernmental levels influences the performance of any one program. Whether it is child care, early childhood education, or substance abuse, most major domestic problems have numerous federal, state, and local programs and tools directed at them with little evidence of coordination or rationalization (U.S. General Accounting Office 1997). The coordination that does occur takes place more from below than above, as local governments and providers struggle to assemble services from the diverse array of funding instruments available—with not only the wide range of grants but also loans and tax expenditures in many areas.

The membership, decision rules, and values of these networks need to be understood by public administrators if they are to gain their cooperation in developing and implementing public policy. As Robert Stoker (1991) suggests, public programs work through implementation regimes featuring actors with mixed motives that have incentives to both cooperate and defect from new public policy initiatives. Public administrators must learn to understand the values and interests of network actors and how to influence their incentives for collective action through collaborative policy development processes and the intelligent design of policy tools and institutions.

Network theory has come into some prominence as a framework to help define the partnership relationships characteristic of third-party governance. Instead of a governmental steering model, policy networks spanning organizational, governmental and public/private boundaries are viewed as the drivers of public goal setting and implementation. In this view, the ex ante goals or policies of one of the participants—that is, government—is not the sole yardstick for accountability. The criteria for assessing networks rest less on an ability to deliver specific outcomes and more on how networks encourage the formation and sustainability of positive interactions across the multiple players sharing the network. Criteria for network management include creating win–win situations that make nonparticipation less attractive, limiting interaction costs, promoting transparency, and securing a commitment to joint undertakings. In this literature, the government's role is not to impose unilateral goals—these would not be effective if they were perceived as being illegitimate by networks. Rather, its role is to work with networks to define goals and to gain cooperation for full implementation. It is acknowledged that government can also serve as a network manager and facilitator, creating or sustaining the conditions for full and open participation (Kickert et al. 1997b).

Network theory provides significant insights about the conditions for legitimate public action. It usefully suggests that policy networks of like-minded actors are a meaningful unit of analysis. It also reminds us that effective and workable networks are not an act of nature but require sustenance and nurturing by network participants and government alike. Nonetheless, network theory has limitations in speaking to the unique accountability issues facing federal policymakers and bureaucrats. Networks can become self-referential and not fully useful to pursue broader public goals that either transcend their boundaries or encompass other interests not represented in the network. Constraining governments to act solely within the boundaries of established networks needlessly limits the scope of public policy to those actions endorsed by what might become highly insular and insulated networks (Linder and Peters 1987).

The interface between governmental tools and networks is an underdeveloped area of research and systematic understanding. Tensions often exist between governmental goals and the tools used by government and the values and practices of networks relied upon to implement programs. The implementation literature tells us that networks are not malleable entities but rather independent communities that often bend and reshape tools to fit their own unique priorities and administrative realities.

Government can and does intervene in various ways to change and shift these networks, but in variable ways that reflect both the differential nature of federal goals and the congruence of network values with those goals. One possible taxonomy of the government–network interface might consist of the following:

- Cooptation and reframing of existing networks—many grant programs are consigned to work within the boundaries of existing networks of state or local providers, with the goal of shifting their priorities through grants and mandates. In one case, by establishing new mandates for the security of drivers' licenses, the 2005 Real ID mandate constitutes an effort to reframe the focus and priorities of state motor vehicle departments from driver safety to homeland security.

- Capture by existing networks—many regulatory and grant programs are effectively captured by existing networks that succeed in reclaiming federal tools to support existing priorities and practices. The finding that federal grants inspire a high level of fiscal substation by state and local governments is a reflection of the successful capture and reprioritization of federal grants (U.S. General Accounting Office 1996).

- Fragmentation of existing networks—many federal tools compartmentalize programs that inspire the multiplication of networks at the local level, leading to major coordination problems for such services as job training.

- Creation of new networks—the Head Start program is but one example where government grants can be used to stimulate the creation of entirely new provider networks to supplement or bypass established networks.

- Undermining existing networks—some federal tools, like vouchers, are intended to challenge and undermine existing provider networks.

As this suggests, the relationships between governmental tools and networks is anything but straightforward. The specific nature of the government–network interface may well be shaped by intentional governmental decisions about the relative authority and influence that networks will be permitted to have in the design and management of governmental tools.

The nature of these relationships will be partly driven by the policy design and governmental role underlying the choice and design of the tool itself. Centralizing tools are likely to strike a more demanding posture for networks, whereas devolutionary tools are likely to be more accommodating to the existing priorities and governance structures in current networks dominating programmatic areas. The governmental role vis-à-vis networks can be conceptualized in three models, as depicted in table 13.1. Different policy tools are needed for more centralized governmental roles in dealing with networks, compared with more decentralized and devolved governmental roles.

Table 13.1 Differential Government–Network Strategies

Aspect	Central Strategy	Partner Strategy	Devolved Strategy
Goals	Federal	Bargained	Third party
Role/third party	Agent	Collaborators	Independent
Tool example	Contract	Categorical grant	Block grant
Provider selection	Competition	Formula	Formula
Oversight	Ex ante	Ex post with federal review	Ex post with delegation to third party

THE KNOWLEDGE, SKILLS, AND CAPACITY NEEDED

As the foregoing suggests, managing within networks and across government–network boundaries is among the most challenging, albeit ill-defined, tasks facing public administration practitioners. Defining the skill sets for the emerging world of third-party governance and collaborative management is a major task ahead for public administration. As Agranoff and McGuire (2003a) conclude, public administration needs a knowledge base on collaborative management that is equivalent to the established literature and research consensus associated with the field of managing through hierarchical organizations.

Many observers conclude that managing in third-party environments place a premium on new kinds of skills for public administrators (Agranoff and McGuire 2003a; Bardach 1998; Cooper 2003; Goldsmith and Eggers 2004; Kettl 2002; Salamon 2002; Stoker 1991). Though trained for the control environments of hierarchical organizations, public managers working in third-party governance environments increasingly confront a world where a premium is placed on other skills and capacities, including the following:

- Activating disparate actors to come together to join in shared governance arrangements, designing and deploying appropriate mixes of governmental tools and other incentives to gain participation and agreement.
- Negotiating and bargaining with independent actors, each with leverage to empower joint enterprise or to undermine it through withholding critical resources.
- Understanding the unique incentives to cooperate in networks of policy actors whose participation is vital to outcomes.
- Providing and communicating compelling goals and measured outcomes to motivate diverse actors to work toward common purposes.

- Building social capital and establishing trust to sustain the capacity of networks to work collaboratively.
- Developing "soft" leadership skills to help steer disparate interests toward consensus-based solutions.
- Establishing policy learning institutions rich in information and feedback mechanisms to improve the steering capacities of loosely connected networks.

Some observers emphasize certain skills as being of particular importance. Goldsmith and Eggers (2004) discuss the critical role played by risk analysis, stressing the importance of ensuring that all parties to a collaborative venture share risks appropriately to avoid exploitative behavior. They also emphasize, along with Kettl (2002) and others, the importance of gaining a deep understanding of the various partners in third-party settings. This means that government procurement officers and program staff alike must understand the capacities and limitations of the private sector before entering into public–private partnerships and contract arrangements—an understanding that, as will be noted below, is not often promoted in graduate public administration programs.

The frustrating experience in recent years with public–private partnerships illustrates the challenges involved in building constructive partnerships between public infrastructure agencies and private businesses with differing goals, incentives, and interests. Though such partnerships ideally can offer significant new support and financing for public objectives for cash-starved governments, in practice Bloomfield (2006) and others note that such arrangements often saddle taxpayers with high-risk, costly obligations for years to come. The classic requisites of effective public–private accountability were often not in place within local governments initiating these complex partnerships, including effective competition, specific performance targets, and transparent accountability practices. Few local governments had the requisite expertise to structure and monitor the long-term contracts that are often involved with infrastructure investments. The estimates of financial savings that often lure governments into arrangements with private firms were often overstated, while the long-term financial risks to governments were understated. The real conflicts of long-term interests and values between public agencies and private businesses threaten the broad promises and language of partnerships that cloak these agreements at the outset.

Leading public managers at the federal, state, and local levels face the prospect of creating incentives and other mechanisms to engage businesses, even though they have no formal exposure to business finance, accounting, or accountability in public administration programs. Agency leaders report that their managers are at a distinct disadvantage, whether it be in administering the corporate income tax or building public–private financial partnerships for infrastructure, because their managers lack a sophisticated understanding of business economies. Private corporate managers may face similar disadvantages if they lack exposure to public budgeting and management accountability.

Public administrators still are facing the fundamental challenge posed by Edward Hamilton (1978, 123) over thirty years ago, when third-party governance was on the emerging frontier of government reform: "We do not know how best to maximize the quantity and quality of governmental product when the point of finance is split and often two or even three levels removed from the point of final output."

FOCUS OF GRADUATE PUBLIC ADMINISTRATION PROGRAMS

Although promising frameworks are emerging to supplement or transcend the traditional focus on hierarchies and public organizations, public administration schools and programs will be challenged to respond to the shifting governance environment of the contemporary practice in the field. These schools and programs must prepare students for this emerging world of governance and enable them to acquire the capacity to become effective designers and managers in third-party governance settings. The nation's ability to make effective adaptations to these more challenging governance settings will in no small part rest on the ability of its academic programs to both prepare students to become effective managers and establish the basis of research to better understand how to achieve public value with diverse governance arrangements.

The adjustment of academic programs to third-party governance is beginning at many institutions, but there is much to do to reorient graduate programs in public administration. The curricula offered by many of the nation's leading graduate public administration programs have traditionally focused on helping students understand and manage large public agencies. The guidance on curricula published by the National Association of Schools of Public Affairs and Administration reflects this orientation. Although this association is careful to say that it does not prescribe specific courses, the common curriculum components contained in its guidance reflect the overall approach taken by most programs, as shown in table 13.2.

To examine the content of specific master of public administration (MPA) programs, I inventoried the core course requirements for nine highest-ranked public management programs in the *U.S. News & World*

Table 13.2 National Association of Schools of Public Affairs and Administration Common Curriculum Components

---

Management of public service organizations
    Human resources
    Budgeting and financial processes
    Information technology, technology applications, and policy
Application of quantitative and qualitative techniques of analysis
    Policy and program formulation, implementation, and evaluation
    Decision making and problem solving
Understanding of the public policy and organizational environment
    Political and legal institutions and processes
    Economic and social institutions and processes
    Organization and management concepts and behavior

Report 2004 survey of public affairs programs.[2] The programs covered generally offer an MPA. Table 13.3 displays the core requirements of these leading public administration programs.

Table 13.3 shows that leading MPA programs provide a rich base of analytic skills—nearly every program provides exposure to statistical analysis and microeconomics. The table also shows courses on organizational theory in most programs. Although organizational theory can accommodate a variety of perspectives, including newer network and tool-based approaches, traditional textbooks in the field focus on the management of large organizations. One popular textbook concentrates for the most part on the study of public organizations, with chapters on organizational goals, decision making, structure, human resources, leadership, organizational culture, teamwork, and organizational change and development (Rainey 2003). One recent survey of textbooks found that the trends toward third-party governance and growing reliance on more indirect tools are largely absent (Cigler 2000).

Other core and elective courses cover important dimensions of management in large organizations. Courses on finance and budgeting, required in most of these programs, provide students with a deeper understanding of how governments as a whole and agencies in particular formulate and execute budgets and how they measure their costs. These are essential skills for understanding and managing in traditional organizational contexts. The human resource management courses required in several programs strengthen students' knowledge of the issues associated with managing people in organizations. Electives in these programs expand the organizational focus to cover information technology, leadership,

Table 13.3 Core Courses in Top-Ranked Public Management Programs

University Party	Introductory	Organization Theory	Ethics	Finance	Human Resources	Policy Process	Economics	Statistics	Law	Third Party
Syracuse	x	x		x		x	x	x		
Georgia	x	x	x	x	x		x	x		
Indiana	x			x			x	x	x	
University of Southern California	x	x	x	x	x		x	x	x	x
State University of New York at Albany	x	x		x			x	x		
University of Kansas	x	x		x	x	x		x	x	
American University	x			x		x	x	x	x	
New York University	x			x		x	x	x		
University of Texas LBJ School		x		x		x	x	x		

Note: This table is based on program requirements listed on university websites, organized by the standard categories in the table. It does not include capstone or policy research courses, which count toward the core in several programs. The table also does not include Harvard University's John F. Kennedy School, which has no core courses for its full two-year master of public administration program. The table does not reflect the University of Georgia's core course on communications or American University's core course on leadership.

organizational change, and other important dimensions of public management in an organizational setting.

Notably, table 13.3 shows that only one leading public administration program—the University of Southern California's program on cross-sectoral governance—has a core course explicitly addressing managing across sectors and institutions. This formal analysis of curriculum may miss informal adaptations by individual faculty to third-party and collaborative governance trends. Indeed, a look at the syllabi for selected introductory and organizational theory courses does indicate some treatment of third-party governance.[3] Some courses are using Salamon's (2002) book *The Tools of Government* as a text in organization theory courses. Though representing an informal response to these trends, there is nonetheless little recognition in formal curricula of the unique challenges and skills needed to manage public programs in collaborative, third-party governance settings.

Consider the following experiences a student would encounter if he or she wished to gain an understanding of leading third-party tools and governance settings:

- *Contracting* is often not covered in public administration programs. Perhaps the student could turn to the business school to gain some perspective of private corporations on public–private partnerships, but public administration course offerings are not providing the overview for public managers challenged to work in these partnerships.
- *Grant design and management* are covered to some extent in intergovernmental management courses, although there is often no dedicated course addressing the important issues associated with grant allocation, fiscal design, and accountability.
- *Regulation* would most likely be included in law school curricula, covering administrative procedures associated with regulation. Public administration programs have very little direct coverage of the important design issues associated with creating and managing different models of regulations, preemptions, and other forms of governmental coercion on private or public sectors.
- *Tax expenditures* are a critical part of federal policy. It is impossible to comprehend such issues as low-income housing or higher education subsidization without understanding the growing role played by tax subsidies in achieving public objectives. However, a student wanting to become familiar with the design and administration of tax expenditures to achieve public goals would be hard-

pressed to find any course that explicitly addressed these anywhere in the university.

- *Financial market intermediation*—the growing use of loans, guarantees, and insurance in achieving public goals—is also largely not covered in MPA programs. A student might be advised to look at business schools to understand financial markets in general but would be stymied in seeking courses that address these important tools.
- *Public–private partnerships* are being used by many states and localities, and some federal agencies, as new ways to partner with the private sector in financing public services and infrastructure. Public budgeting and finance courses can provide insights into public finance issues, but students are not gaining exposure through these courses to the rules, incentives, and constraints associated with various kinds of private financing alternatives.

Enterprising students may very well be able to cobble together an educational program including third-party governance challenges and institutional responses. For example, many public administration programs offer extensive courses on the nonprofit sector that can be valuable for students wishing to be exposed to these increasingly critical actors and their networks. Students may seek exposure to private finance incentives through courses on corporate finance and accounting in business schools. Students can gain exposure to the institutions and incentives facing each level of government in our system through courses in our public administration and policy programs. However, for the most part, universities have not yet developed a synthesis that draws together an integrated curriculum focusing on third-party governance relationships.

AN AGENDA FOR CHANGE

How should the courses and skills we teach in public administration programs shift to accommodate and, indeed, guide the evolving world of practice? Students will need to be provided with new understandings and skills in at least the following areas:

- Acquiring a realistic understanding of the various roles played by different sectors in major areas of the public policy endeavor. Understanding governmental processes and structures will always be central. Students will also have to gain a working knowledge of other sectors that have become important players in the delivery of public programs, including nonprofits, for-profit corporations, partnerships, government-sponsored enterprises, and other kinds of entities engaged in the emerging public service field.

- Understanding nonbureaucratic models such as networks, public–private partnerships, performance partnerships, and other kinds of cooperative institutional arrangements to achieve public goals in diverse settings.

- Gaining a working knowledge of the major tools of government used by all levels of government, including an understanding of the major design options and their consequences for each tool. Policy design is the only opportunity government will have to influence the outcomes achieved from such indirect tools as tax expenditures and certain kinds of vouchers.

- Obtaining the skills necessary to negotiate with other sectors and networks, performance metrics, financial incentives, and other features of third-party arrangements.

Although public administration programs will have to take the lead, they will face the formidable task of bringing together the various areas of expertise that are relevant to modern governance from across the many different schools and departments on most large campuses. As Agranoff and McGuire (2003a) note, various theories and frameworks from many disciplines provide important perspectives on collaboration and third-party governance. Such frameworks certainly include important areas of inquiry within public administration itself, including implementation analysis and network theory.

Other disciplines have useful frameworks that can provide insight. Economics, to name one, has contributed to the study of complex public policy delivery through pioneering contributions from microeconomics. Principal–agent theory provides a heuristic concept that helped chart some of the dilemmas of third-party governance (Pratt and Zeckhauser 1991). Notwithstanding the apparent dominance of principals, agents have critical leverage to influence these relationships, owing to their monopolies over information and access to services and clients. Far from sharing goals with principals, agents are opportunistic and independent actors that will shirk their contractual responsibilities when it is cost-effective for them to do so, with untold effects on program goals. As such, these concepts do presage the accountability dilemmas faced in third-party governance environments and they do suggest appropriate units of analysis for conceptualizing the risks in these relationships. However, these concepts still are unproven for many third-party settings beyond those of simple contracts, which form the model for these concepts. For instance, multiple principals define expectations for agents delivering public services for many larger programs, such as grants or regulations. Accountability does not simply flow from multiple agents to a single principal; rather, each agent, such as a state or a nonprofit, must answer to multiple principals, including its own boards, legislatures, advisory groups, and citizenry.

Bridging the heretofore-separate worlds of public and private administration and management is also an important part of the academic challenge. In this regard, insights from business programs about the managerial environment and incentives facing business when approaching public ventures will prove important to deepening our understanding of public governance challenges.

ONE MODEL FOR CURRICULUM REFORM

What models exist to help public administration programs retool their course offerings to address third-party governance trends? The following discussion is based on changes now under way at George Mason University's MPA program. Because George Mason is in the Washington region, its students are mostly practitioners employed by all levels of government, as well as by nonprofit and for-profit organizations. Many of these students report that they are being challenged to work with tools and sectors that are not covered by conventional theories of organization or traditional courses. Employers similarly have asked the university to fill gaps in understanding and skills in collaborative management. Senior leaders in local government in Northern Virginia have suggested that their own managers need better training in understanding and negotiating with private firms to strengthen public accountability for public–private partnerships.

These steps represent one model for developing a focus on third-party governance:[4]

- Create a core course on third-party governance that addresses trends in the distribution of public authority and consequences for public policy and management. This course introduces students to overall trends in the distribution of authority in the U.S. system, as well as to models and literatures providing overviews of the challenges posed by third-party governance for public policy development and implementation. The course draws extensively on the tools of government literature, as well as network theory and contributions from related fields such as principal–agent theories.
- Redesign the organizational theory core course with more focus on networks and other more decentralized models of public action.

Though not abandoning the traditional focus on organizational design and structure, this course broadens the focus to more explicitly address theories of interorganizational relationships such as vertical and horizontal networks, as well as other models for collaborative governance.

- Institute a managerial economics course that exposes students to concepts underscoring the challenges associated with creating incentives and overseeing third parties, including the literatures on principal–agent relationships and moral hazard.
- Offer specific courses on key governmental tools used in third-party governance, including separate courses on contracting, grant design and management, regulation, and financial market intermediation. A course on intergovernmental management focuses on the key issues associated with managing across levels of government through a variety of tools, including grants, mandates, technical assistance, and intergovernmental agreements and compacts.
- Add a compact course on the revenue side of government to supplement traditional budgeting courses, with a focus on both tax policy and tax expenditures. Public administration programs rarely treat the revenue side of government with the same attention and emphasis as the spending side, notwithstanding the blurring of lines between revenue and spending tools and issues.
- Create a capstone course in which students are required to use tools and third network frameworks to assess significant third-party government policy and management issues involving the intersection of multiple tools and sectors. Fertile areas that are rich for assessing these issues include low-income housing, higher education assistance, and critical infrastructure protection. Each of these areas involves multiple governmental and private-sector actors engaged through many programs and governance tools.

In recognition of the cross-sectoral nature of governance, MPA programs ideally should engage in partnerships with other schools across the campus, most notably with the business school. Joint MPA–master of business administration degrees, such as the one at the University of Texas at Austin, are examples of a dual-degree program that trains students to be conversant and literate in both the public and private sectors.

This model represents one approach to synchronizing public administration graduate education with modern governance trends. The relative emphasis will vary, based on the student population and environment of each school. Thus, a program in the Washington area would focus more on the governmental tools deployed by federal agencies, but a program in another area of the country might well emphasize collaborative governance issues faced at the local level. And a program focusing on state governance might strike an entirely different balance in its course offerings.

Curriculum reform is not the only task on the agenda. Course materials need to be enhanced to enrich the teaching about tools and third-party networks. Documented case studies can help students gain a better understanding of how public officials currently wrestle with third-party governance issues in different programmatic areas. Ideally, such cases would illustrate how various aspects of structure and administrative behavior by all parties can influence outcomes either favorably or unfavorably. Though some case study series, such as the Electronic Hallways series, do include third-party governance cases, more needs to be done to illustrate the issues across different policy areas.[5]

More broadly, case studies need to be grouped to stimulate and support the development of new frameworks defining the interaction between government and networks. The research agenda involves nothing less than developing frameworks and taxonomies that systematically relate governmental actions to the diverse public and private actors that are instrumental for public outcomes. Students and practitioners alike will gain immeasurably from analytic models that enable them to locate their actual policy and administrative experiences in some kind of conceptual space.

In this regard, a deeper literature on the governmental toolbox needs to be promoted. Although the literature on contracting and public–private partnerships has been enhanced in recent years (Cooper 2003; Donahue and Nye 2002; Rosenau 2000; Savas 2000), the literature on other tools remains either underdeveloped or out of date. The literature on credit, tax expenditures, and government-sponsored enterprises has always been sparse. The literature on grants and regulation has been far more fertile, but serious updating is in order. The grant design and implementation literature has atrophied in the past twenty-five years, reflecting such factors as the abolition of the Advisory Commission on Intergovernmental Relations and the ideological divide that has encroached on most of these decisions in recent years.

This literature will be of great service to a revitalized academic enterprise focused on third-party governance and tools. However, it should also be of high value to public officials, particularly to those who serve as staff in agencies, budget offices, and legislatures. They wrestle with tool selection and design trade-offs, often without referring to it in those terms. One major step to address the needs of the practitioner community would be to generate a series of workbooks and primers. Distilling the best of the literature from theory and practice, such publications would crystallize institutional knowledge in the academic and policy communities into a single readable volume that would be readily accessible by hard-pressed public officials. Given the central role played by the design of policy tools, such workbooks and primers will be the functional equivalent of management textbooks for managers in the contemporary environment.

Some new initiatives to address these issues are, in fact, under way. Programs such as that at the University of Southern California and George Mason have introduced third-party governance courses as part of the core required for their master's degree. One promising new initiative is the Cross-Sector Governance Consortium between the universities of Arizona, Washington, and Southern California. This partnership is dedicated to promoting curriculum reform, new research, and training opportunities for public managers in the area of cross-sectoral collaborations and networks (Eller College of Management 2006). A group within the National Academy of Public Administration has been meeting to move forward with new texts, case studies, and practitioner support and training to enhance the collective capacity to manage within third-party governance settings.[6]

Ultimately, theory in the field of public administration needs to be rejoined with practice. Don Kettl (2002, 17) captures the fundamental dilemma facing those in the field when he says that "public administration without a guiding theory is risky; administrative theory without a connection to action is meaningless." A public administration profession that has public service as a core value must heed this call. A profession that speaks to the needs of public officials stands a chance of not only becoming more relevant to the world of practice but also repositioning itself to once again lead with timely, relevant, and compelling concepts and research.

Recent developments offer some encouragement. A more robust academic literature on collaboration and third-party governance is being developed. Moreover, there is a growing awareness in both the academic and practitioners' communities of the daunting challenges posed by the new governance models. Public administration programs should capitalize on these developments to recast their curricula to more directly and explicitly address these challenges in their courses and pedagogy. In doing so, academic programs themselves will have to become more collaborative within universities to fully reflect the important intellectual disciplines and sectoral studies whose contributions are essential to fully understanding the complex governance challenges facing the U.S. system.

NOTES

1. The Chesapeake Bay Project is at www.chesapeakebay.net/info/overview.cfm.

2. The top ten schools were reviewed, but Harvard University's John F. Kennedy School had no core requirements for their two-year MPA program.

3. These were course syllabi reviewed for selected courses at George Mason and Indiana University public administration programs.

4. Some of these changes, such as the core course and tools-related courses, have now been incorporated into George Mason's curriculum, while others represent future changes that are in the proposal stage.

5. See Daniel J. Evans, "The Electronic Hallway," School of Public Affairs, University of Washington, available at www.hallway.org.

6. The National Academy of Public Administration group includes Lester Salamon, Thomas Stanton, Jonathan Breul, Sallyanne Payton, and this author.

Chapter 14

Surprising Findings, Paradoxes, and Thoughts on the Future of Collaborative Public Management Research

Rosemary O'Leary and Lisa Blomgren Bingham

In this chapter, we review a number of surprising findings our contributors have made in their studies of public managers in collaboration. These findings, and the work that supports them, lead us to identify a number of dimensions along which collaboration paradoxically leads to conflict. We briefly review a framework for addressing this conflict in collaborative networks. Then we close with a call for building on the contributions of this book by engaging in assessment and evaluation of the work of collaborative public managers across the policy continuum, from upstream in policy development to midstream in its implementation and downstream in policy enforcement. Within this call, we include evaluating how well collaborative networks manage conflict; this is a core component of collaboration.

As the authors of the chapters in this book demonstrate, public managers who work collaboratively find themselves not solely as unitary leaders of unitary organizations. Instead, they often find themselves facilitating and operating in multiorganizational arrangements to solve problems that cannot be solved, or solved easily, by single organizations. Collaborative public management may include participatory governance: the active involvement of citizens in government decision making.

The review of the literature in chapter 1 emphasizes that collaborative public management is not new a new phenomenon. In chapter 12, Emerson revisits this point, emphasizing that collaboration as a process is rooted in two competing political traditions: classic liberalism and civic republicanism. Classic liberalism, Emerson writes, with its emphasis on private interest, views collaboration as a process that aggregates private preferences into collective choices through self-interested bargaining. Organizations enter into collaborative agreements to achieve their own goals, negotiating among competing interests and brokering coalitions among competing value systems, expectations, and self-interested motivations. Conversely, civic republicanism, according to Emerson, with its emphasis on a commitment to something larger than the individual (whether that be a neighborhood or the state), views collaboration as an integrative process that treats differences as the basis for deliberation in order to assist at "mutual understanding, a collective will, trust and sympathy [and the] implementation of shared preferences" (March and Olsen 1989, 126, as quoted by Thomson and Perry 2006, 20). These two competing themes can be found throughout this book and account for some of the schism in how public management scholars study collaboration.

The review of the literature in chapter 1 also emphasizes that whatever the motivation behind collaboration, there is no one best way to organize for collaboration and that the most studied factors involved in collaboration include structural and motivational dimensions, the nature of shared goals, the degree of risk or reward, the degree of involvement, the extent of interpersonal trust, shared norms, the quality and amount of shared resources, and the presence of formal agreements. The authors of the chapters in this volume build on these factors and at the same time yield numerous surprising findings.

In chapter 8, the first surprising finding by Van Slyke is that public agencies contract with nonprofit agencies in part because of the perceived legitimacy of the nonprofit organization. Tied in with this, approximately 75 percent of the public managers in Van Slyke's study perceived nonprofit organizations as having higher levels of public trust than their own agencies. Next, public agencies report the perception that nonprofits can better think "out of the box" and have stronger creative capacity. Also, public agencies contract with nonprofit agencies in part because nonprofits are not subject to the same media scrutiny as government, especially as it relates to failure.

According to Van Slyke, collaboration between public and nonprofit organizations evolves in tandem with trust. In other words, he hypothesizes that trust is an antecedent to highly collaborative activities. This is echoed by Tschirhart, Amezcua, and Anker in chapter 2; they note that trust among the participants they studied was frequently mentioned as an important requirement for effective collaboration.

Tschirhart, Amezcua, and Anker hypothesize that the earliest participants in a resource-sharing arrangement may play critical roles in shaping the membership in the sharing system. These authors suggest that if collaborative managers find themselves struggling to develop or sustain a resource-sharing arrangement, they should consider how much of their difficulty is related to differences of opinion on the attributes of the resource they are attempting to share.

A surprising finding from McGuire in chapter 5 is that contrary to earlier research on interagency collaboration in emergency management, the size of the county as measured by the total population is not a statistically significant determinant of collaborative activity in the average-performing county. Tied in with this, professionalism in emergency management is associated with greater levels of collaborative activity. McGuire finds that the greater the number of functions for which an agency has trained, the greater the level of collaborative activity undertaken by that agency. Formal education at a university is not significantly associated with collaborative activity in the highest-performing counties.

McGuire also emphasizes the surprising finding that a command-and-control model of management is not associated with collaboration. Concomitantly, where one sits in an organization may partially determine whether and how one collaborates outside that organization. Emergency management directors whose primary responsibility is first response collaborate less than directors from other types of agencies. The good news, according to McGuire: Collaboration can be learned and collaborative capacity can be developed.

Waugh's most important surprising finding in chapter 9 concerns the paradox that, following Hurricane Katrina, speeches frequently mentioned the need for "nimble" organizations; yet these calls were usually followed by greater centralization of decision making. In fact, the emergency managers in Waugh's study had more difficulty engaging in collaborative behavior with larger events. Contrasted to this, the education managers described in chapter 6 by Hicklin, O'Toole, Meier, and Robinson engaged in higher levels of collaboration when faced with larger organizational shocks.

From Waugh we learn that the personality and training of collaborators matter, perhaps more than other variables. This meshes with Hicklin, O'Toole, Meier, and Robinson's finding that a superintendent's overall level of networking prior to a hurricane is a significant predictor of how collaborative they will be in an emergency. Both chapters emphasize that individual-level patterns of behavior have organizational consequences concerning the extent of collaboration.

A surprising finding concerning whether collaboration saves money comes from chapter 7, where Brudney, Cho, and Wright explain that though state agencies with high collaboration scores were more likely to contract out, they find no relationship between such collaboration and cost savings, and they do not find a relationship between collaboration and quality results. Ryu and Rainey ask a different question in chapter 10, focusing instead on whether collaboration makes money for those served by a collaborative service delivery agency. Their surprising finding is that local service delivery areas with collaborative structures increased the hourly wage of adult participants by as much as 54 cents. Graddy and Chen conclude in chapter 4 that client outcomes are more likely to be improved when organizations choose their collaborative partners based on programmatic needs. Also important is a shared vision among partners. Paying attention to who participates and why is key. Graddy and Chen note that the contractual requirement to partner is associated with improved interorganizational relationships.

The chapters in this volume yield surprising findings in the area of motivation to collaborate. Graddy and Chen suggest in chapter 4 that reputation enhancement is the most important reason, as well as organizational legitimacy. Fleishman, in chapter 3, finds that the desire to leverage resources to achieve common goals is of paramount importance for nonprofit environmental groups. Fleishman takes this observation one step further by suggesting that public managers who want to encourage collaboration should emphasize common ground and shared interests. They also should avoid burdensome bureaucratic procedures, maintain legitimacy, and be attentive to the needs of partners.

In chapter 11, Alexander and O'Leary give us the surprising finding that collaboration and competition can go hand in hand. Just because a public manager is collaborating does not mean that he or she is not competing. In fact, collaboration can be a form of cooptation.

SURPRISING RESEARCH QUESTIONS

Some of the most valuable surprising findings in this book come from unanswered questions raised by the chapter authors. What is the difference on the ground between forced and voluntary collaboration (McGuire in chapter 5)? When do organizations suffer from collaboration (Tschirhart, Amezcua, and Anker in chapter 2)? What are the necessary skills for the collaborative public manager operating in a networked contract environment (Van Slyke in chapter 8)?

What type of education yields more collaboration (McGuire in chapter 5)? How can emergency managers be taught to be more collaborative in their work, seeing the incident management system as a tool rather than a rule (Waugh in chapter 9)? How do we train people to adapt, improvise, and work in a world of shared authority and resources (Waugh in chapter 9; Hicklin, O'Toole, Meier, and Robinson in chapter 6)? How do we foster a public management view that values the interdisciplinary collaborative approach as well as an understanding of the need to adapt, improvise, and learn (Waugh in chapter 9)?

How do we measure the success of collaborative public management (Emerson in chapter 12)? Is collaborative public management a means to an end or an end in itself (Emerson)? Are collaborative principles in tension with efficient management principles (Emerson)?

Posner writes in chapter 13 that the curriculum offered in many of the nation's leading graduate public administration programs has traditionally focused on helping students understand and manage large public agencies. How do we adjust our master of public administration, public affairs, and public policy curricula to reflect the realities of collaborative public management? How do we teach nonbureaucratic models of public administration such as networks, public–private partnerships, performance partnerships, and other kinds of collaborative institutional arrangements to achieve public goals in diverse settings?

COLLABORATIVE PUBLIC MANAGEMENT AND CONFLICT

A surprising finding running throughout this volume is the paradox that collaboration may yield conflict. One of the major challenges of collaborative public management concerns the management of conflict. The theme of conflict manifests itself in each chapter of this book in different ways.

In their study of resource sharing among agencies in chapter 2, Tschirhart, Amezcua, and Anker reflect several times on the conflict that may come with sharing. Conflict may arise when there are different priorities among the sharing agencies. The degree of conflict may affect the sustainability of the collaborative system. The members of a network might be selected to reduce conflict. And conflict resolution systems may be needed to address tensions between partners.

The increasing levels of contracting out by states noted by Brudney, Cho, and Wright in chapter 7 often yields conflicts. The authors note that in 2004, 58 percent of the state governments contracted with other governments, 68 percent contracted with nonprofit organizations, and

85 percent contracted with for-profit organizations. Contract management as an occupation has grown in recent years, in part as an attempt to prevent and resolve contractual conflicts. As the number of contracts rises, the number of lawyers involved in these transactions rises—yet another source of conflict, as attorneys zealously seek to represent their clients' best interests.

Van Slyke, in his study of relational contracting in chapter 8, finds that trust is inextricably linked to conflict. Trust is affected by the manner in which conflict is managed, but it also affects the way conflict is managed. As trust increases between contracting partners, collaboration increases. As collaboration increases, conflicts tend to be resolved through dialogue and other more informal dispute resolution mechanisms.

Partner selection in collaborative endeavors, as analyzed by Graddy and Chen in chapter 4, reflects the paradox of collaboration yielding conflict. They find that partnerships between organizations with different visions are difficult to initiate and sustain because fundamentally different missions can create interorganizational conflicts. For example, nonprofit service delivery organizations often distrust the profit motives of business organizations. The authors highlight the importance of careful selection of collaborative partners to minimize conflict. From this one might hypothesize that the collaborative employment training programs studied by Ryu and Rainey in chapter 10, which yielded higher earnings for clients, would also yield conflict among partner agencies that would need to be managed.

Conflict is embedded in the world of a collaborative public emergency manager, according to McGuire in chapter 5. Acting collaboratively means operating across organizational and sectoral boundaries that are not easily traversed. In many respects, compared with managers in other public-sector fields, the emergency manager may have the most complex organizational context because many nongovernmental organizations are at the heart of successful emergency and disaster planning, response, and recovery. Emergency managers must work with professionals who come from agencies with strong, well-established cultures defined more in terms of command-and-control management than collaboration and cooperation, such as police officers and firefighters. Emergency management collaboration also transcends other programmatic areas—including health, public safety, and community development—requiring managers to seek out information and expertise from multiple sources for multiple purposes. All of this potentially contributes to the paradox of conflict within collaboration.

In chapter 6 Hicklin, O'Toole, Meir, and Robinson study collaboration under crisis conditions fraught with conflict: the mandated collaboration thrust upon Texas school systems in response to hurricanes Rita and Katrina in September 2005. These systems took on the challenge of absorbing the large number of students who evacuated from the paths of the hurricanes with diverse and extensive needs reaching well beyond what school districts are normally expected to address. This conflict was further compounded by the fact that the plethora of regulations, curricula, and standard operating procedures governing the local schools were set at the state level. Because most of the evacuees migrated across state lines, the interstate dimension produced additional collaborative management conflicts that were not able to be resolved without cross-jurisdictional effort.

In his study of mechanisms for collaboration in emergency management in chapter 9, Waugh examines the challenges of emergency networks during a terrorist attack and points out that any such efforts are characterized by ad hoc actions, major uncertainties, and conflicting priorities. Tied in with this, additional network conflict would most likely come from the involvement of large numbers of nongovernmental response and recovery organizations, as well as the involvement of a large number of government agencies that cannot share authority. Further exacerbating the potential conflicts is the fact that in some local governments, authority is shared among two or more officials and emergency plans may not resolve the issues. There are also cultural conflicts when nonhierarchical organizations, such as volunteer organizations, have to interact with very hierarchical ones.

In the area of environmental collaboration, in chapter 3 Fleishman points out that conflict sometimes arises when the goals and objectives of certain organizations in a collaborative network are truly incompatible. Conflict also may arise when organizations' motivations change over time. The incentives that initially brought an organization into the collaboration may not keep it there.

In their study of the birth and evolution of the U.S. Institute for Environmental Conflict Resolution (USIECR) in chapter 11, Alexander and O'Leary analyze the network of environmental mediators created by the USIECR and conclude that conflict sometimes arose when decisions were made as to who was "in" the network and who was not. Conflict also arose at times when determinations were made as to who within the network would be chosen to mediate a case. Finally, conflict arose as the USIECR sought to find its place among the network of federal environmental agencies, with the older, more established organizations sometimes feeling defensive and guarding their power.

In chapter 12, Emerson writes that public managers are exploring cooperative networks and partnerships with stakeholders, but conflicts may arise when they are not familiar with or skilled in interest-based negotiation or multiparty negotiation. Likewise, conflicts may emerge when public policy mediators or public engagement facilitators hired to work with networks may not be fully versed in the "wicked" nature of a particular policy problem they are being asked to mediate. There are also conflicting views of the normative and the instrumental use of collaboration.

In chapter 13, Posner discusses the conflict that has emerged as policymakers and agencies adopt a wide range of tools that distribute responsibility and authority for financing and results across a variety of independent third parties, including state and local governments, nonprofits, and private companies. The modern government program now deploys a wide range of more indirect governance tools—including grants, contracts, credit, insurance, and regulations—to leverage the participation and compliance of these collaborative partners. The model of a hierarchical organization that controls the policy formulation, financing, and implementation of programs has largely been cast aside. Various forms of collaboration across governmental and sectoral boundaries have increasingly defined the practice of public administration in recent decades. This emergence of third-party governance as a primary strategy for achieving public objectives has created conflicts by testing the skills and knowledge of public administrators with new challenges in policy development and implementation. The new environment for public programs is more complex, uncertain, conflictual, and less predictable and controllable than ever before.

All the chapters in this book give credence to, and insights about, the paradox that with collaboration may come conflict. Indeed, in their monograph on managing networks, Milward and Provan (2006) write that one of the most important tasks for network managers is to try to minimize the occurrence of conflict and try to resolve it successfully if and when it does occur. They conclude that although network organizations generally commit to achieving network-level goals, conflict among network participants is inevitable (see also O'Leary and Bingham 2008.)

Managing and resolving conflicts in networks and other collaborative forms of governance is no small task. Networks by definition are complex conglomerations of diverse organizations and individuals. The characteristics that add to the complexity of network disputes as illuminated by some of the chapters in this book are numerous. Let us look at some of them.

There are multiple members. Network disputes typically involve many individuals and organizations. Each member brings their own interests that must be met. If their interests are not met, members may leave the network. For example, see chapters 2 and 3.

Network members bring both different and common missions. There must be some commonality of purpose to provide incentives to become a member of a network. Yet each organization also has it own unique mission that must be followed. These can at times clash with the mission of the network. For example, see chapters 5, 6, and 9.

Each network organization has a different organization culture. Culture is to the organization what character is to the individual. Just as each individual is unique, so is each organization's culture. Diversity among network organizations' cultures may present conflict management challenges within the network itself. For example, see chapters 4 and 10.

Network organizations have different methods of operation. They will differ in degrees of hierarchy. They will differ in degrees of management control. These and other differences may affect what a network can and cannot accomplish and the speed at which it is accomplished. For example, see chapter 9.

Network members have different stakeholder groups and different funders. To satisfy their diverse constituencies, network members will have different perspectives on appropriate directions and activities. Some of these preferences will overlap; some will not. For example, see chapters 11 and 13.

Network members have different degrees of power. Not all members of a network are created equal. Despite network rules that may give an equal vote to each member, some are typically more powerful than others. For example, see chapters 8, 11, and 12.

There are often multiple issues. Networks are typically formed to address complex problems that are not easily solved by one organization. Complex problems bring with them multiple issues and subissues, which in turn typically yield multiple challenges for conflict management. For example, see chapters 6, 7, and 12.

There are multiple forums for decision making. Public decisions may be made by networks. At the same time, the same public issue may be debated and dealt with in the legislature, in the courts, or in the offices of career public servants. Whether and how a decision is made by a network can be a source of conflict. For example, see chapters 6 and 13.

Networks are both interorganizational and interpersonal. The networks studied in the management literature typically are spider webs of organizations. But each organization typically is represented in the network by one or more agents of that organization. Just as networked organizations may clash, so too may networked individuals. For example, see chapters 2 and 8.

There are a variety of governance structures available to networks. How the network chooses to govern itself, lead members, develop consensuses, and create conventions for dialogue and deliberative processes are all exceedingly important and demanding responsibilities. Just designing the network's governance rules can be an exceedingly complex procedure. For example, see chapters 3, 5, and 9.

Networks may encounter conflict with the public. Increasingly, collaborative public management networks are engaging citizens through a variety of means. Because networks often address issues of concern to the public, conflict may emerge. For example, see chapters 12 and 13.

ANOTHER PARADOX OF COLLABORATIVE MANAGEMENT

Connelly, Zhang, and Faerman (2008) write of another paradox involved in being a collaborative manager. As managers work both within their own organizations and in networks, they are challenged in very different ways. These challenges demand different skill sets from managers. Borrowing from Connelly, Zhang, and Faerman, let us consider some of the most compelling paradoxes of being a collaborative manager inspired by the chapters in this book.

Collaborative managers must work with both autonomy and interdependence. As the leader of a single program or organization, a manager often works with independence, setting the rules and calling the shots. As a member of a collaborative network, a manager is typically now one of many managers with numerous intertwining interests that must be met.

Collaborative managers and their networks have both common and diverse goals. Each member of a network has goals that typically are unique to that member's organization or program. At the same time, as members of a network, managers typically share common goals.

Collaborative managers must work both with a smaller number and greater variety of groups that are increasingly more diverse. When organizations combine to form a network, they become one body—hence the smaller number. Yet within this one body typically are a great variety of organizations with different cultures, missions, and ways of operating—hence the greater diversity.

Collaborative managers need to be both participative and authoritative. Behavior within a network is typically participative because the members make decisions concerning the direction of the group. Yet as the head of a single program or organization, a manager is expected at times to take command and call the shots as he or she sees them. (Connelly, Zhang, and Faerman emphasize that "authoritative" is the key word here, not "authoritarian," which connotes a more dictatorial style.) Figure 14.1

demonstrates how assertiveness and cooperativeness come together in the skill set of the collaborative manager.

Collaborative managers need to see both the forest and the trees. A manager of a single program or organization needs to master the details and fine points of what he or she does on a daily basis. At the same time, as a member of a network, he or she needs to think holistically and laterally.

Collaborative managers need to balance advocacy and inquiry. Every manager has an obligation to promote, support, and act in favor of his or her organization. Yet behavior and especially decision making in a network, because of the intertwining interests, suggest the need for probing and questioning in order to gather the information necessary to act in the best interests of the network.

So what is a collaborative manager to do? Connelly, Zhang, and Faerman emphasize that these paradoxes should be accepted, embraced, and transcended, not resolved. These paradoxes are fundamental challenges of working both in and outside networks. Yet these paradoxes also suggest that a manager needs to consciously and assertively seek to handle the inevitable conflicts that will arise given these tensions.

Carpenter and Kennedy (2001) developed the idea of the spiral of unmanaged conflict that is directly applicable to conflict in collaborative

Figure 14.1 How Assertiveness and Cooperativeness Come Together in the Skill Set of the Collaborative Manager

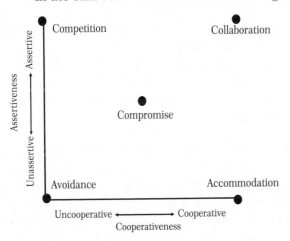

Source: Thomas 1976. Reprinted by permission of Leaetta Hough-Dunnette.

public management. Borrowing from Carpenter and Kennedy, if conflict in collaborative public management is not managed properly, the results are predictable: The problem emerges, sides form, positions harden, communication stops, resources are committed, the conflict goes outside the network, perceptions become distorted, and eventually a sense of crisis emerges. The conflict spiral is not inevitable, but it is predictable when conflict is not managed at an early stage. The earlier conflict is managed, the better.

Thus, collaborative managers need to be conflict managers and conflict resolvers. Conflict resolution is effectively group problem solving. Many guiding principles from the conflict resolution literature can assist in managing conflicts in networks (for a complete discussion, see O'Leary and Bingham 2008). These include

- reframing (redefining) conflicts as mutual problems to be solved together (Bunker 2006; Deutsch and Coleman 2000);
- educating each other in order to better understand the problem (Chaiken, Gruenfeld, and Judd 2000; Dukes, Piscolish, and Stephens 2000);
- developing a conflict management plan that addresses procedures, substance, and relationships (Strauss 1999; Carpenter and Kennedy 2001);
- involving the members of the network in designing the process and developing a solution (Carpenter 1999; Carlson 1999; Gruber 2000);
- balanced representation (Laws 1999; Coleman 2000; Lewicki and Wiethoff 2000; Gray, Lewicki, and and Elliot 2003);
- insisting that network members participate directly, fully, and in good faith (Krauss and Morsella 2000; Zartman and Rubin 2000; Moffitt and Bordone 2005);
- maintaining transparency (Lewicki et al. 2003) and timeliness (Coleman and Deutsch 2000); and
- the implementability of agreements (Susskind, McKearnan, and Thomas-Larmer 1999).

Tied in with this, collaborative managers need to know how to bargain and how to negotiate. There is a rich literature on interest-based bargaining and negotiation that can be applied to conflicts in networks. Interest-based bargaining is a negotiating strategy that focuses on satisfying as many interests or needs as possible for all negotiators (Fisher, Ury, and Patton 1991). It is a problem-solving process used to reach an integrative solution rather than distributing rewards in a win/lose manner. It is not a process of compromise. The basic tenet of interest-based bargaining is issue resolution through interest satisfaction. These principles are directly applicable to managing the conflicts that arise in collaborative public management.

THE FINAL PARADOX

We began this book by giving an overview of the history of the literature and theory on collaborative public management. It is significant that our analysis of the best works in this area did not include books and articles on "collaborative governance," a term used to describe the integration of reasoned discussions by citizens and other residents into the decision making of public representatives (see the website of the Institute for Local Government's Collaborative Governance Initiative, www.ca-ilg.org).

The public administration and public management literatures generally fall into two categories, as introduced by Emerson in chapter 12—one focusing on collaboration among organizations, and the other focusing on civic engagement and ways for citizens to participate in governance. However, these are two related parts of the same puzzle, for collaborative public management networks are increasingly engaging citizens through a variety of means. Though some scholars of the new, networked governance talk about the importance of negotiation and collaboration skills, conflict management, and consensus building to get the public's work done, for the most part, paradoxically, they do not look closely at either the processes for collaboration, termed "new governance processes" (Bingham, Nabatchi, and O'Leary 2005), or at the tools and methods for evaluating them. There is a need to assess collaborative processes, focusing on their impact on the people they were meant to serve. These evaluation tools are in their earliest stages of development.

Assessing collaboration is of necessity an interdisciplinary enterprise. The relevant criteria and metrics come not only from the policy analysis and program evaluation literatures. They also come from political science, social psychology, conflict management, negotiation, dispute resolution, planning, and other fields.

There is much to be learned by the fields of public management and public administration, by examining both the formative and summative evaluation strategies, processes, effects, and outcomes for collaborative public management and collaborative governance already used by other disciplines. The appropriate variables and metrics could be organized based on the relation of collaboration to the policy process. The relevant criteria for success will vary depending upon whether collaboration occurs upstream, midstream, or downstream in the policy process (Bingham 2006; O'Leary and Bingham 2003). The *upstream* use of new governance involves the earliest stage of the policy process, which entails the identification of a policy problem and the ordering of policy preferences. It involves the creation of policy and the quasi-legislative process of crafting ordinances, regulations, and language to establish the rules to be enforced downstream. *Midstream* uses include efforts to implement these rules through permits and projects that bring the policy choices into practice. *Downstream* uses involve the enforcement of public laws, for example, adjudicating compliance with conditions approved in the permitting process.

There is a substantial literature on collaboration in environmental conflict resolution and policy consensus processes that has a direct bearing on collaborative public management and collaborative governance (Bingham and O'Leary 2006). Environmental conflict resolution entails the creation of a collaborative network of governmental stakeholders from federal, state, and local governments, tribal sovereign governments, nongovernmental organizations, citizen groups, and the private sector. It incorporates elements of civic engagement. The upstream/midstream/downstream framework has proven useful in this context, as we delineated in *The Promise and Performance of Environmental Conflict Resolution* (O'Leary and Bingham 2003). In that volume, we developed the following list based on work we analyzed and synthesized. For assessing success upstream in the policy process, we suggested incorporating public values; improving decision quality; resolving conflict; building trust; educating the public; ensuring socioeconomic representativeness; consultation and/or outreach with the wider public; diversity of participants and views represented; integration of concerns; information exchange; mutual learning; effectiveness; efficiency and equity; cost avoidance; project/decision acceptability as legitimate; mutual respect; social capital; increased overall knowledge; increased individual stakeholder knowledge; identifying threats, goals, and management actions; adequacy of a plan to achieve goals; and certainty of agreement on implementation.

For midstream uses, we identified positive net benefits, measurable objectives, cost-effective implementation, financial feasibility, a fair distribution of costs among parties, flexibility, incentive compatibility, improved problem-solving capacity, enhanced social capital, clear documentation protocols, reduction in conflict and hostility, improved relations, cognitive and affective shift, an ability to resolve subsequent disputes, durable agreements, comprehensive or complete agreements, party capacity improved, and government decision-making improved. For downstream uses, we identified participant procedural justice, the comparative satisfaction of different categories of disputants, reducing or narrowing issues, referrals, and voluntary use rates.

Many of these criteria, developed to assess collaboration in one context, have a direct bearing on evaluating the success of collaboration in the new governance of networks and expanded civic engagement. These criteria should be examined to determine their applicability and to expand upon them. Indicators and measures also need to be developed.

Public managers need a new framework for thinking about how to measure the results of collaboration, and there is much to be learned from other disciplines. The major test confronting the fields of public management and public administration, therefore, is not only to broaden and deepen our research. Our major challenge is to reach out, build upon, and learn from other disciplines in order to build knowledge, fully understand, and comprehensively evaluate the challenges for public management in a world of shared power.

References

Adamek, Raymond J., and Bebe F. Lavin. 1975. Inter-Organizational Exchange: A Note on the Scarcity Hypothesis. In *Inter-organizational Theory*, ed. Anant R. Neghand. Kent, OH: Kent State University Press.

Agranoff, Robert. 2005. Managing Collaborative Performance: Changing the Boundaries of the State? *Public Performance and Management Review* 29, no. 1:18–45.

———. 2006. Inside Collaborative Networks: Ten Lessons for Public Managers. *Public Administration Review* 66, no. 10:56–65.

———. 2007. *Managing within Networks: Adding Value to Public Organizations*. Washington, DC: Georgetown University Press.

Agranoff, Robert, and Michael McGuire. 1998. Multinetwork Management: Collaboration and the Hollow State in Local Economic Policy. *Journal of Public Administration Research and Theory* 8, no. 1:67–91.

———. 2001. Big Questions in Public Network Management Research. *Journal of Public Administration Research and Theory* 11, no. 3:295–326.

———. 2003a. *Collaborative Public Management: New Strategies for Local Governments*. Washington, DC: Georgetown University Press.

———. 2003b. Inside the Matrix: Integrating the Paradigms of Intergovernmental and Network Management. *International Journal of Public Administration* 26, no. 12:1401–22.

Ahuja, Gautam. 2000. Collaboration Networks, Structural Holes, and Innovation: A Longitudinal Study. *Administrative Science Quarterly* 45, no. 3:425–55.

Aldrich, Howard. 1976. Resource Dependence and Interorganizational Relations: Local Employment Service Offices and Social Services Sector Organizations. *Administration & Society* 7, no. 4:419–54.

———. 1979. *Organizations and Environments*. Englewood Cliffs, NJ: Prentice Hall.

———. 2001. *Organizations Evolving*. Thousand Oaks, CA: Sage.

Aldrich, Howard, and C. Marlene Fiol. 1994. Fools Rush In? The Institutional Context of Industry Creation. *Academy of Management Review* 19, no. 4:645–70.

Aldrich, Howard, and Martha A. Martinez. 2001. Many Are Called, But Few Are Chosen: An Evolutionary Perspective for the Study of Entrepreneurship. *Entrepreneurship, Theory and Practice*, Summer, 41–56.

Alexander, David. 2003. Towards the Development of Standards in Emergency Management Training and Education. *Disaster Prevention and Management* 12, no. 2:113–12.

Alexander, Jennifer, Renee Nank, and Camilla Stivers. 1999. Implications of Welfare Reform: Do Nonprofit Survival Strategies Threaten Civil Society? *Nonprofit and Voluntary Sector Quarterly* 28, no. 4:452–75.

Alter, Catherine, and Jerald Hage. 1993. *Organizations Working Together.* Newbury Park, CA: Sage.

Apogee Research Inc. 1992. *State Government Privatization in 1992: An Updated Opinion Survey of State Governments on Their Use of Privatization.* Bethesda, MD: Apogee Research.

Artz, Kendall W., and Thomas H. Brush. 2000. Asset Specificity, Uncertainty, and Relational Norms: An Examination of Coordination Costs in Collaborative Strategic Alliances. *Journal of Economic Behavior & Organization* 41:337–62.

Ashforth, Blake E., and Barry W. Gibbs. 1990. The Double Edge of Organizational Legitimation. *Organization Science* 1, no. 2:177–94.

Auger, Deborah A. 1999. Privatization, Contracting, and the States: Lessons from State Government Experience. *Public Productivity and Management Review* 14 (March): 435–54.

Austin, James E. 2000. *The Collaboration Challenge.* San Francisco: Jossey-Bass.

Baker, George, Robert Gibbons, and Kevin J. Murphy. 2002. Relational Contracts in Strategic Alliances. Unpublished working paper.

Bannon, Anne Louise. 2006. Adapting to Working Together: Can DHS Do It? *Homeland Protection Professional*, July, 42.

Bardach, Eugene. 1998. *Getting Agencies to Work Together: The Practice and Theory of Managerial Craftsmanship.* Washington, DC: Brookings Institution Press.

Barnow, Burt S. 2000. Exploring the Relationship between Performance Management and Program Impact: A Case Study of the Job Training Partnership Act. *Journal of Policy Analysis and Management* 19, no. 1:118–41.

Barnow, Burt S., and Christopher T. King. 2003. *The Workforce Investment Act in Eight States: Overview of Findings from a Field Network Study: Interim Report.* Contract Report to U. S. Employment and Training Administration, U.S. Department of Labor, Contract AK-12224-01-60. Albany: Nelson A. Rockefeller Institute of Government, State University of New York at Albany.

Barnow, Burt S., and Jeffrey A. Smith. 2004. Performance Management of U. S. Job Training Programs: Lessons from the Job Training Partnership Act. *Public Finance and Management* 4, no. 3:247–87.

Bartle, John R., and Ronnie LaCourse Korisec. 2000. Procurement and Contracting in State Government, 2000. In *Government Performance Project.* Syracuse, NY: Syracuse University Press.

Battigalli, Pierpaolo, and Giovanni Maggi. 2002. Rigidity, Discretion, and the Costs of Writing Contracts. *American Economic Review* 92, no. 4:798–817.

Becker, Fred W. 2001. *Problems in Privatization Theory and Practice in State and Local Governments.* Lewiston, NY: Edward Mellen Press.

Becker, Fred, and Valerie Patterson. 2005. Public-Private Partnerships: Balancing Financial Returns, Risks and Roles of Partners. *Public Performance and Management Review* 29, no. 2:125–44.

Benkler, Yochai. 2004. Sharing Nicely: On Shareable Goods and the Emergence of Sharing as a Modality of Economic Production. *Yale Law Journal* 114, nos. 1–2:273–358.

Benson, J. Kenneth. 1975. The Interorganizational Network as a Political Economy. *Administrative Science Quarterly* 20(2): 229–49.

Bernheim, B. Douglas, and Michael D. Whinston. 1998. Incomplete Contracts and Strategic Ambiguity. *American Economic Review* 88, no. 4:902–32.

Berry, Frances S., Ralph S. Brower, Sang Ok Choi, Wendy Xinfang Goa, HeeSoun Jang, Myungjung Kwon, and Jessica Ward. 2004. Three Traditions of Network Research: What the Public Management Research Agenda Can Learn from Other Research Communities. *Public Administration Review* 64, no. 5:539–52.

Berry, Frances S., and Ralph S. Brower. 2005. Intergovernmental and Intersectoral Management: Weaving Networking, Contracting Out, and Management Roles into Third-Party Government. *Public Performance and Management Review* 29, no. 1:7–17.

Bingham, Gail, Juliana Birkhoff, and Janet Stone. 1997. Building Bridges between Research and Practice. *Resolve* 28. www.resolve.org/publications/reports.

Bingham, Lisa Blomgren. 1997. Mediating Employment Disputes: Perceptions of Redress at the United States Postal Service. *Review of Public Personnel Administration* 17, no. 2:20–30.

———. 2006. The New Urban Governance: Processes for Engaging Citizens and Stakeholders. *Review of Policy Research* 23, no. 4:815–26.

Bingham, Lisa Blomgren, Tina Nabatchi, and Rosemary O'Leary. 2005. The New Governance: Practices and Processes for Stakeholder and Citizen Participation in the Work of Government. *Public Administration Review* 65, no. 5:547–58.

Bingham, Lisa Blomgren, and Rosemary O'Leary. 2006. Conclusion: Parallel Play, Not Collaboration: Missing Questions, Missing Connections. *Public Administration Review* 66, no. 6:159–67.

Bloom, Howard S., Carolyn J. Hill, and James A. Riccio. 2003. Linking Program Implementation and Effectiveness: Lessons from a Pooled Sample of Welfare-to-Work Experiments. *Journal of Policy Analysis and Management* 22, no. 4:551–75.

Bloom, Howard S., Larry L. Orr, Stephen H. Bell, George Cave, Fred Doolittle, Winston Lin, and Johannes M. Bos. 1996. The Benefits and Costs of J.T.P.A. Title II-A Programs: Key Findings from the National Job Training Partnership Act Study. *Journal of Human Resources* 32, no. 3:549–76.

Bloomfield, Pamela. 2006. The Challenging Business of Long-Term Public-Private Partnerships: Reflections on Local Experience. *Public Administration Review* 66, no. 3:400–11.

Boddy, David, Douglas MacBeth, and Beverly Wagner. 2000. Implementing Collaboration between Organizations: An Empirical Study of Supply Chain Partnering. *Journal of Management Studies* 37, no. 7:1003–17.

Bogason, Peter, and Theo Toonen. 1998. Comparing Networks. Symposium in *Public Administration* 76:205–407.

Bohte, John, and Kenneth J. Meier. 2000. The Marble Cake: Introducing Federalism into the Government Growth Equation. *Publius: The Journal of Federalism* 30 (Summer): 35–46.

Boin, Arjen. 2004. The Development of Public Institutions: Reconsidering the Role of Leadership. In *Why Public Organizations Become Institutions: An Interdisciplinary Discussion of Research Questions, Theoretical Frameworks and Initial Findings*. Department of Public Administration, Leiden University, Leiden.

Boin, Arjen, and Tom Christensen. 2004. Reconsidering Leadership and Institutions in the Public Sector. A Question of Design? Paper prepared for European Group on Public Administration Annual Conference, Ljubljana.

Boulding, Kenneth E. 1959. National Images and International Systems. *Journal of Conflict Resolution: A Quarterly for Research Related to War and Peace* 3, no. 2:120–31.

Bowling, Cynthia J. 2006. American State Administrators Project: Publications Inventory. Department of Political Science, Auburn University.

Bowling, Cynthia J., and Deil S. Wright. 1998a. Change and Continuity in State Administration: Administrative Leadership across Four Decades. *Public Administration Review* 58 (September–October): 429–44.

———. 1998b. Public Administration in the Fifty American States: A Half-Century Revolution. *State and Local Government Review* 30 (Winter): 50–62.

Bowling, Cynthia J., Chung-Lae Cho, and Deil S. Wright. 2004. Establishing a Continuum from Minimizing to Maximizing Bureaucrats: State Agency Head Preferences for Governmental Expansion—A Typology of Administrator Growth Pastures, 1964–1998. *Public Administration Review* 64 (July–August): 447–68.

Bowling, Cynthia J., Christine Kelleher, Jennifer Jones, and Deil S. Wright. 2006. Cracked Ceilings, Firmer Floors, and Weakening Walls: Trends and Patterns in Gender Representation among Executives in American State Governments, 1970–2004. *Public Administration Review* 66 (November–December): 821–34.

Boyne, George A. 1998. The Determinants of Variations in Local Service Contracting: Garbage In, Garbage Out? *Urban Affairs Review* 34:149–62.

Boyne, George A., and Richard M. Walker. 2005. Introducing the "Determinants of Performance in Public Organizations" Symposium. *Journal of Public Administration Research and Theory* 15, no. 4:483–88.

Bozeman, Barry. 1987. *All Organizations Are Public: Bridging Public and Private Organizational Theories*. San Francisco: Jossey-Bass.

Brown, Trevor L., and Matthew Potoski. 2005. Transaction Costs and Contracting: The Practitioner Perspective. *Public Performance and Management Review* 28, no. 3:326–51.

Brown, Trevor L., Matthew Potoski, and David M. Van Slyke. 2006. Managing Public-Service Contracts: Aligning Values, Institutions, and Markets. *Public Administration Review* 66, no. 3:53–67.

———. 2007. Trust and Contract Completeness in the Public Sector. *Local Government Studies* 33, no. 4:607–23.

————. Forthcoming. Changing Modes of Service Delivery: How Past Choices Structure Future Choices. *Environment and Planning C: Government and Policy*.

Brudney Jeffrey L., Chung-Lae Cho, Yoo-Sung Choi, and Deil S. Wright. 2006. Collaborative Governance: Service Delivery Performance through Multi-Sector Contracting: The Case of American State Administrative Agencies, 1998 and 2004. Paper presented at European Group on Public Administration and the American Society for Public Administration International Conference on Public Sector Performance, Leuven, June 1–3.

Brudney Jeffrey L., Sergio Fernandez, Jay Eungha Ryu, and Deil S. Wright. 2005. Exploring and Explaining Contracting Out: Patterns among the American States. *Journal of Public Administration Research and Theory* 15 (April): 393–419.

Brudney, Jeffrey, F. Ted Hebert, and Deil S. Wright. 1999. Reinventing Government in the American States: Measuring and Explaining Administrative Reform. *Public Administration Review* 59, no. 1:19–30.

Brudney, Jeffrey L., and Deil S. Wright. 2002. Revisiting Administrative Reform in the American States: The Status of Reinventing Government during the 1990s. *Public Administration Review* 62 (May–June): 353–61.

Bryson, John M., Barbara C. Crosby, and Melissa Middleton Stone. 2006. The Design and Implementation of Cross-Sector Collaborations: Propositions from the Literature. *Public Administration Review* 66, no. 6 (Special Issue): 44–55.

Buck, Dick A., Joseph E. Trainor, and Benigno E. Aguirre. 2006. A Critical Evaluation of the Incident Command System and NIMS. *Journal of Homeland Security and Emergency Management* 3, no. 3: article 1.

Bunker, Barbara Benedict. 2006. Managing Conflict through Large Group Methods. In *The Handbook of Conflict Resolution: Theory and Practice*, ed. Morton Deutsch and Peter Coleman. San Francisco: Jossey-Bass.

Carlson, Chris. 1999. Convening. In *The Consensus-Building Handbook: A Comprehensive Guide to Reaching Agreement*, ed. Lawrence Susskind, Sarah McKearnan, and Jennifer Thomas-Larmer. Thousand Oaks, CA: Sage.

Carpenter, Sarah, and W. J. D. Kennedy. 2001. *Managing Public Disputes*, 2nd ed. San Francisco: Jossey-Bass.

Carpenter, Susan. 1999. Choosing Appropriate Consensus-Building Techniques and Strategies. In *The Consensus-Building Handbook: A Comprehensive Guide to Reaching Agreement*, ed. Lawrence Susskind, Sarah McKearnan, and Jennifer Thomas-Larmer. Thousand Oaks, CA: Sage.

Carroll, Glenn R. 1984. Organizational Ecology. *Annual Review of Sociology* 10:71–93.

Chaiken, Shelly L., Deborah H. Gruenfeld, and Charles M. Judd. 2000. Persuasion in Negotiations and Conflict Situations. In *The Handbook of Conflict Resolution: Theory and Practice*, ed. Morton Deutsch and Peter Coleman. San Francisco: Jossey-Bass.

Charalambides, Leonidas C. 1984. Shared Capacity Resource Reallocation in a

Decentralized Service System. *Journal of Operations Management* 5, no. 1:57–74.

Chaserant, Camille. 2003. Cooperation, Contracts and Social Networks: From a Bounded to a Procedural Rationality Approach. *Journal of Management and Governance* 7:163–86.

Chi, Keon S. 1993. Privatization in State Government: Options for the Future. *State Trends and Forecasts* 2 (November): 1–24.

Chi, Keon S., Kelley A. Arnold, and Heather M. Perkins. 2003. Privatization in State Government: Trends and Issues. *Spectrum: The Journal of State Government* 76 (Fall): 12–21.

Chi, Tailan. 1994. Trading in Strategic Resources: Necessary Conditions, Transaction Cost Problems, and Choice of Exchange Structure. *Strategic Management Journal* 15, no. 4:271–90.

Cho, Chung-Lae, and Deil S. Wright. 2004. The Devolution Revolution in Intergovernmental Relations in the 1990's: Changes in Cooperative and Coercive State-National Relations as Perceived by State Administrators. *Journal of Public Administration Research and Theory* 14 (October): 469–94.

———. 2007. Perceptions of Federal Aid Impacts on State Agencies: Patterns, Trends, and Variations Across the 20th Century. *Publius: The Journal of Federalism* 37 (Winter): 103–30.

Choi, Yoo-Sung, Chung-Lae Cho, Deil S. Wright, and Jeffrey L. Brudney. 2005. Dimensions of Contracting for Service Delivery by American State Administrative Agencies. *Public Performance and Management Review* 29 (September): 46–66.

Choi, Yoo-Sung, and Deil S. Wright. 2004. Contracting Out as Administrative Reform: Conceptualizing Components and Measuring Dimensions of Contracting as a Feature in the Global Transformation of Governance. *Korea Local Administration Review* (Seoul) 18 (June): 199–232.

Cigler, Beverly A. 2000. A Sampling of Introductory Public Administration Texts. *Journal of Public Affairs Education* 6, no. 1:45–53.

Cohen, Wesley M., and Daniel A. Levinthal. 1990. Absorptive Capacity: A New Perspective on Learning and Innovation. *Administrative Science Quarterly* 35:128–52.

Coleman, Peter T. 2000. Power and Conflict. In *The Handbook of Conflict Resolution: Theory and Practice*, ed. Morton Deutsch and Peter Coleman. San Francisco: Jossey-Bass.

Coleman, Peter T., and Morton Deutsch. 2000. Some Guidelines for Developing a Creative Approach to Conflict. In *The Handbook of Conflict Resolution: Theory and Practice*, ed. Morton Deutsch and Peter Coleman. San Francisco: Jossey-Bass.

Comfort, Louise. 1999. *Shared Risk: Complex Systems in Seismic Response*. Oxford: Pergamon Press.

———. 2006. The Politics of Policy Learning: Catastrophic Events in Real Time. Paper presented at annual meeting of American Political Science Association, Philadelphia, August 31–September 3.

Connelly, David R., Jing Zhang, and Sue Faerman. 2008. The Paradoxical Nature of Collaboration. In *Big Ideas in Collaborative Public Management*, ed. Lisa Blomgren Bingham and Rosemary O'Leary. Armonk, NY: M. E. Sharpe.

Cook, Alethia H. 2006. *The 1995 Oklahoma City Bombing: Bureaucratic Response to Terrorism and a Method for Evaluation*. Unpublished manuscript.

Cooper, Phillip J. 2003. *Governing by Contract: Challenges and Opportunities for Public Managers*. Washington, D.C.: CQ Press.

Corts, Kenneth S., and Jasjit Singh. 2004. The Effect of Repeated Interaction on Contract Choice: Evidence from Offshore Drilling. *Journal of Law, Economics, and Organization* 20, no. 1:230–60.

Courty, Pascal, and Gerald Marschke. 2003. Performance Funding in Federal Agencies: A Case Study of a Federal Job Training Program. *Public Budgeting and Finance* 23, no. 3:22–48.

Cutter, Susan L., Bryan J. Boruff, and W. Lynn Shirley. 2003. Social Vulnerability to Environmental Hazards. *Social Science Quarterly* 84, no. 2:242–61.

D'Amico, Ron, Deborah Kogan, Suzanne Kreutzer, Andrew Wiegand, Alberta Baker, Gardner Carrick, and Carole McCarthy. 2001. *A Report on Early State and Local Progress towards W.I.A. Implementation*. Contract Report to U. S. Department of Labor, Contract G-7681-9-00-87-30. Oakland and Bethesda, MD: Social Policy Research Associates and Technical Assistance and Training Corporation.

Das, T. K., and Bing-Sheng Teng. 1998. Between Trust and Control: Developing Confidence in Partner Cooperation in Alliances. *Academy of Management Review* 23, no. 3:491–512.

———. 2001. Trust, Control, and Risk in Strategic Alliances: An Integrated Framework. *Organization Studies* 22, no. 2:251–83.

DeHoog, Ruth Hoogland. 1984. *Contracting Out for Human Services: Economic, Political, and Organizational Perspectives*. Albany: State University of New York Press.

DeHoog, Ruth Hoogland, and Lester M. Salamon. 2002. Purchase of Service Contracting. In *The Tools of Government: A Guide to the New Governance*, ed. Lester M. Salamon. New York: Oxford University Press

Deutsch, Morton, and Peter T. Coleman, eds. 2000. *The Handbook of Conflict Resolution: Theory and Practice*. San Francisco: Jossey-Bass.

Devlin, Godfrey, and Mark Bleackley. 1988. Strategic Alliances: Guidelines for Success. *Long Range Planning* 21:18–23.

DHS (U.S. Department of Homeland Security). 2004. *National Incident Management System*. Washington, DC: U.S. Government Printing Office.

Dicke, Lisa A. 2002. Ensuring Accountability in Human Services Contracting: Can Stewardship Theory Fill the Bill? *American Review of Public Administration* 32 (December): 455–70.

Dickinson, Katherine P., Terry R. Johnson, and Richard W. West. 1987. An Analysis of the Sensitivity of Quasi-Experimental Net Impact Estimates of CETA Programs. *Evaluation Review* 11, no. 4:452–72.

Dillman, Don. 2000. *Mail and Internet Surveys: The Tailored Design Method,* 2d ed. New York: John Wiley & Sons.

DiMaggio, Paul J., and Walter W. Powell. 1983. Institutional Isomorphism and Collective Rationality in Organizational Fields. *American Sociology Review* 48:147–60.

Donahue, John D., and Joseph S. Nye. 2002. *Market-Based Governance: Supply Side, Demand Side, Upside, and Downside.* Washington, D.C.: Brookings Institution Press.

Dowling, John, and Jeffrey Pfeffer. 1975. Organizational Legitimacy: Social Values and Organizational Behavior. *Pacific Sociological Review* 18, no. 1:122–36.

Doz, L. Yves, and Gary Hamel. 1998. *Alliance Advantage: The Art of Creating Value through Partnering.* Boston: Harvard Business School Press.

Drabek, Thomas E. 1983. Alternative Patterns of Decision Making in Emergent Disaster Response Networks. *International Journal of Mass Emergencies and Disasters* 1 277–305.

———. 1985. Managing the Emergency Response. *Public Administration Review* 45:85–92.

———. 1987. *The Professional Emergency Manager: Structures and Strategies for Success.* Boulder, CO: Institute of Behavioral Science, University of Colorado.

———. 2001. Coordinating Disaster Responses: A Strategic Perspective. *American Society of Professional Emergency Planners* 8, no. 1:29–40.

Drabek, Thomas E., Rita Braito, Cynthia C. Cook, James R. Powell, and David Rogers. 1982. Selecting Samples of Organizations: Central Issues and Emergent Trends. *Pacific Sociological Review* 25, no. 3:377–400.

Drabek, Thomas E., and David A. McEntire. 2002. Emergent Phenomena and Multiorganizational Coordination in Disasters: Lessons from the Research Literature. *International Journal of Mass Emergencies and Disasters* 20, no. 2:197–224.

Dukes, E. Franklin. 2004. What We Know about Environmental Conflict Resolution: An Analysis Based on Research. *Conflict Resolution Quarterly* 22, nos. 1–2.

Dukes, E. Franklin, Marina A. Piscolish, and J. B. Stephens. 2000. *Reaching for Higher Ground in Conflict Resolution.* San Francisco: Jossey-Bass.

Dynes, Russell R. 1994. Community Emergency Planning: False Assumptions and Inappropriate Analogies. *International Journal of Mass Emergencies and Disasters* 12, no. 2:141–58.

Dyer, H. Jeffrey, and Harbir Singh. 1998. The Relational View: Cooperative Strategy and Sources of Interorganizational Competitive Advantage. *Academy of Management Review* 23, no. 4:660–79.

Elazar, Daniel J. 1962. *The American Partnership: Intergovernmental Cooperation in the Nineteenth-Century United States.* Chicago: University of Chicago Press.

Eller College of Management. 2006. Press release. Tucson, December 19.

Elling, Richard C. 2004. Administering State Programs; Performance and Politics. In *Politics in the American States: A Comparative Analysis*, 8th ed., edited by Virginia Fray and Russell L. Hanson. Washington, DC: CQ Press.

Emerson, Kirk, and Christine Carlson. 2003. An Evaluation System for State and Federal Conflict Resolution Programs. In *The Promise and Performance of Environmental Conflict Resolution*, ed. Rosemary O'Leary and Lisa Blomgren Bingham. Washington, DC: Resources for the Future.

Emerson, Kirk, Tina Nabatchi, Rosemary O'Leary, and John Stephens. 2003. The Challenges of Environmental Conflict Resolution. In *The Promise and Performance of Environmental Conflict Resolution*, ed. Rosemary O'Leary and Lisa Blomgren Bingham. Washington, DC: Resources for the Future.

Ewalt, Jo Ann G. 2004. Alternative Governance Structures for Welfare Provider Networks. In *The Art of Governance: Analyzing Management and Administration*, ed. Patricia W. Ingraham and Laurence E. Lynn Jr. Washington, DC: Georgetown University Press.

Fernandez, Sergio. 2005. Accounting for Performance in Contracting for Services: Are Successful Contractual Relationships Controlled or Managed? Paper presented at National Public Management Research Conference, Los Angeles.

Ferris, James M. 1993. The Double-Edged Sword of Social Service Contracting: Public Accountability versus Nonprofit Autonomy. *Nonprofit Management & Leadership* 3, no. 4:363–76.

Finnemore, Martha, and Kathryn Sikkink. 1998. International Norm Dynamics and Political Change. *International Organization* 52, no. 4:887–917.

FIRESCOPE. 2006. MACS Procedures Manual. MACS 410-1. Available at www.firescope.org.

Fisher, Roger, William Ury, and Bruce Patton. 1991. *Getting to Yes*, 2nd ed. New York: Penguin Press.

Fosler, R. Scott. 2002. *Working better Together: How Government, Business, and Nonprofit Organizations Can Achieve Public Purposes through Cross-Sector Collaboration, Alliances, and Partnerships*. Washington, DC: Independent Sector.

Foster, Mary K., and Agnes G. Meinhard. 2002a. A Contingency View of the Responses of Voluntary Social Service Organizations in Ontario to Government Cutbacks. *Canadian Journal of Administrative Sciences* 19, no. 1:27–41.

———. 2002b. A Regression Model Explaining Predisposition to Collaborate. *Nonprofit and Voluntary Sector Quarterly* 31, no. 4:549–64.

Fountain, Jane E. 1998. Social Capital: Its Relationship to Innovation in Science and Technology. *Science and Public Policy* 25, no. 2:103–15.

Frumkin, Peter, and Joseph Galaskiewicz. 2004. Institutional Isomorphism and Public Sector Organizations. *Journal of Public Administration Research and Theory* 14, no. 3:283–307.

Fugate, Craig. 2006. The State of Federal Emergency Management (Plenary), 31st Annual Natural Hazards Research and Applications Workshop, Boulder, CO, July 9–12.

Fung, Archon. 2006. Varieties of Participation in Complex Governance. *Public Administration Review* 66, no. 6:66–75.

Galaskiewicz, Joseph. 1985. Interorganizational Relations. *Annual Review of Sociology*, 11:281–304.

Gazley, Beth. 2008a. Beyond the Contract: The Scope and Nature of Informal Government-Nonprofit Partnerships. *Public Administration Review* 68, no. 1:141–54.

———. 2008b. Intersectoral Collaboration and the Motivation to Collaborate: Toward an Integrated Theory. In *Big Ideas in Collaborative Public Management*, ed. Lisa Blomgren Bingham and Rosemary O'Leary. Armonk, NY: M. E. Sharpe.

Gazley, Beth, and Jeffrey L. Brudney. 2007. The Purpose (and Perils) of Government-Nonprofit Partnership. *Nonprofit and Voluntary Sector Quarterly* 36, no. 3:389–415.

Gillespie, David F., and Calvin L. Streeter. 1987. Conceptualizing and Measuring Disaster Preparedness. *International Journal of Mass Emergencies and Disasters* 5:155–76.

Goldsmith, Stephen, and William D. Eggers. 2004. *Governing by Network: The New Shape of the Public Sector*. Washington, DC: Brookings Institution Press.

Govindarajan, V., and Joseph Fisher. 1990. Strategy, Control Systems, and Resource-Sharing: Effects on Business Unit Performance. *Academy of Management Journal* 33, no. 2:259–85.

Graddy, Elizabeth A., and Bin Chen. 2006. Influences on the Size and Scope of Networks for Social Service Delivery. *Journal of Public Administration Research and Theory* 16, no. 4:533–52.

Graddy, Elizabeth, and James Ferris. 2006. Public-Private Alliances: Why, When, and to What End? In *Institutions and Planning*, ed. N. Verma. Oxford: Elsevier.

Granovetter, Mark. 1985. Economic Action and Social Structure: The Problem of Embeddedness. *American Journal of Sociology* 91:481–510.

Gray, Andrew. 2003. *Collaboration in Public Services: The Challenge for Evaluation*. New Brunswick, NJ: Transaction.

Gray, Barbara. 1989. *Collaborating: Finding Common Ground for Multiparty Problems*, 1st ed. San Francisco: Jossey-Bass.

———. 2000. Assessing Inter-Organizational Collaboration: Multiple Conceptions and Multiple Methods. In *Perspectives on Collaboration*, ed. David Faulkner and Mark De Rond. Oxford: Oxford University Press.

Gray, Barbara, Roy Lewicki, and Michael Elliot. 2003. *Making Sense of Intractable Environmental Conflicts: Concepts and Cases*. Washington, DC: Island Press.

Gray, Barbara, and Donna J. Wood. 1991. Collaborative Alliances: Moving from Practice to Theory. *Journal of Applied Behavioral Science* 27, no. 1:3–22.

Greene, Jeffrey D. 1994. How Much Privatization? A Research Note on the Use of Privatization by Cities in 1982 and 1992. *Policy Studies Journal* 24, no. 4:632–64.

———. 1996. Does Privatization Make a Difference? The Impact of Private Contracting on Municipal Efficiency. *International Journal of Public Administration* 17, no. 7:1299–1325.

———. 2002. *Cities and Privatization: Prospects for the New Century.* Upper Saddle River, NJ: Prentice Hall.

Grodzins, Morton. 1960. The Federal System. In *Goals for Americans: The Report of the President's Commission on National Goals.* Englewood Cliffs, NJ: Prentice-Hall.

Grønbjerg, Kirsten A. 1990. *Managing Nonprofit Funding Relations: Case Studies of Six Human Service Organizations.* New Haven, CT: Institution for Social and Policy Studies.

———. 1993. *Understanding Nonprofit Funding: Managing Revenues in Social Services and Community Development Organizations,* 1st ed. San Francisco: Jossey-Bass.

Gruber, Howard E. 2000. Creativity and Conflict Resolution. In *The Handbook of Conflict Resolution: Theory and Practice,* ed. Morton Deutsch and Peter Coleman. San Francisco: Jossey-Bass.

Gujarati, Damodar N. 2003. *Basic Econometrics.* Boston: McGraw-Hill.

Gulati, Ranjay. 1995a. Does Familiarity Breed Trust? The Implications of Repeated Ties for Contractual Choice in Alliances. *Academy of Management Journal* 38, no. 1:85–112.

———. 1995b. Social Structure and Alliance Formation Patterns: A Longitudinal Analysis. *Administrative Science Quarterly* 40:619–52.

———. 1998. Alliances and Networks. *Strategic Management Journal* 19:293–317.

Guo, Chao, and Muhittin Acar. 2005. Understanding Collaboration among Nonprofit Organizations: Combining Resource Dependency, Institutional, and Network Perspectives. *Nonprofit and Voluntary Sector Quarterly* 34, no. 3:340–61.

Guriev, Sergei, and Dmitry Kvasov. 2005. Contracting on Time. *American Economic Review* 95, no. 5:1369–85.

Hall, Thad E., and Laurence J. O'Toole Jr. 2000. Structures for Policy Implementation: An Analysis of National Legislation, 1965–66 and 1993–94. *Administration and Society* 31, no. 6:667–86.

———. 2004. Shaping Formal Networks through the Regulatory Process. *Administration and Society* 36, no. 2:186–207.

Hamilton, Edward K. 1978. On Non-Constitutional Management of a Constitutional Problem. *Daedalus* 107 (Winter): 111–28.

Hanf, Kenneth, Benny Hjern, and David O. Porter. 1978. Local Networks of Manpower Training in the Federal Republic of Germany and Sweden. In *Interorganizational Policy Making: Limits to Coordination and Central Control,* ed. Kenneth Hanf and Fritz W. Scharpf. London: Sage.

Hannan, Michael T., and John Freeman. 1977. The Population Ecology of Organizations. *American Journal of Sociology* 82, no. 5:929–64.

Hansen, Randy R. 2006. Letter to the Editor Regarding Incident Command System (ICS). *Journal of Homeland Security and Emergency Management* 3, no. 4.

Hardin, Russell. 2002. *Trust and Trustworthiness*. New York: Russell Sage Foundation.

Hart, Oliver, and John Moore. 1999. Foundation of Incomplete Contracts. *Review of Economic Studies* 66:115–38.

Heclo, Hugh. 1978. Issue Networks and the Executive Establishment. In *The New American Political System*, ed. Anthony King. Washington, DC: American Enterprise Institute.

Heinrich, Carolyn J. 2000. Organizational Form and Performance: An Empirical Investigation of Nonprofit and For-Profit Job-Training Service Providers. *Journal of Policy Analysis and Management* 19, no. 2:233–61.

———. 2003. Measuring Public Sector Performance and Effectiveness. In *Handbook of Public Administration*, ed. B. Guy Peters and Jon Pierre. Thousand Oaks, CA: Sage.

———. 2004. Improving Public Sector Performance Management: One Step Forward, Two Steps Back? *Public Finance and Management* 4, no. 3:317–51.

Heinrich, Carolyn J., and Laurence E. Lynn Jr. 2000. Governance and Performance: The Influence of Program Structure and Management on Job Training Partnership Act (JTPA) Program Outcomes. In *Governance and Performance: New Perspectives*, ed. Carolyn J. Heinrich and Laurence E. Lynn Jr. Washington, DC: Georgetown University Press.

Hennessey, Thomas J., Jr. 1998. "Reinventing" Government: Does Leadership Make the Difference? *Public Administration Review* 58, no. 6:522–32.

Henry, Nicholas. 2002. Is Privatization Passé? The Case for Competition and the Emergence of Intersectoral Administration. *Public Administration Review* 62 (May–June): 374–78.

Hensler, Deborah. 2000. ADR Research at the Crossroads. 2000. *Journal of Dispute Resolution* 71:71–78.

Hill, Carolyn J. 2004. Can Casework Design Choices Improve Outcomes for Clients Who Are Difficult to Employ? Evidence from Welfare-to-Work Offices. In *The Art of Governance: Analyzing Management and Administration*, ed. Patricia W. Ingraham and Laurence E. Lynn Jr. Washington, DC: Georgetown University Press.

———. 2006. Casework Job Design and Client Outcomes in Welfare-to-Work Offices. *Journal of Public Administration Research and Theory* 16, no. 2:263–88.

Hill, Carolyn J., and Laurence E. Lynn Jr. 2004. Is Hierarchical Governance in Decline? Evidence from Empirical Research. *Journal of Public Administration Research and Theory* 15, no. 2:173–95.

Holcomb, Pamela, and Burt S. Barnow. 2004. Serving People with Disabilities through the Workforce Investment Act's One-Stop Career Centers. http://urban.org/authors/authortopic.cfm?&expertid=6012&topicid=96&page=1.

Hox, J. J. 1995. *Applied Multilevel Analysis*. Amsterdam: TT-Publikaties. http://www.ioe.ac.uk/multilevel/.

Hsu, Spencer S. 2006. First the Flood, Now the Fight. *Washington Post*, August 30.

Hughes, Jonathan T. 2001. Building Functional Communities: Concepts for Reframing Social and Fiscal Policy. *International Journal of Value-Based Management* 14, no. 1:35–57.

Hull, Christopher J., with Benny Hjern. 1987. *Helping Small Firms Grow: An Implementation Approach*. London: Croom Helm.

Huxham, Chris, ed. 1996. *Creating Collaborative Advantage*. London: Sage.

———. 2003. Theorizing Collaboration Practice. *Public Management Review* 5, no. 3:401–23.

Huxham, Chris, and Siv Vangen. 2000. Ambiguity, Complexity and Dynamics in the Membership of Collaboration. *Human Relations* 53, no. 6:771–806.

Hybels, Ralph C. 1995. On Legitimacy, Legitimation, and Organizations: A Critical Review and Integrative Theoretical Model. *Academy of Management Journal* 38:241–45.

Imperial, Mark T. 2005. Using Collaboration as a Governance Strategy: Lessons from Six Watershed Management Programs. *Administration and Society* 37, no. 3:281–320.

Ingraham, Patricia W. 2005. You Talking to Me? Accountability and the Modern Public Service. John Gaus Lecture, presented at annual meeting of American Political Science Association. Reprinted in *PS: Political Science and Politics* 39 (January): 17–21.

Ingram, Helen. 1977. Policy Implementation through Bargaining: The Case of Federal Grants-in-Aid. *Public Policy* 25, no. 4:499–526.

Inkpen, Andrew C., and Steven C. Currall. 2004. The Co-Evolution of Trust, Control, and Learning in Joint Ventures. *Organization Science* 15, no. 5:586–99.

Irwin, Robert L. 1989. The Incident Command System (ICS). In *Disaster Response: Principles of Preparation and Coordination*, ed. Erik Auf der Heide. Saint Louis: C. V. Mosby.

Isett, Kimberly Roussin, and Keith G. Provan. 2005. The Evolution of Dyadic Interorganizational Relationships in a Network of Publicly Funded Nonprofit Agencies. *Journal of Public Administration Research and Theory* 15, no. 1:149–65.

Jahawar, I. M., and Gary L. McLaughlin. 2001. Toward a Descriptive Stakeholder Theory: An Organizational Life Cycle Approach. *Academy of Management Review* 26, no. 3:397–414.

Jap, Sandy D. 2001. Pie-Sharing in Complex Collaboration Contexts. *Journal of Marketing Research* 38, no. 1:86–99.

Jeffries, Frank L., and Richard Reed. 2000. Trust and Adaptation in Relational Contracting. *Academy of Management Review* 25, no. 4:873–82.

Jennings, Edward T., Jr., and Jo Ann G. Ewalt. 1998. Interorganizational Coordination, Administrative Consolidation, and Policy Performance. *Public Administration Review* 58, no. 5:417–28.

Johnston, Jocelyn M., and Barbara S. Romzek. 1999. Contracting and Accountability in State Medicaid Reform: Rhetoric, Theories, and Reality. *Public Administration Review* 59, no. 5:383–99.

Kakalik, James, Deborah Hensler, Daniel McCaffrey, Martin Oshiro, Nicholas M. Pace, and Mary E. Vaiana. 1998. *Discovery Management: Further Analysis of the Civil Justice Reform Act, Evaluation Data*. Santa Monica, CA: RAND Corporation.

Kamarck, Elaine C. 2004. Applying 21st-Century Government to the Challenge of Homeland Security. In *Collaboration: Using Networks and Partnerships*, ed. John M. Kamensky and Thomas J. Burlin. Lanham, MD: Rowman & Littlefield.

Kamensky, John M., and Thomas J. Burlin, eds. 2004. *Collaboration: Using Networks and Partnerships*. Lanham, MD: Rowman & Littlefield.

Kanter, Rosabeth M. 1994. Collaborative Advantage: The Art of Alliances. *Harvard Business Review*, July–August, 96–108.

Kaufman, Herbert. 1985. *Time, Chance, and Organizations*. Chatham, NJ: Chatham House Publishers.

Kearney, Richard C., Berry M. Feldman, and Carmine P. F. Scavo. 2000. Reinventing Government: City Manager Attitudes and Actions. *Public Administration Review* 60, no. 6:535–48.

Kelman, Stephen J. 1990. *Procurement and Public Management: The Fear of Discretion and the Quality of Government Performance*. Washington, DC: AEI Press.

———. 2002. Contracting. In *The Tools of Government: A Guide to the New Governance*, ed. Lester M. Salamon. New York: Oxford University Press.

———. 2005. Public Management Needs Help! *Academy of Management Journal* 48, no. 6:967–69.

Kendra, James M., and Tricia Wachtendorf. 2003. Elements of Resilience after the World Trade Center Disaster: Reconstituting New York City's Emergency Operations Center. *Disasters* 27, no. 1:37–53.

Kerr, James W. 2004. Letters: Incident Command System. *AUSA: Army Magazine*, March 1.

Kettl, Donald F. 1988a. *Government by Proxy*. Washington, DC: CQ Press.

———. 1988b. Performance and Accountability: The Challenge of Government by Proxy for Public Administration. *American Review of Public Administration* 18, no. 1:9–28.

———. 1993. *Sharing Power: Public Governance and Private Markets*. Washington, DC: Brookings Institution Press.

———. 2000. The Transformation of Governance: Globalization, Devolution, and the Role of Government. *Public Administration Review* 60 (November–December): 488–97.

———. 2002. *The Transformation of Governance: Public Administration for Twenty-First Century America*. Baltimore: Johns Hopkins University Press.

———. 2003. Contingent Coordination: Practical and Theoretical Puzzles for Homeland Security. *American Review of Public Administration* 33 (September): 253–77.

———. 2005a. *The Global Public Management Revolution*, 2nd ed. Washington, DC: Brookings Institution Press.

———. 2005b. *The Next Government of the United States: Challenges for Perfor-*

mance in the 21st Century. Transformation of Organizations Series. Washington, DC: IBM Center for the Business of Government.

Kickert, Walter J.M., Erik-Hans Klijn, and Joop F. M. Koppenjan. 1997a. Introduction: A Management Perspective on Policy Networks. In *Managing Complex Networks*, ed. Walter J. M. Kickert, Erik-Hans Klijn, and Joop F.M. Koppenjan. London: Sage.

———, eds. 1997b. *Managing Complex Networks: Strategies for the Public Sector*. London: Sage.

Kickert, Walter J. M., and Joop F. M. Koppenjan. 1997. Public Management and Network Management: An Overview. In *Managing Complex Networks*, ed. Walter J. M. Kickert, Erik-Hans Klijn, and Joop F. M. Koppenjan. London: Sage.

Klijn, Erik-Hans. 1996. Analyzing and Managing Policy Processes in Complex Networks: A Theoretical Examination of the Concept Policy Network and Its Problems. *Administration and Society* 28:90–119.

———. 1997. Policy Networks: An Overview. In *Managing Complex Networks: Strategies for the Public Sector*, ed. Walter J. M. Kickert, Erik-Hans Klijn, and Joop F. M. Koppenjan. London: Sage.

———. 2005. Networks and Inter-organizational Management: Challenging, Steering, Evaluation, and the Role of Public Actors in Public Management. In *The Oxford Handbook of Public Management*. Oxford: Oxford University Press.

Klingner, Donald E., John Nalbandian, and Barbara Romzek. 2002. Politics, Administration, and Markets: Conflicting Expectations and Accountability. *American Review of Public Administration* 32 (June): 117–44.

Kogan, Deborah, Katherine P. Dickinson, Ruth Fedrau, Michael J. Midling, and Kristin E. Wolff. 1997. *Creating Workforce Development Systems That Work: An Evaluation of the Initial One-Stop Implementation Experience: Final Report*. Contract report to U.S. Department of Labor, Contract F-4957-5-00-80-30. Oakland: Social Policy Research Associates.

Kooiman, Jan. 1993. Governance and Governability: Using Complexity, Dynamics and Diversity. In *Modern Governance: New Government-Society Interactions*, ed. Jan Kooiman. London: Sage.

———. 2000. Societal Governance: Levels, Models, and Orders of Social-Political Interaction. In *Debating Governance*, ed. Jon Pierre. New York: Oxford University Press.

Koontz, Tomas M., Toddi A. Steelman, JoAnn Carmin, Katrina Smith Korfmacher, Cassandra Moseley, and Craig W. Thomas. 2004. *Collaborative Environmental Management: What Roles for Government?* Washington, DC: Resources for the Future.

Kouwenhoven, Vincent. 1993. Public-Private Partnerships. In *Modern Governance: New Government-Society Interactions*, ed. Jan Kooiman. London: Sage.

Kramer, Ralph M. 1994. Voluntary Agencies and the Contract Culture: Dream or Nightmare? *Social Service Review* 68, no. 1:33–60.

Krauss, Robert M., and Ezequiel Morsella. 2000. Communication and Conflict.

In *The Handbook of Conflict Resolution: Theory and Practice*, ed. Morton Deutsch and Peter Coleman. San Francisco: Jossey-Bass.

Kvaloy, Ola, and Trond E. Olsen. 2004. Endogenous Verifiability in Relational Contracting. Unpublished working paper.

Lasker, Roz D., Elisa S. Weiss, and Rebecca Miller. 2001. Partnership Synergy: A Practical Framework for Studying and Strengthening the Collaborative Advantage. *Milbank Quarterly* 79, no. 2:179–205.

Laws, David. 1999. Representation of Stakeholding Interests. In *The Consensus-Building Handbook: A Comprehensive Guide to Reaching Agreement*, ed. Laurance Susskind, Sarah McKearnan, and Jennifer Thomas-Larmer. Thousand Oaks, CA: Sage.

Leach, William D. L. 2006. Collaborative Public Management and Democracy: Evidence from Western Watershed Partnerships. *Public Administration Review* 66, no. 6:100–10.

Leach, William D. L., and Paul A. Sabatier. 2005. To Trust an Adversary: Integrating Rational and Psychological Models of Collaborative Policymaking. *American Political Science Review* 99, no. 4:491–503.

Lehman, Christopher K. 1989. The Forgotten Fundamental: Successes and Excesses of Direct Government. In *Beyond Privatization: The Tools of Government Action*, ed. Lester M. Salamon and Michael S. Lund. Washington, DC: Urban Institute Press.

Levin, Jonathan. 2003. Relational Incentive Contracts. *American Economic Review* 93, no. 3:835–57.

Levine, Sol, and Paul E. White. 1961. Exchange as a Conceptual Framework for the Study of Interorganizational Relationships. *Administrative Science Quarterly* 5:583–610.

Levinthal, G. S. 1980. What Should Be Done with Equity Theory? New Approaches to the Study of Fairness in Social Relationships. In *Social Exchange: Advances in Theory and Research*, ed. Kenneth J. Gergen, Martin S. Greenberg, and. Richard H. Willis. New York: Plenum Press.

Lewicki, Roy J., Bruce Barry, David M. Saunders, and John W. Minton. 2003. *Negotiation*, 4th ed. Boston: Irwin.

Lewicki., Roy J., and Carolyn Wiethoff. 2000. Trust, Trust Development, and Trust Repair. In *The Handbook of Conflict Resolution: Theory and Practice*, ed. Morton Deutsch and Peter T. Coleman. San Francisco: Jossey-Bass.

Light, Paul C. 1999. *The New Public Service*. Washington, DC: Brookings Institution Press.

Lindell, Michael K., Carla Prater, and Ronald W. Perry. 2006. *Introduction to Emergency Management*. Hoboken, NJ: John Wiley & Sons.

Linden, Russell M. 2002. *Working across Boundaries: Making Collaboration Work in Government and Nonprofit Organizations*. San Francisco: Jossey-Bass.

Linder, Stephen H., and B. Guy Peters. 1987. Relativism, Contingency, and the

Definition of Success in Implementation Research. *Policy Studies Review* 7, no. 1:116–27.

Lowndes, Vivian, and Chris Skelcher. 2004. Like a House and Carriage or a Fish on a Bicycle: How Well Do Local Partnerships and Public Participation Go Together? *Local Government Studies* 30, no. 1:51–73.

Lynn, Laurence E., Jr. 2004. What Is Public Administration? *Management Matters: Public Management Research Associations Newsletter* 2 (July): 1–4.

Lynn, Laurence E., Jr., Carolyn J. Heinrich, and Carolyn J. Hill. 2001. *Improving Governance: A New Logic for Empirical Research.* Washington, DC: Georgetown University Press.

Macneil, Ian R. 1978. Contracts: Adjustments of Long-Term Economic Relations under Classical, Neoclassical, and Relational Contract Law. *Northwestern University Law Review* 72: 855–905.

Mandell, Myrna P., and Toddi A. Steelman. 2003. Understanding What Can Be Accomplished through Interorganizational Innovations: The Importance of Typologies, Context and Management Strategies. *Public Management Review* 5, no. 2:197–224.

March, James G., and Johan P. Olsen. 1989. *Rediscovering Institutions: The Organizational Basis of Politics.* New York: Free Press.

Marino, Jonathan. 2006. DHS Keeping Close Eye on Rebuilding Funds, Official Says. www.GovExec.com, August 30.

Mattessich, Paul, and Barbara Monsey. 1992. *Collaboration: What Makes It Work?* Saint Paul: Amherst H. Wilder Foundation.

Mayer, Roger C., James H. Davis, and F. David Schoorman. 1995. An Integrative Model of Organizational Trust. *Academy of Management Review* 20, no. 3:709–34.

McEntire, David A. 1998. *Towards a Theory of Coordination: Umbrella Organization and Disaster Relief in the 1997–98 Peruvian El Niño Disaster.* Quick Response Report 105. Boulder, CO: Natural Hazards Research and Information Applications Center, University of Colorado.

———. 2002. Coordinating Multi-Organisational Responses to Disaster: Lessons from the March 28, 2000, Fort Worth Tornado. *Disaster Prevention and Management* 11, no. 5:369–79.

———. 2007. *Disaster Response and Recovery.* Hoboken, NJ: John Wiley & Sons.

McGuire, Michael. 2000. Collaborative Policy Making and Administration: The Operational Demands of Local Economic Development. *Economic Development Quarterly* 14, no. 3:276–91.

———. 2002. Managing Networks: Propositions on What Managers Do and Why They Do It. *Public Administration Review* 62, no. 5:599–609.

———. 2003. Is It Really So Strange? A Critical Look at the "Network Management Is Different from Hierarchical Management" Perspective. Paper presented at Seventh National Public Management Research Conference, Washington, October 9–11.

———. 2006. Collaborative Public Management: Assessing What We Know and How We Know It. *Public Administration Review* 66, no. 6 (Supplement): 33–43.

Meier, Kenneth J., and Jeff Gill. 2000. *What Works: A New Approach to Policy Analysis*. Boulder, CO: Westview Press.

Meier, Kenneth J., and Laurence J. O'Toole Jr. 2001. Managerial Strategies and Behavior in Networks: A Model with Evidence from U.S. Public Education. *Journal of Public Administration Research and Theory* 11 (July): 271–95.

———. 2003. Public Management and Educational Performance: The Impact of Managerial Networking. *Public Administration Review* 63, no. 6:689–99.

———. 2005. Managerial Networking: Issues of Measurement and Research Design. *Administration and Society* 37, no. 5 (November): 523–41.

———. 2008. Management Theory and Occam's Razor: How Public Organizations Buffer the Environment. Paper presented at annual meetings of American Political Science Association, Philadelphia, August 31–September 3.

Meier, Kenneth J., Laurence J. O'Toole Jr., and Sean Nicholson-Crotty. 2004. Multilevel Governance and Organizational Performance: Investigating the Political-Bureaucratic Labyrinth. *Journal of Policy Analysis and Management* 23, no. 1:31–47.

Meyers, Marcia K., Norma M. Riccucci, and Irene Lurie. 2001. Achieving Goal Congruence in Complex Environments: The Case of Welfare Reform. *Journal of Public Administration Research and Theory* 11, no. 2:165–201.

Milward, H. Brinton, and Keith G. Provan. 2000. How Networks Are Governed. In *Governance and Performance: New Perspectives*, ed. Carolyn J. Heinrich and Laurence E. Lynn Jr. Washington, DC: Georgetown University Press.

———. 2006. *A Manager's Guide to Choosing and Using Collaborative Networks*. Washington, DC: IBM Center for the Business of Government.

Mitchell, Shannon M., and Stephen M. Shortell. 2000. The Governance and Management of Effective Community Health Partnerships: A Typology for Research, Policy, and Practice. *Milbank Quarterly* 78, no. 2:241–89.

Moffitt, M. L., and R. C. Bordone, eds. 2005. *The Handbook of Dispute Resolution*. San Francisco: Jossey-Bass.

Mosher, Frederick C. 1980. The Changing Responsibilities and Tactics of the Federal Government. *Public Administration Review* 40 (November–December): 541–48.

Moynihan, Donald P. 2005a. *Leveraging Collaborative Networks in Infrequent Emergency Situations*. Washington, DC: IBM Center for the Business of Government.

———. 2005b. The Use of Networks in Emergency Management. Paper presented at Annual Meeting of American Political Science Association, Washington, September 1–4.

Mulroy, Elizabeth A., and Sharon Shay. 1997. Nonprofit Organizations and Innovation: A Model of Neighborhood-Based Collaboration to Prevent Child Mistreatment. *Social Work* 42, no. 5:515–25.

National Environmental Conflict Resolution Advisory Committee. 2005. *Final Report Submitted to the U.S. Institute for Environmental Conflict Resolution.* www.ecr.gov/necrac/pdf/NECRAC_Report.pdf.

National Institute for Dispute Resolution. 1987. *Statewide Offices of Mediation: Experiments in Public Policy.* Washington, DC: Dispute Resolution Forum.

Neal, David M. 2000. Developing Degree Programs in Disaster Management: Some Reflections and Observations. *International Journal of Mass Emergencies and Disasters* 18, no. 3:417–37.

Neal, David M., and Brenda D. Phillips. 1995. Effective Emergency Management: Reconsidering the Bureaucratic Approach. *Disasters* 19, no. 4:327–37.

Nilsson, Carl-Henric. 1997. Cross-Sectoral Alliances, Trick or Treat? The Case of Scania. *International Journal of Production Economics* 52:147–60.

Nutt, Paul C. 1999. Public-Private Differences and the Assessment of Alternatives for Decision-Making. *Journal of Public Administration Research and Theory* 9, no. 2:305–49.

Nutt, Paul C., and Robert W. Backoff. 1993. Transforming Public Organizations with Strategic Management and Strategic Leadership. *Journal of Management* 19, no. 2:299–347.

Office of Emergency Services. 2001. *They Will Come: Post-Disaster Volunteers and Local Governments.* Sacramento: Office of Emergency Services, State of California.

O'Leary, Rosemary, and Lisa Blomgren Bingham, eds. 2003. *The Promise and Performance of Environmental Conflict Resolution.* Washington, DC: Resources for the Future.

O'Leary, Rosemary, and Lisa Blomgren Bingham. 2008. *A Manager's Guide to Resolving Conflicts in Collaborative Networks.* Washington, DC: IBM Center for the Business of Government.

O'Leary, Rosemary, Catherine Gerard, and Lisa Blomgren Bingham. 2006. Introduction to the Symposium on Collaborative Public Management. *Public Administration Review* 66, no. 6:6–9.

Oliver, Christine. 1990. Determinants of Interorganizational Relationships: Integration and Future Directions. *Academy of Management Review* 15, no. 2:241–65.

———. 1997. The Influence of Institutional and Task Environment Relationship on Organizational Performance: The Canadian Construction Industry. *Journal of Management Studies* 34, no. 1:99–124.

O'Neill, Michael. 2002. *Nonprofit Nation: A New Look at the Third America.* San Francisco: Jossey-Bass.

Orr, Patricia, Kirk Emerson, and Dale L. Keyes. 2008. Environmental Conflict Resolution Practice and Performance: An Evaluation Framework. *Conflict Resolution Quarterly* 25, no. 3:283–301

Orr, Patricia, Dale L. Keyes, Kirk Emerson, and Kathy McKnight. 2008. Environmental Conflict Resolution: Evaluating Performance Outcomes and Contributing Factors. In press.

Ostrom, Elinor. 1990. *Governing the Commons: The Evolution of Institutions for Collective Action.* Cambridge: Cambridge University Press.

O'Toole, Laurence J., Jr. 1985. Diffusion of Responsibility: An Interorganizational Analysis. In *Policy Implementation in Federal and Unitary Systems,* ed. Kenneth Hanf and A. J. Toonen. Dordrecht: Martinus Nijhoff.

———. 1996. Hollowing the Infrastructure: Revolving Loan Programs and Network Dynamics in the American States. *Journal of Public Administration Research and Theory* 6, no. 2:225–42.

———. 1997. Treating Networks Seriously: Practical and Research-Based Agendas in Public Administration. *Public Administration Review* 57, no. 1:45–52.

———. 2000. Different Public Managements? Implications of Structural Context in Hierarchies and Networks. In *Advancing Public Management: New Developments in Theory, Methods, and Practice,* ed. Jeffrey L. Brudney, Laurence J. O'Toole Jr., and Hal G. Rainey. Washington, DC: Georgetown University Press.

O'Toole, Laurence J., Jr., and Kenneth J. Meier. 1999. Modeling the Impact of Public Management: The Implications of Structural Context. *Journal of Public Administration Research and Theory* 9 (October): 505–26.

———. 2003. Plus Ça Change: Public Management, Personnel Stability, and Organizational Performance. *Journal of Public Administration Research and Theory* 13 (January): 43–64.

———. 2004a. Desperately Seeking Selznick: Cooptation and the Dark Side of Public Management in Networks. *Public Administration Review* 64, no. 6:681–93.

———. 2004b. Public Management in Intergovernmental Networks: Matching Structural Networks and Managerial Networking. *Journal of Public Administration Research and Theory* 14, no. 4:469–94.

Page, Stephen. 2003. Entrepreneurial Strategies for Managing Interagency Collaboration. *Journal of Public Administration Research and Theory* 13, no. 3:311–40.

Palmer, K. 2005a. Consultant Urges Performance-Based Contracting. *Government Executive,* April 4. Available at www.govexec.com.

———. 2005b. "Outside Experts Emphasize Contracting Relationships. *Government Executive,* April 20. Available at www.govexec.com.

———. 2006. Best Bets: Top Contracting Shops Share Their Secrets. *Government Executive,* August 15. Available at www.govexec.com.

Patton, Ann. 2007. Collaborative Emergency Management. In *Emergency Management: Principles and Practice for Local Government,* 2nd ed., edited by William L Waugh, Jr., and Kathleen Tierney. Washington, DC: International City/County Management Association.

Peters, B. Guy. 1998. With a Little Help from Our Friends: Public-Private Partnerships as Institutions and Instruments. In *Partnerships in Urban Governance,* ed. John Pierre. New York: St. Martin's Press.

Pfeffer, Jeffrey, and Gerald Salancik. 1978. *External Control of Organizations: A Resource Dependence Perspective.* New York: Harper & Row.

Pierre, John, ed. 1998. *Partnerships in Urban Governance*. New York: St. Martin's Press.

Polyani, Michael. 1967. *The Tacit Dimension*. Garden City, NY: Anchor.

Posner, Paul, Robert Yetvin, Mark Schneiderman, Christopher Spiro, and Andrea Barnett. 2000. A Survey of Voucher Use: Variations and Common Elements. In *Vouchers and the Provision of Public Services*, ed. C. Eugene Steuerle. Washington, DC: Brookings Institution Press.

Powers, John R. 2003. Managing the Response to a Major Terrorist Event. *Homeland Defense Journal*, February 24, 16–19.

Pratt, John W., and Richard J. Zeckhauser. 1991. Principals and Agents: An Overview. In *Principals and Agents: The Structure of Business*, ed. John W. Pratt and Richard J. Zeckhauser. Cambridge, MA: Harvard Business School Press.

Pressman, Jeffrey L. 1975. *Federal Programs and City Politics: The Dynamics of the Aid Process in Oakland*. Berkeley: University of California Press.

Pressman, Jeffrey L., and Aaron Wildavsky. 1973. *Implementation*. Berkeley: University of California Press.

Prizzia, Ross. 2003. An International Perspective on Privatization: The Need to Balance Economic and Social Performance. *American Review of Public Administration* 33 (September): 316–72.

Provan, Keith G., and H. Brinton Milward. 1991. Institutional-Level Norms and Organizational Involvement in a Service-Implementation Network. *Journal of Public Administration Research and Theory* 1, no. 4:391–417.

———. 1995. A Preliminary Theory of Interorganizational Effectiveness: A Comparative Study of Four Community Mental Health Systems. *Administrative Science Quarterly* 40, no. 1:1–33.

———. 2001. Do Networks Really Work? A Framework for Evaluating Public-Sector Organizational Networks. *Public Administration Review* 61, no. 4:414–23.

Quarantelli, Enrico L. 1997. Ten Criteria for Evaluating the Management of Community Disasters. *Disasters* 21, no. 1:39–56.

Raab, Jörg. 2002. Where Do Policy Networks Come From? *Journal of Public Administration Research and Theory* 12, no. 4:581–622.

Radin, Beryl A., Robert Agranoff, Ann O'M. Bowman, Gregory C. Buntz, Steven J. Ott, Barbara S. Romzek, and Robert H. Wilson. 1996. *New Governance for Rural America: Creating Intergovernmental Partnerships*. Lawrence: University Press of Kansas.

Rainey, Hal G. 1997. *Understanding and Managing Public Organizations*, 2nd ed. San Francisco: Jossey-Bass.

———. 2003. *Understanding and Managing Public Organization*, 3rd ed. New York: John Wiley & Sons.

Rainey, Hal G., and Barry Bozeman. 2000. Comparing Public and Private Organizations: Empirical Research and the Power of A Priori. *Journal of Public Administration Research and Theory* 10, no. 2:447–69.

Rapp, Cynthia A., and Carolyn M. Whitfield. 1999. Neighborhood-Based Services:

Organizational Change and Integration Prospects. *Nonprofit Management & Leadership* 9, no. 3:261–76.

Rehfuss, John A. 1989. *Contracting Out in Government: A Guide to Working with Outside Contractors to Supply Public Services*. San Francisco: Jossey-Bass.

Rethemeyer, R. Karl. 2005. Conceptualizing and Measuring Collaborative Networks. *Public Administration Review* 65 (January–February): 117–21.

Rhodes, R. A. W. 1997. *Understanding Governance*. Buckingham, U.K.: Open University Press.

———. 2002. Putting People Back into Networks. *Australian Journal of Political Science* 37, no. 3:399–416.

Riccucci, Norma M. 2005. Street-Level Bureaucrats and Intrastate Variation in the Implementation of Temporary Assistance for Needy Families Policies. *Journal of Public Administration Research and Theory* 15, no. 1:89–111.

Rittel, Horst, and Melcin Webber. 1973. Dilemmas in a General Theory of Planning. *Policy Sciences* 4:155–69.

Ritti, R. Richard, and Jonathan H. Silver. 1986. Early Processes of Institutionalization: The Dramaturgy of Exchange in Interorganizational Relations. *Administrative Science Quarterly* 31, no. 1:25–42.

Rogers, David L. and David A. Whetten. 1982. *Interorganizational Coordination: Theory, Research, and Implementation*. Ames: Iowa State University Press.

Rosenau, Pauline V. 2000. *Public-Private Policy Partnerships*. Cambridge, MA: MIT Press.

Rubin, Claire B., with Martin D. Saperstein and Daniel G. Barbee. 1985. *Community Recovery from a Major Disaster*. Boulder, CO: Institute of Behavioral Science, University of Colorado.

Sabatier, Paul. 1993. Policy Change over a Decade or More. In *Policy Change and Learning: An Advocacy Coalition Approach*, ed. Paul Sabatier and Hank Jenkins-Smith. Boulder, CO: Westview Press.

Saidel, Judith R. 1991. Resource Interdependence: The Relationship between Public Agencies and Nonprofit Organizations. *Public Administration Review* 51, no. 6:543–53.

———. 1994. The Dynamics of Interdependence between Public Agencies and Nonprofit Organizations. *Research in Public Administration* 3:210–29.

Salamon, Lester M. 1981. Rethinking Public Management: Third-Party Government and the Changing Forms of Governmental Action. *Public Policy* 29 (Summer): 255–75.

———, ed. 1989. *Beyond Privatization: The Tools of Government Action*. Washington, DC: Urban Institute Press.

———. 2002. *The Tools of Government: A Guide to the New Governance*: New York: Oxford University Press.

Sandfort, Jodi R. 2000. Moving Beyond Discretion and Outcomes: Examining Public Management from the Front Lines of the Welfare System. *Journal of Public Administration Research and Theory* 10, no. 4:729–56.

Savas, Emanuel S. 1982. *Privatizing the Public Sector*. Chatham, NJ: Chatham House.

———. 1987. *Privatization: The Key to Better Government*. Chatham, NJ: Chatham House.

———. 2000. *Privatization and Public-Private Partnerships*. Chatham, NJ: Chatham House.

Saxton, Todd. 1997. The Effects of Partner and Relationship Characteristics on Alliance Outcomes. *Academy of Management Journal* 40, no. 2:443–61.

Scardaville, Michael. 2003. Principles the Department of Homeland Security Must Follow for an Effective Transition. *Heritage Foundation Backgrounder*, February 28, 1–8.

Scharpf, Fritz. 1978. Interorganizational Policy Studies: Issues, Concepts, and Perspectives. In *Interorganizational Policy Making: Limits to Coordination and Central Control*, ed. Kenneth Hanf and Fritz W. Scharpf. London: Sage.

Schneider, Mark, John Scholz, Mark Lubell, Denisa Mindruta, and Matthew Edwardsen. 2003. Building Consensual Institutions: Networks and the National Estuary Program. *American Journal of Political Science* 47, no. 1:143–58.

Schneider, Saundra K. 1995. *Flirting with Disaster: Public Management in Crisis Situations*. Armonk, NY: M. E. Sharpe.

Schneider, Saundra K., and William G. Jacoby. 1996. Influences of Bureaucratic Policy Initiatives in the American States. *Journal of Public Administration Research and Theory* 6 (October): 495–522.

Sclar, Elliot D. 2000. *You Don't Always Get What You Pay For: The Economics of Privatization*. Ithaca, NY: Cornell University Press.

Scott, W. Richard. 2003. *Organizations: Rational, Natural, and Open Systems*. Upper Saddle River: Prentice-Hall.

Selden, Sally Coleman, Jessica Sowa, and Jodi Sandfort. 2002. *The Impact of Nonprofit Collaboration in Early Childhood Education on Management and Program Outcomes*. Paper presented at Annual Meeting of Association of Nonprofit Organizations and Voluntary Action, Montreal, November 14–16.

———. 2006. The Impact of Nonprofit Collaboration in Early Child Care and Education on Management and Program Outcomes. *Public Administration Review* 66, no. 3:412–25.

Sharfman, Mark P., Barbara Gray, and Aimin Yan. 1991. The Context of Interorganizational Collaboration in the Garment Industry: An Institutional Perspective. *Journal of Applied Behavioral Science* 27, no. 2:181–208.

Shaw, Mary M. 2003. Successful Collaboration between the Nonprofit and Public Sectors. *Nonprofit Management & Leadership* 14, no. 1:107–20.

Shleifer, Andrei, and Robert W. Vishny. 1998. *The Grabbing Hand: Government Pathologies and Their Cures*. Cambridge, MA: Harvard University Press.

Siegel, Gilbert B. 1999. Where Are We on Local Government Service Contracting? *Public Productivity and Management Review* 14 (March): 365–89.

Simon, Herbert A. 1997. *Administrative Behavior*, 4th ed. New York: Free Press.

Simonin, Bernard L. 1997. The Importance of Collaborative Know-How: An Empirical Test of the Learning Organization. *Academy of Management Journal* 40, no. 5:1150–74.

Singer, Peter W. 2003. *Corporate Warriors: The Rise of The Privatized Military*. Ithaca, NY: Cornell University Press.

Singh, Jitendra V., David J.Tucker, and Agnes G. Meinhard. 1991. Institutional Change and Ecological Dynamics. In *The New Institutionalism in Organizational Analysis*, ed. Paul J. DiMaggio and Walter W. Powell. Chicago: University of Chicago Press.

Smith, Steven Rathgeb, and Michael Lipsky. 1993. *Non-Profits for Hire: The Welfare State in the Age of Contracting*. Cambridge, MA: Harvard University Press.

Snavely, Keith, and Martin B. Tracy. 2000. Collaboration among Rural Nonprofit Organizations. *Nonprofit Management & Leadership* 11, no. 2:145–65.

Society of Professionals in Dispute Resolution. 1987. Best Practices for Government Agencies. http://acrnet.org/acrlibrary/more.php?id=13_0_1_0_M.

Stanley, Ellis M., and William L. Waugh Jr. 2001. Emergency Managers for the New Millennium. In *Handbook of Crisis and Emergency Management*, ed. Ali Farazmand. New York: Marcel Dekker.

State of Texas. 1994. *The Application for an Employment and Training One-Stop Career Center System Implementation/Planning and Development*. Austin: Office of the Governor, State of Texas.

Steenbergen, Marco R., and Bradford S. Jones. 2002. Modeling Multilevel Data Structures. *American Journal of Political Science* 46, no. 1:218–37.

Stephenson, Max O., Jr. 1991. Wither the Public-Private Partnership? A Critical Overview. *Urban Affairs Quarterly* 27:109–27.

Stiles, Jan. 2001. Managing Strategic Alliances' Success: Determining the Influencing Factors of Intent within Partnerships. In *Effective Collaboration: Managing the Obstacles to Success*, ed. Jens Genefke and Frank McDonald. New York: Palgrave.

Stinchcombe, Arthur L. 1965. Social Structure and Organizations. In *Handbook of Organizations*, ed. J. G. March. Chicago: Rand McNally.

Stoker, Gerry. 2004. *Modernizing British Local Government. From Thatcherism to New Labour*. Basingstoke, U.K.: Palgrave Macmillan.

Stoker, Robert. 1991. *Reluctant Partners: Implementing Federal Policy*. Pittsburgh: University of Pittsburgh Press.

Strauss, David A. 1999. Designing a Consensus-Building Process Using a Graphic Road Map. In *The Consensus-Building Handbook: A Comprehensive Guide to Reaching Agreement*, ed. Lawrence Susskind, Sarah McKearnan, and Jennifer Thomas-Larmer. Thousand Oaks, CA: Sage.

Suchman, Mark C. 1995. Managing Legitimacy: Strategic and Institutional Approaches. *Academy of Management Review* 20, no. 3:571–610.

Sullivan, Helen, and Chris Skelcher. 2002. *Working across Boundaries: Collaboration in Public Services*. Basingstoke, U.K.: Palgrave Macmillan.

Susskind, Lawrence, Sarah McKearnan, and Jennifer Thomas-Larmer, eds. 1999. *The Consensus-Building Handbook: A Comprehensive Guide to Reaching Agreement.* Thousand Oaks, CA: Sage.

Tadelis, Steven. 2002. Complexity, Flexibility, and the Make-or-Buy Decision. *American Economic Association Papers and Proceedings* 92, no. 2:433–37.

Takahashi, Lois M., and Gayla Smutny. 2002. Collaborative Windows and Organizational Governance: Exploring the Formation and Demise of Social Service Partnerships. *Nonprofit and Voluntary Sector Quarterly* 31, no. 2:165–85.

Thacher, David. 2004. Interorganizational Partnerships as Inchoate Hierarchies: A Case Study of the Community Security Initiative. *Administration and Society* 36, no. 1:91–127.

Thomas, Craig W. 1999. Linking Public Agencies with Community-Based Watershed Organizations: Lessons from California. *Policy Studies Journal* 27, no. 3:544–64.

Thomas, Kenneth. 1976. Conflict and Conflict Management. In *Handbook of Industrial and Organizational Psychology*, ed. Marvin D. Dunnette. New York: John Wiley & Sons.

Thompson, James D. 1967. *Organizations in Action.* New York: McGraw-Hill.

Thomson, Ann Marie. 2001. Collaboration: Meaning and Measurement. PhD diss., Indiana University.

Thomson, Ann Marie, and James L. Perry. 2006. Collaboration Processes: Inside the Black Box. *Public Administration Review* 66, no. 6 (Supplement): 20–32.

Tierney, Kathleen J., Michael K. Lindell, and Ronald W. Perry. 2001. *Facing the Unexpected: Disaster Preparedness and Response in the United States.* Washington, DC: Joseph Henry Press.

Tirole, Jean. 1999. Incomplete Contracts: Where Do We Stand? *Econometrica* 67:741–81.

Upjohn Institute. 1994. *P.Y. 94 Standardized Program Information Report (S.P.I.R.) Public Use File: Record Layout.* CD-ROM. Kalamazoo, MI: Upjohn Institute.

U.S. General Accounting Office. 1996. *Federal Grants.* Washington, DC: U.S. Government Printing Office.

———. 1997. *Managing for Results: Using the Results Act to Address Mission Fragmentation and Program Overlap.* Washington, DC: U.S. Government Printing Office.

———. 2002. Welfare Reform: Interim Report on Potential Ways to Strengthen Federal Oversight of State and Local Contracting. Report GAO-02-245. Washington, DC: U.S. Government Printing Office.

U.S. Institute for Environmental Conflict Resolution. 2006. ECR Performance Evaluation: An Inventory of Indicators. http://ecr.gov/multiagency/pdf/INV20061010.pdf.

Van Bueren, Ellen M., Erik-Hans Klijn, and Joop F. M. Koppenjan. 2003. Dealing with Wicked Problems in Networks: Analyzing an Environmental Debate from a Network Perspective. *Journal of Public Administration Research and Theory* 13 (April): 193–212.

Van de Ven, Andrew H., Dennis C. Emmett, and Richard Koening Jr. 1975. Frameworks for Interorganizational Analysis. In *Interorganizational theory*, ed. Anant R. Negandhi. Kent, OH: Kent State University Press.

Vangen, Siv, and Chris Huxham. 2003. Nurturing Collaborative Relations: Building Trust in Interorganizational Collaboration. *Journal of Applied Behavioral Science,* 39, no. 1): 5–31.

Van Horn, Carl E. 2006. Power, Politics, and Public Policy in the States. In *The State of The States*, 4th ed., edited by Carl E. Van Horn. Washington, DC: CQ Press.

Van Slyke, David M. 2003. The Mythology of Privatization in Contracting for Social Services. *Public Administration Review* 63, no. 3:277–96.

———. 2007. Agents or Stewards: Using Theory to Understand the Government–Nonprofit Social Service Contracting Relationship. *Journal of Public Administration Research and Theory* 17, no. 2:157–87.

Van Slyke, David M., and Robert W. Alexander. 2006. Public Service Leadership: Opportunities for Clarity and Coherence. *American Review of Public Administration* 36, no. 4:362–74.

Van Slyke, David M., and Charles A. Hammonds. 2003. The Privatization Decision: Do Public Managers Make a Difference? *American Review of Public Administration* 33 (June): 136–63.

Vigoda-Gadot, Eran. 2003. *Managing Collaboration in Public Administration: The Promise of Alliance among Governance, Citizens and Businesses.* Westport, CT: Praeger.

Wachtendorf, Tricia. 2004. Improvising 9/11: Organizational Improvisation Following the World Trade Center Disaster. PhD diss., University of Delaware.

Waddock, Sandra A. 1988. Building Successful Social Partnerships. *Sloan Management Review*, 17–23.

Walker, Henry A., George M. Thomas, and Morris Zelditch Jr. 1986. Legitimation, Endorsement, and Stability. *Social Forces* 64, no. 3:620–43.

Waugh, William L., Jr. 1993. Co-ordination or Control: Organizational Design and the Emergency Management Function. *International Journal of Disaster Prevention and Management* 2 (December): 17–31.

———. 1994. Regionalizing Emergency Management: Counties as State and Local Government. *Public Administration Review* 54 (May–June): 253–58.

———. 2000. *Living with Hazards, Dealing with Disasters*. Armonk, NY: M. E. Sharpe.

———. 2002. Organizational Culture, Communication, and Decision-Making: Making Multi-Organizational, Inter-Sector and Intergovernmental Operations Work. Paper presented at National Conference on Catastrophic Care for the Nation, National Disaster Medical System, Atlanta, April 13–17.

———. 2003. Terrorism, Homeland Security and the National Emergency Management Network. *Public Organization Review* 3:373–85.

———. 2006. The Political Costs of Failure in the Responses to Hurricanes Katrina and Rita. *Annals of the Academy of Political and Social Science* 604 (March): 10–25.

Waugh, William L., Jr., and Gregory Streib. 2006. Collaboration and Leadership for Effective Emergency Management. *Public Administration Review* 66, no. s1:131–40.

Waugh, William L., Jr., and Richard T. Sylves. 2002. Organizing the War on Terrorism. *Public Administration Review*, Special Issue (September): 145–53.

Weick, Karl E. 1979. *The Social Psychology of Organizing.* New York: McGraw-Hill.

———. 1995. *Sensemaking in Organizations.* Thousand Oaks, CA: Sage

———. 2001. *Making Sense of the Organization.* Malden, MA: Blackwell.

Weidner, Edward W. 1960. *Intergovernmental Relations as Seen by Public Officials.* Minneapolis: University of Minnesota Press.

Wenger, Dennis E., Enrique L. Qaurantelli, and Russell R. Dynes. 1986. *Disaster Analysis: Local Emergency Offices and Arrangements.* Final Project Report 37. Newark: Disaster Research Center, University of Delaware.

Whitaker, Gordon P., and Rosalind Day. 2001. How Local Governments Work with Nonprofit Organizations in North Carolina. *Popular Government*, Winter 2001, 25–32.

White House. 2006. *The Federal Response to Hurricane Katrina: Lessons Learned.* Washington, DC: White House.

Whitener, Ellen M., Susan E. Brodt, M. Audrey Korsgaard, and Jon M. Werner. 1998. Managers as Initiators of Trust: An Exchange Relationship Framework for Understanding Managerial Trustworthy Behavior. *Academy of Management Review* 23, no. 3:513–30.

Willer, David, ed. 1999. *Network Exchange Theory.* Westport, CT: Praeger.

Williamson, Oliver E. 1991. Comparative Economic Organization: The Analysis of Discrete Structural Alternatives. *Administrative Science Quarterly* 36:269–96.

———. 1996. *The Mechanisms of Governance.* New York: Oxford University Press.

———. 2005. The Economics of Governance. *American Economic Association Papers and Proceedings* 95, no. 2:1–18.

Wise, Charles R. 1990. Public Service Configurations and Public Organizations: Public Organization Design in the Post-Privatization Era. *Public Administration Review* 50 (March–April): 141–55.

———. 2002. Organizing for Homeland Security. *Public Administration Review* 62, no. 2:131–44.

Wondolleck, Julia M., and Steven L. Yaffee. 2000. *Making Collaboration Work: Lessons from Innovation in Natural Resource Management.* Washington, DC: Island Press.

Wright, Deil S., and Chung-Lae Cho. 2000. State Administration and Intergovernmental Interdependency: Do National Impacts on State Agencies Contribute to Organizational Turbulence? In *Handbook of State Administration*, ed. John J. Gargan. New York: Marcel Dekker.

———. 2001. American State Administrators Project (ASAP) Overview: Major Features of the ASAP Surveys, 1964–1998. Odum Institute for Research in Social Science, Chapel Hill, NC. Unpublished, available on request.

Wright, Ned, and Wayne Randle. 2006. Federal Incident Response Support Team (FIRST). *IAEM Bulletin*, September, 13–14.

Yamagishi, Toshio, and Midori Yamagishi. 1994. Trust and Commitment in the United States and Japan. *Motivation and Emotion* 1, no. 2:129–66.

Yin, Robert K. 2003. *Case Study Research: Design and Methods*. Thousand Oaks, CA: Sage.

Zartman, I. William, and Jeffrey Z. Rubin, eds. 2000. *Power and Negotiation*. Ann Arbor: University of Michigan Press.

Zucker, Lynne G. 1989. Combining Institutional Theory and Population Ecology: No Legitimacy, No History. *American Sociological Review* 54, no. 4:542–45.

Contributors

Robert Alexander is a doctoral candidate in public administration at the Maxwell School of Syracuse University.

Alejandro Amezcua is a doctoral student in public administration at the Maxwell School of Syracuse University.

Alison Anker is a doctoral candidate in public administration at the Maxwell School of Syracuse University.

Lisa Blomgren Bingham is the Keller-Runden Professor of Public Service at the School of Public and Environmental Affairs at Indiana University–Bloomington.

Jeffrey L. Brudney is the Albert A. Levin Chair of Urban Studies and Public Service at Cleveland State University's Maxine Goodman Levin College of Urban Affairs.

Bin Chen is assistant professor in the School of Public Affairs, Baruch College of the City University of New York.

Chung-Lae Cho is assistant professor of public administration at Ewha Woman's University, Seoul.

Kirk Emerson is director of the U.S. Institute for Environmental Conflict Resolution.

Rachel Fleishman is a doctoral candidate in public administration at the Maxwell School of Syracuse University.

Beth Gazley is assistant professor of public and environmental affairs at Indiana University–Bloomington.

Elizabeth A. Graddy is professor and senior associate dean for faculty and academic affairs at the School of Policy, Planning, and Development at the University of Southern California.

Alisa Hicklin is assistant professor of political science at the University of Oklahoma.

Michael McGuire is associate professor of public and environmental affairs at Indiana University–Bloomington.

Kenneth J. Meier is distinguished professor of political science and the Charles H. Gregory Chair in Liberal Arts at Texas A&M University, and professor of public management at Cardiff University in Wales.

Rosemary O'Leary is distinguished professor of public administration, Phanstiel Endowed Chair in Strategic Management and Leadership, codirector of the Collaborative Governance Initiative, and codirector of the Program on the Analysis and Resolution of Conflicts at the Maxwell School of Syracuse University.

Laurence J. O'Toole Jr. is the Margaret Hughes and Robert T. Golembiewski Professor of Public Administration and head of the Department of Public Administration and Policy at the School of Public and International Affairs at the University of Georgia. He is also professor of comparative sustainability policy studies at Twente University in the Netherlands.

Paul L. Posner, formerly managing director for federal budget and intergovernmental issues at the U.S. Government Accountability Office, is the director of the public administration program at George Mason University.

Hal G. Rainey is Alumni Foundation Distinguished Professor in the Department of Public Administration and Policy at the School of Public and International Affairs at the University of Georgia.

Scott E. Robinson is associate professor of government and public service at the Bush School at Texas A&M University.

Jay Eungha Ryu is assistant professor of public administration at Ohio University.

Mary Tschirhart is the director of the Campbell Public Affairs Institute and associate professor of public administration at the Maxwell School of Syracuse University.

David M. Van Slyke is associate professor of public administration at the Maxwell School of Syracuse University.

William L. Waugh Jr. is professor of public administration and urban studies at Georgia State University.

Deil S. Wright is alumni distinguished professor of political science at the University of North Carolina.

Index

Carlson, Christine, 216
Carpenter, Sarah, 265–66
Centers for Disease Control and
Prevention (CDC), 2
CEQ. *See* President's Council on
Environmental Quality (CEQ)
Charalambides, Leonidas C., 26
Charlotte Harbor National Estuary
Program, 37t
Chen, Bin, 57. *See also* partner
selection and interorganizational
collaborations (social service
agencies in Los Angeles County)
Cho, Chung-Lae. *See* contracting
patterns and performance for
service delivery
"civic switchboard" model, 174–75
Clean Water Act (1987 amendments to), 35
coalitions, defining, 10
collaboration and competing
political traditions, 225, 255–56
Collaborative Action and Dispute
Resolution (CADR) of the U.S.
Department of the Interior, 216,
220
"collaborative know-how," 19
collaborative public management, 1–
12, 255–69; addressing conflict,
259–64, 265–67; antecedents to
collaboration, 8–9; challenges
and paradoxes for collaborative
managers, 12, 264–67; the continuum of collaborative service
arrangements, 5, 5f; cross-sectoral
(public-private partnerships), 5–6;
the current interest in U.S. and
elsewhere, 96; defining, 3, 139;
as different from "cooperation"/
"coordination," 5; examples of
intergovernmental relations
and federal policymaking, 3–4;

examples of policymaking/
implementation outside the U.S.,
4; four elements of collaboration,
4–5; identifying success using
upstream/midstream/downstream
framework, 267–69; learning
from public management/public
administration fields, 267–69;
multidimensional/multitheore-
tical nature of, 6; real-world
examples of new developments,
2–3; recent scholarship on, 1–12;
research on partnership failure,
7; skill sets for collaborative
managers, 264–65, 265f; studies
of the goals/outcomes of, 6–7;
surprising findings from contributors' studies, 255–59; theories on
collaboration and strategic
decision making across sectors,
7–8; types of collaborative
structures, 9–11
collaborative structures, 9–11
command-and-control models and
emergency management, 11, 91,
159, 164, 165–67, 168f, 172–73,
257; Incident Command System
(ICS), 167, 168f, 172–73; incident management systems, 165–
67, 168f, 172–73
Community Family Preservation
Networks (CFPN) in Los Angeles
County, 60–61. *See also* partner
selection and interorganizational
collaborations (social service
agencies in Los Angeles County)
"Conceptualizing and Measuring
Collaborative Networks"
(Rethemeyer), 131
conflict resolution: addressing
conflict, 259–64, 265–67; and
contracting patterns/perfor-

environmental conflict resolution
(synthesizing practice and performance in the field) (*continued*)
evaluations of court-based ADR
programs, 219; and evolution of
ECR field, 216–19, 230; examples of ECR activity at federal
level, 218; examples of synthesis
and "parallel play," 215–16;
and the "OMB-CEQ ECR Joint
Memorandum on Environmental
Conflict Resolution," 225–30,
231n2; perceived distinctions/
tensions between collaborative
practice and performance, 224–
25; performance guidance and
recommendations for performance evaluation (OMB-CEQ
memorandum), 229–30; and the
Policy Consensus Initiative, 216,
220–23, 231n1; synthesizing an
operating model for ECR, 219–
23; synthesizing practice and
performance in policy, 223–30
environmental organizations. *See*
organizational participation
(motivations and obstacles)
Environmental Policy and Conflict
Resolution Act (1998), 197, 218
EPA. *See* U.S. Environmental
Protection Agency (EPA)
estuary partnerships, 35–38, 37t.
See also organizational participation (motivations and obstacles);
U.S. Environmental Protection
Agency (EPA)
Ewalt, Jo Ann G., 179, 186

Faerman, Sue, 264–65
Fairman, David, 231n1
Family Preservation (FP) Program
in Los Angeles County, 60. *See*

also partner selection and
interorganizational collaborations
(social service agencies in Los
Angeles County)
Federal Emergency Management
Agency (FEMA): and collaborative mechanisms, 159–60, 162,
163, 167, 172–73; development
of an ICS system, 167; Environmental and Historic Preservation
program, 92; and Federal Incident Response Support Team,
163; golden age and the "all
hazards" perspective, 159–60;
post–September 2001 changes,
157–58, 172–73; process of
rebuilding, 162; training, 73, 79–
80, 80t, 83–85, 84t, 86–89, 87t,
88t. *See also* emergency management and collaborative mechanisms
Federal Energy Regulatory
Commission's Dispute Resolution
Services, 220
Federal Highway Administration's
Office of Project Development
and Environmental Review, 220
Federal Incident Response Support
Team, 163
federalism, American, 3–4
FEMA. *See* Federal Emergency
Management Agency (FEMA)
Fernandez, Sergio, 147
FIRESCOPE project (Firefighting
Resources of Southern California
Organized for Potential Emergen-
cies), 167
Fleishman, Rachel. *See* organiza-
tional participation (motivations
and obstacles)
Florida Conflict Resolution Consor-
tium, 220

national SoVI scores, 76, 77t; comparison of sample counties with U.S. counties, 75–76, 75t; conflict and organizational tasks of the public emergency manager, 260; control variables, 80t, 81–82, 84t, 85; data collection (web-based questionnaire/survey), 74–75; data set, 75; and Department of Homeland Security, 161–62; the dependent variable, 76–79, 78t; descriptive statistics for explanatory variables, 79–82, 80t; and development of social capital, 90; discussion of variables and hypotheses, 74–82; education and training variables, 73–74, 79–81, 80t, 83–85, 84t, 90, 92; the eleven collaborative activities, 76, 78t; establishing valid measure of collaboration, 79; and FEMA training, 73, 79–80, 80t, 83–85, 84t, 86–89, 87t, 88t; generalizability of the sample, 75–76; and the IAEM training program, 74, 79–80, 80t, 84t, 85; implications for emergency management/ collaborative public management, 90–93; and interagency collaborative capacity, 90–91; and mandated collaboration, 92; the new professional model of emergency management, 71–74, 159–63; OLS results, 82–86, 84t; professionalization as associated with greater levels of collaborative activity, 84t, 85–86, 90, 257; structural variables (organizational structure), 73, 74, 80t, 81, 84t, 85; SWLS regression model results, 83, 86–89, 87t, 88t; and types of collaborative organiza

tions, 78t; unit of analysis, 74–75; conclusions/findings, 90–93, 257, 258, 259

The Promise and Performance of Environmental Conflict Resolution (O'Leary and Bingham), 220–21, 268

Provan, Keith G.: on collaboration and conflict, 262; on firefighting and command-and-control approaches, 167; on four network types, 10; on relational contracting, 135n4, 138–39, 148; warnings regarding ICS and emergency management, 175

public administration education for the third-party governance era, 233–53, 259; challenges for public administrators/managers, 235–37, 242–43, 262; common curriculum components (National Association of Schools of Public Affairs and Administration), 243–44, 244t; core courses in top-ranked public management programs, 243–46, 245t; defining skill sets for third-party governance and collaborative management, 237–38, 241–43, 247–48; differential government-network strategies, 240, 241t; the emergence of third-party governance, 233–35, 262; existing models for curriculum reform, 249–52; the government-network interface, 237–41, 241t; how third-party governance complicates public management, 235–37, 236f; insights provided by network theory, 238–39; needed case studies/research agenda, 251; needed literature on the

public administration education for
the third-party governance era
(*continued*)
governmental toolbox, 251–52;
possible areas of study, 246–47;
reorienting graduate public
administration programs, 243–49,
251–52; and theories/frameworks
from other disciplines, 248–49;
third-party environments and the
three faces of governance, 236–
37, 236f; third-party governance
and accountability issues, 235,
238
Public Administration Review
(*PAR*), 215
public organization start-ups
(collaborative approaches to
USIECR's evolution), 197–213,
261; actor-based strategies, 200;
and adaptive management, 200;
agency-based strategies, 200, 212;
the birth and early evolution of
public-sector organizations, 198–
99; boundary-buffering behaviors,
210–11; boundary-spanning
behaviors, 211–12; and client/
customer interactions, 205–6,
211–12; and collaborators/exter-
nal stakeholders, 205; and competition, 204, 212, 258; differences
of public-sector/private-sector
organizational environments,
198–99; and dynamic qualities,
208–10; and economic forces,
206; establishing "chains of
evidence," 202; explanation of
propositions/predictions, 200–
201, 212; external forces influencing USIECR's evolution,
203–7, 203f, 213n2; and fixed

(original) qualities, 207–8; the
founding statute's language and
publicness, 208; institutionalization and public-sector organizations, 199; internal forces
influencing USIECR's evolution,
207–10, 213n2; interview
protocols and questions, 201,
213n2; interview subjects, 201,
202t; and legal factors, 206–7;
legitimacy-seeking strategies,
199–200, 210–12; and the
"liability of newness," 198, 199;
and organizational culture
(cultural and institutional influences), 200–201, 209–10, 212;
personnel characteristics, 209;
political factors (USIECR evolution, Congress, and the OMB),
204–5; predictions regarding
USIECR's early strategic management, 200–201, 212; results of
the initial analysis, 202–10, 203f,
213n2; size and location factors,
207–8; sources of data and
methods, 201–2; and strategic
collaborative behaviors, 210–12;
and strategic management,
199–200; and targeting of key
political/budgetary stakeholders,
200, 212; and targeting of
potential clients and promoters
of professional norms, 200,
212; and USIECR's neutrality
value, 210; and USIECR's
unique set of circumstances,
200–201
public-private partnerships (cross-
sectoral collaboration), 5–6

Quarantelli, Enrique L., 98

resource sharing (*continued*)
and the social network of organizations, 26–27; and strategic
resources, 18; and tangibility of
shared resource, 19–20, 23t, 24,
27; and trust, 24, 256
Rethemeyer, R. Karl, 131
Robinson, Scott E. *See* disaster
response and collaborative public
management in Texas school
districts
Rowe, Andy, 231n1
Ryu, Jay Eungha. *See* "one-stop
service" approach in employment
and training programs (Texas)

Salamon, Lester M., 119, 234, 246
Sandfort, Jodi, 5
Scardaville, Michael, 163–64
Scharpf, Fritz, 32
Schneider, Saundra K., 98
Sechrest, Lee, 231n1
Selden, Sally Coleman, 5
September 2001 terrorist attacks
and the national emergency
management system, 157–58,
164–65, 172–73
service delivery: conflict resolution
and contracting patterns/perfor-
mance for, 259–60; network
formation model for, 55–57;
relational contracting and
government-nonprofit relationships, 143–45. *See also* contracting patterns and performance for
service delivery
Shirley, W. Lynn, 76
social capital, 90, 113
social network theory, 57, 238–39
social service agencies. *See* contracting patterns and perfor-

mance for service delivery;
partner selection and interorganizational collaborations
(social service agencies in Los
Angeles County)
Social Vulnerability Index (SoVI),
76, 77t
Sowa, Jessica, 5
Standardized Program Information
Report (SPIR) reporting system,
180
Stanley, Ellis M., 71–72, 90
states/state agencies: alternative
dispute resolution (ADR) pro-
grams, 219–20; contracting for
service delivery, 118–21. *See also*
contracting patterns and perfor-
mance for service delivery
State University of New York at
Albany, 245
Steelman, Toddi A., 9–10
Stiles, Jan, 8
Stinchombe, Arthur L., 199
Stoker, Robert, 238
Stone, Melissa Middleton, 120–21,
128, 129, 150–51
strategic management, 199–200.
See also public organization start-
ups (collaborative approaches to
USIECR's evolution)
Streeter, Calvin L., 98–99
substantively weighted least squares
(SWLS) analysis, 83, 86–89, 87t,
88t
Syracuse University public manage-
ment program, 245

Temporary Assistance for Needy
Families (TANF), 156n2
Texas. *See* disaster response and
collaborative public management